21ST CENTURY CORPORATE BOARD

Books of Related Interest

William G. Bowen ■ *Inside the Boardroom: Governance by Directors and Trustees*

Louis Braiotta Jr. ■ *Audit Committee Handbook*

Copyright © 1997 by John Wiley & Sons, Inc.

Library of Congress Cataloging in Publication Data:

Ward, Ralph D.
    21st century corporate board / by Ralph D. Ward.
      p.   cm.
    Includes bibliographical references.
    ISBN 0-471-15679-5 (cloth : alk. paper)
      1. Directors of corporations—United States. 2. Corporate
governance—United States. 3. Chief executive officers—United
States. I. Title.
    HD2745.W375 1996
658.4'22—dc20
                                      96-21408
                                        CIP

Printed in the United States of America

10 9 8 7 6 5 4 3 2

21st Century Corporate Board

Ralph D. Ward

John Wiley & Sons, Inc.

New York • Chichester • Brisbane • Toronto • Singapore • Weinheim

To Tammy, Maud, and Ada, who make everything possible;
for Mom.
And of course, to Judy the boss.

Contents

Preface

In editing a national magazine on corporate boards over the past six years, I've had a ringside seat for the wildest era of corporate governance change since the New Deal. We've had some sharp, insightful authors reporting on this turmoil for us (God bless 'em), but too many other writers on corporate boards stick with a handful of useful clichés. The most common:

- Change is sweeping America's boardrooms.
- Directors are not the pushovers they used to be.
- Boards are getting tough with CEOs.

As with most clichés, these are true at their core, but they seem to be repeated again and again to the exclusion of any deeper insight. Worse, they beg the response; so what? What *if* the board is changing, growing tougher, more independent? Who says corporate boards even matter?

Well, the Securities and Exchange Commission does. Some of their recent decisions make clear that they now consider the board a key player in any corporate wrongdoing. Congress does. The Private Securities Litigation Reform Act of 1995 made tort relief for directors a major priority (and also mandated crucial new board oversight duties). Indeed, passage of the law was considered so vital that Congress made it President Bill Clinton's first veto override. Regulators believe that boards matter. Federal environmental laws put directors on the spot for assuring corporate compliance programs—with penalties that can wreck a multinational corporation. Major shareholders think the board matters. Big pension funds now target the board with proxy resolutions, view board contacts as urgent, and increasingly use the board as its corporate liaison. Institutional investors own half of all outstanding stock, and their priorities move the market.

CEOs *really* know that their boards matter. In recent years, they've seen their formerly safe haven of cronies change in disturbing ways. Like a once harmless child maturing into a truculent adolescent, CEOs' boards have grown away from them in ways hard to understand. The CEO once ruled without question or challenge. But now the board asks more questions, evaluates the CEO's performance, and digs into all levels of the company. Being nice to the board and attending to their perks isn't enough anymore. Suddenly, the CEO's directors want—and have the power to demand—results.

Most of all, *directors* now realize that boards matter. The effect on boards has been both intimidating and stimulating, as with any new, great personal responsibility. In a sense, corporate directors, even if they are moonlighting CEOs, are experiencing their first day on the job. The corporate board of directors has woken up from a long nap to discover itself in charge of corporate America, and like the truculent adolescent mentioned above, they are still a bit uncertain of themselves.

As we enter the next century, our boards of directors are rushing to complete a transformation bigger than any in corporate governance history. They are literally creating a new corporate form—the independent, yet powerful, board of directors. Though lacking major ownership of the company, and without the power of top inside executives, the board is transforming itself into a distinct force for governance accountability. This change was slow and evolutionary for decades. However, it suddenly burst upon the business world in revolutionary form just a few years ago, in the boardroom of a certain troubled automaker.

It was a shock to the business world. The board of General Motors actually fired the boss! With the United States in a recession, sales, market share, and profits were down dangerously. The management team, despite repeated warnings from the board, seemed incapable of coping with the dangers facing GM, with the CEO certain the storm clouds would soon pass. But with each day the situation grew more dangerous, and major investors demanded tough action. Finally, a director who served as the informal leader of the board spearheaded a coup against the boss, who was fired. This director, with the support of shareholders, took over as chairman of GM and named a bright top executive as the new CEO. Together, they launched a restructuring that soon turned GM around. Who would have thought it possible? General Motors! And the board of *General Motors leading the insurrection!*

Amazing indeed . . .

PART I

How Corporate Boards Got This Way

1

Roger Smith Loses Some
Important Friends

The directors' boardroom on the 25th floor of the General Motors building in New York was a classic in boardroom decor. Despite the ritualistic pomp we associate with major corporate boards, GM's boardroom was like many others in stressing elegant simplicity. A large and handsome, but unostentatious, mahogany board table centered the room. Thickly upholstered leather chairs surrounded the table, each bearing a metal nameplate for a particular director. The lighting was subdued. The walls were paneled with teak (Ross Perot had joked about the forests that fell to panel the room).

Behind the chair's seat, at the head of the table, was a modern intrusion, an audiovisual screen. But the walls surrounding the boardroom displayed portraits of illustrious past chairmen of General Motors. One of these was company founder William C. Durant. Billy Durant was a hyperactive, winning salesman and stock juggler who started assembling GM in 1908 by buying up every carmaker he could find. Usually he went with stock-for-stock deals, which kept debt low. Durant was an innovator, but not a manager, and he'd had his own troubles with the GM Board of Directors. In 1992, as the image of the long-dead Durant looked down from his boardroom portrait, he might have sympathized with the problems GM Chairman and CEO Robert Stempel faced with the current board.

The board of directors that General Motors assembled over the 1980s and into the 1990s was among the most impressive in corporate America. John G. Smale, a director since 1982, had retired in 1990 as chairman of Procter & Gamble, though he still held an emeritus position. He was noted in the business world as a consumer products marketing innovator. Edmund Pratt was chairman emeritus of Pfizer, and J. Willard Marriott was chairman and CEO of his namesake corporation. Dennis Weatherstone chaired J. P. Morgan & Company, which was also GM's investment banker. Thomas Wyman chaired S. G. Warburg & Company, and had also served as chairman of CBS. Charles Fisher III, chairman of NBD Bancorp, was a scion of the Fisher family, which had been prominent in Detroit's financial and auto world for decades. Other eminent outsiders included former Reagan Labor Secretary Ann McLaughlin and former Republican Party Chair Anne Armstrong.

Long dominated by insiders, over the 1980s GM's board had joined the trend of other major U.S. boards in trimming its size and share of inside members. The 1965-model GM board had 29 directors, 17 of them insiders, including nonagenarians Alfred P. Sloan and Charles S. Mott. By 1992, the board totaled only 17 directors, by coincidence the same as the number of insiders alone 27 years earlier. By the start of the 1990s, though, there remained a strong inside contingent on the GM board, including Chairman Stempel, former Chairman Roger Smith, President Lloyd Reuss, and Executive Vice Presidents F. Alan Smith and John "Jack" Smith. The growing number of outsiders had shifted the tone of the board, making it more independent and estimable. In fact, when then-Chairman Roger Smith in 1988 tried to add three more insiders back to the board, he was rebuffed, one of the first hints that Smith had lost the board's support.

Of course, events during Roger Smith's tenure could well have shaken the GM board's faith in management. The 1985–86 buyout fiasco with Ross Perot's Electronic Data Systems company had been the first event to leave a bad taste in their mouths. Roger Smith had sold the board on the need of buying up EDS to launch GM's information systems into the twenty-first century. Perot had joined the GM board as part of the deal. But Smith and Perot were soon publicly squabbling, with Perot telling anyone who would listen that GM was one sick company—and that the board was a group of passive "pet rocks." By 1986 the marriage was in collapse. Smith and Perot cobbled together an agreement to buy out Perot's GM/ EDS stock (and get him off the board), but at a price of nearly three-quarters of a billion dollars. Perot claims that he fully expected the board to rebel over signing such a giveaway and was dumbfounded when they approved.

The GM board received other hints that the company was not being managed as well as it should. Smith had launched a massive reorganization in 1984 to consolidate GM operations. Although the need for radical change was obvious, the reorganization was proving an overblown, expensive failure. In the 1980s, Smith sought to jump-start the next century with robotics, acquisitions, new plants, and even a new company, Saturn. These moves had drained the one thing that had always seen GM through—its cash cushion. From an $8.6 billion cash balance at the end of 1984, the company was *losing* a billion dollars per quarter by the beginning of 1992. These losses did not really accelerate until the 1990 recession, but the drop in market share had been steady and depressing. GM held 45% of the U.S. car market at the start of the 1980s, but by 1992 its share had slipped to barely one-third.

Director John Smale had long been a CEO loyalist (he backed Smith in the controversial $3.5 billion decision to launch Saturn). An attentive board member, in the late 1980s he was doing his own poking around in the far-flung GM organization. This was done informally and without a definite agenda, like a casual buyer kicking the tires of a GM product, according to the *Washington Post*.[1] Smale visited plants, browsed financials, and talked with managers several layers deep within the company.

Like TV's Lieutenant Columbo, Smale was unobtrusive, but perceptive. He kept uncovering aspects of GM that did not look healthy. Although the company's market share was shrinking, Smith was actually adding expensive new capacity. Ultimately, if all plant and equipment were running flat out, GM would be able to build almost twice as many cars as it could sell. This created enormous built-in inefficiency. The 1984 reorganization, though launched for all the right reasons, had brought massive turmoil, but no apparent cost savings. The old GM had functioned, to a degree, in an inefficient, muddling-through sort of way. But the new GM, which

---

1. "An Outside Director's Coup inside GM," Maryann Keller, *Washington Post*, April 12, 1992, p. H1.

rejuggled and combined the firm's 35 operating units, had broken down this ad hoc structure and let the operating ecosystem run amok. Rather than forge a new, high-tech GM, it had proved only that "there was something worse than the old GM."[2]

There was also muttering out in the field. The GM system enforced dirt-eating loyalty to one's superiors, especially the Big Superior at the head of the board table. Yet a few voices hinted that all was not well. That costs were out of control. That shareholders were grumbling. That company products were flawed and unpopular.

Smale's walkabouts also helped him make a lot of new contacts, both inside and outside the GM structure. One such inside contact was Elmer Johnson. In 1983, Smith had lured Johnson, a noted attorney from the Chicago office of Kirkland & Ellis, to join GM as general counsel. Johnson, a noted corporate litigator, was a respected expert in dealing with the delicacies of shareholder suits and governance law. He was an innovative legal thinker on the subject of boards and effective governance. Roger Smith may have been seeking someone who could refresh the board processes at GM the way he had hoped buying EDS would shake up GM management. And, with shareholders growing more pugnacious, it could not hurt to have one of the best governance attorneys around on his team. Smith hinted that Johnson just might have a shot at ultimately running General Motors. Rather than just counsel corporations, why not manage one?

But Elmer Johnson had also proven himself an able consigliere in a number of delicate board and management matters, helping ease out chairmen at International Harvester and Firestone. Although Smith knew Johnson was skilled in helping boards defend themselves from shareholders, he was also adept in helping boards oust their underperforming CEOs.

Smith named Johnson to the GM board in 1987. Johnson took Smith's call for fresh, effective governance seriously, and in 1988 he opposed Smith on continuing to pour cash into the Saturn project. But Roger Smith drew a distinct line between his concepts of "innovation" and "loyalty." Saturn was Smith's dream child, and an attack on the new nameplate was an attack on him. Smith won

---

2. *Comeback,* Paul Ingrassia and Joseph B. White, Simon & Schuster, 1994, p. 96.

his Saturn battle, and within a year, Elmer Johnson was back at Kirkland & Ellis.

But John Smale had discovered a few other faces in the board-room who shared his concerns. Tom Wyman, who joined the GM board in 1985, had been squeezed out as chairman of CBS. He was increasingly unhappy with the performance of GM's board, privately sharing some of Ross Perot's criticisms. Dennis Weatherstone, chairman of J. P. Morgan, GM's investment banker, was another, as was J. Willard Marriott after he joined the board in 1989. These outside directors were recognized business and civic leaders, noted for their independence and good ideas. Roger Smith said he had courted them to his board for precisely these qualities, and no one doubted him. Smith wanted tough, savvy innovators for his board, not yes-men (or yes-women).

These were becoming important qualities on corporate boards of the time. Through most of U.S. business history, boards had been either control mechanisms for the founders and financiers or sleepy, insider-dominated serfdoms of the CEO. Smith, ever the innovator, sought a board for the next century, made up of men and women powerful and talented enough to become a real force in governance of the company. But once they were on the GM board, these leaders made an interesting discovery. Roger Smith wanted them to share their ideas and energy to help him do what he *intended to do anyway*. Whether the idea was good, bad, overreaching, or 20 years too early did not matter.

So some of the best corporate directors in the United States had made it to the board of the world's biggest company only to find they could do little good. Indeed, some events of the era left them exposed to shareholder liability suits. When Roger Smith proposed buying EDS in 1985, Elmer Johnson warned directors that the tricky transaction could leave them vulnerable to suits by disgruntled stockholders. He advised the board to seek its own outside counsel and introduced them to a friend, noted corporate attorney Ira Millstein. The directors did not have to travel far. Millstein's office, one of the most handsome in the prestigious law firm of Weil, Gotshall, & Manges, was also in the New York GM building, several floors up.

Millstein was one of New York's foremost corporate attorneys, handling litigation for such blue chips as General Electric, Westinghouse, and Bethlehem Steel. He had previously helped GM win a major consumer suit over alleged defects in the company's X-cars and had proven himself a sharp, vigorous litigator. He aided Elmer Johnson in negotiating with Perot, including the ultimate buyout agreement, and suggested that the board appoint an oversight committee of outside directors to pass judgment on EDS matters. This special committee was based on a nucleus of the board's audit committee and, by the time of the Perot buyout, had expanded to include most of the outside board members.

These outside directors were pleased with the value of Millstein's work and retained him to continue serving as an independent counsel for the board, a capacity separate from the GM legal structure. Some of the outsiders were also impressed with Millstein's ideas on corporate governance.

Although the takeovers of the 1980s had brought some new accountability to management (as well as value to shareholders, another Millstein precept), it was rough, erratic justice. A more solid, long-term solution was for shareholders to flex their muscles through active corporate boards, the legal body designated to ride herd on management. Millstein lectured and wrote on the topic during the 1980s, and he had built close relationships with some of the most active institutional investors, including the enormous $40 billion California Public Employee Retirement System (CalPERS). In a 1989 profile, *Institutional Investor* observed, "Millstein believes that, ideally, management should be answerable to shareholders and directors . . . . He feels he can urge the process along."[3] Millstein offered valuable legal advice to the board's outsiders and also opened their horizons to the changes that were stirring in corporate governance. Liability laws, angry institutional shareholders, and government regulators were making life too dangerous for do-nothing boards. Shareholders demanded "certifying" boards, in his phrase. That is, boards to whom management was truly accountable and boards that in turn answered to investors. Millstein's work with the GM board must have had some effect. Late in the 1980s, Roger Smith took the GM building elevator up to Millstein's floor to personally chew him out for interfering with his board.[4]

Elmer Johnson had brought one further change to the top

---

3. "Ira Millstein Turns Up the Heat," *Institutional Investor*, November 1989, p. 103.
4. *Comeback*, Ingrassia and White, p. 178.

levels of GM that also caught John Smale's eye. He mentored another attorney who joined the GM legal staff in the mid-1980s, Harry Pearce. Pearce had likewise been involved in defending a number of cases for GM, including his first civil case, fighting an action against the Corvair in 1970. His 1984 and 1985 work in battling the X-car recall case cemented his reputation as a winner, and he joined GM in 1985.

Pearce was a tough courtroom counsel, "the trial lawyer's trial lawyer," who once so frazzled an opposing expert witness that the poor fellow started chewing his tie.[5] A master of technical detail, smart and ambitious, Pearce was promoted to the position of GM general counsel after Johnson joined the board. Pearce reshaped the GM legal department in a way that many wished the corporation would flush out the whole GM system. He cut a third of the department's 150 lawyers and replaced career hacks with tough talent from the outside. As with his mentor Elmer Johnson, Pearce developed close links with the board. He served the outside directors as a valuable negotiator and liaison with executives below the CEO's immediate team. The board's continuing relationship with Ira Millstein also brought the two attorneys together, and they hit it off strongly. Though Elmer Johnson departed from GM in 1988, he left the board with some governance and legal talent that would bring interesting results in the future.

---

5. "Harry Pearce for the Defense," *Business Week*, May 17, 1994, p. 44.

2

Robert Stempel and the Revenge
of the "Car Guys"

As Roger Smith wound down the 1980s, as well as his career
with GM, he found his board increasingly feisty. In 1987 alone,
GM's share of the domestic car market dropped five points. Smith's
1988 failure to pack the board with three more insiders had shaken
him, and word leaked out that the directors were not quite the "pet
rocks" they had been a couple of years earlier. The Chevrolet-Pon-
tiac-Canada segment of GM's reorganization was a money pit, losing $3 billion per year. Lloyd Reuss, the vice president in charge of
CPC and an inside director, assured the board that a turnaround
was imminent, but he seemed ever harder to believe. John Smale
was growing increasingly impatient for Smith to leave and, according to rumor, tried stirring a boardroom "dump Roger" revolt
about this time. But the other outside directors preferred to wait
Smith out until his 1990 retirement, and the move came to nothing.[1]

The last year of Smith's tenure was the most volatile. First, he
had talked the board into upping his retirement pension to $1.2
million yearly, a $500,000 increase. The directors, making an early
effort to bond with shareholders, submitted the pension boost to
an investor vote. Although the increase passed easily, 13% of shareholders voted "no," a dangerously high level of dissent for a proxy
proposal. Worse, the media and shareholder groups condemned the

---

1. *Comeback,* Paul Ingrassia and Joseph B. White, Simon & Schuster, 1994,
   p. 288.

move for coming in the teeth of sluggish results. The board did a slow burn.

Smith's succession planning also troubled the core of activist outside directors. Succession was a vital issue. Aside from the delicate internal politics, GM, like most corporations, combined the offices of chief executive officer and chairman of the board, so a bad pick would be doubly disastrous. Several of the major public pension funds, including CalPERS and the New York state employees' pension fund, sent inquiries to Smith asking what criteria the board would use in selecting a successor. By implication, the queries made clear that more of the current quality of leadership was not welcome. Smith released a response for the board—without showing it to the directors—dryly noting that executive succession "is the board's responsibility," and no one else's business.

Robert Stempel, GM president and a director since 1987, had the inside track and was named heir apparent in April 1990. Stempel had a reputation as a hardworking, yet humane, reformer. He was one of the most genuinely nice people in the upper echelons of the auto industry and cared about the welfare of his employees. He was loyal to the team of subordinates who worked with him—particularly Lloyd Reuss.

Stempel, however, had one unusual characteristic for a chair of General Motors—he was a "car guy." In Motown-speak, this meant that he had worked his way up in the company from the engineering side, starting at Oldsmobile in 1958. At GM, however, tradition since the 1950s had been to combine the chair/CEO position in a "finance guy," an executive who came up through GM's estimable financial operations. But Bob Stempel, despite wide operational experience, remained a car guy, one of the few top executives at GM who could still tear down and fix one of the company's products. The board likely thought that he was just enough of an "outsider from the inside" to tear down and repair their ailing corporate colossus.

The designation of Bob Stempel as GM chairman-elect brought general rejoicing from those in the auto industry, who often have a weak spot for someone who actually knows about gear ratios. Even Ross Perot, by now safely past his GM interlude, gushed that "this is a terrific day for General Motors."[2] However, the out-

---

2. "Top Production Manager Picked to Head GM," *Washington Post*, April 4, 1990, p. C1.

side directors were concerned over Stempel's pick for a number two, Lloyd Reuss. Reuss was also a car guy, who had worked his way up through engineering and assembly positions to the top production job, that of North American operations. Two car guys in the two top slots disturbed some members of the board.

But the information sniffed out by Smale and others on the board was even worse. Reuss, though a sunny, can-do sort, seemed to have popped up like an auto-industry Forrest Gump at all the recent production disasters in GM history. In 1970 he was project engineer on the Chevy Vega. This car's seizure-prone aluminum engine and habit of showing rust while still on dealer lots almost ruined the Chevrolet nameplate. Reuss spearheaded a failed $2.5 billion automation program at Buick, and as production chief for the ill-fated 1988 GM-10 midsized car, dedicated each factory to building only one divisional model. When his guess on model sales proved wrong, there was no practical way to rejuggle the mix without spending millions. "Reuss's rise at GM was remarkable," wrote *Wall Street Journal* reporters Paul Ingrassia and Joseph White. "He had walked away unscathed from the scene of disasters that would have destroyed his career at almost any other company."[3]

The GM board thus resisted naming Reuss as Stempel's president. They preferred John "Jack" Smith. Smith was in charge of GM international operations and had proven pivotal in moving GM Europe from a money-losing sinkhole into a strong profit center. Better still, he was a finance guy. But Stempel insisted to the board that he needed to have his own team working under him, and ultimately the directors relented. However, Jack Smith was named to the board as vice chairman for international operations. And Reuss, though named GM president, was denied the usual added title of chief operating officer. The directors were making it clear that the Roger Smith days were over.

---

3. *Comeback,* Ingrassia and White, p. 165.

3

"The Market Will Save Us"

In July 1990, Roger Smith, in one of his last official acts as GM chairman, drove the first Saturn auto off the assembly line in Spring Hill, Tennessee. Almost literally, he then drove off into retirement, though he stayed on the GM board, where his presence irritated the outside directors. On August 1, 1990, Robert Stempel officially took over as chairman and CEO of General Motors Corporation. With his team in place and a willingness to make some major changes, he could look forward to almost a decade to leave his mark. But the next day, August 2, the forces of Iraqi dictator Saddam Hussein invaded Kuwait. The resultant oil shock sent fuel prices temporarily into the rafters and triggered a stock-market plunge. The U.S. economy, which for months had been slowing, tipped abruptly into a full-blown recession. Auto sales sagged.

General Motors now found itself in a fix that no amount of tricky bookkeeping could obscure. Chevy dealer orders in January 1991 were half the level of a year earlier. Steadily losing market share and profitability during the booming 1980s, GM was all the more vulnerable to a recession.

The board's outside directors soon made it clear to Robert Stempel that they would support him in taking bold measures to restructure the company, with an unspoken message that they *expected* him to take such measures. Early indications looked positive. In November 1990, Stempel cut a massive 111,000 units from fourth-quarter production and announced the closing of seven GM assembly plants for a restructuring charge of $2.1 billion. In February 1991 he cut the common stock dividend almost in half. Major cuts were also announced for GM's salaried staff, a move that many (even Ross Perot) had been urging for years. Lloyd Reuss led a planning effort for longer-term reorganization, a complex North American Vehicle Organization (NAVO) strategy. For a time it seemed that the radical housecleaning demanded for GM had come to pass.

But by the spring of 1991, the board found Stempel's ardor for change cooling. The Persian Gulf War had ended quickly and resoundingly, bringing the nation a spiritual lift. Most experts predicted that the current recession would thus be a brief one. Besides, Stempel brought a quirky humaneness to his job. He hesitated to make really major cuts, even if necessary, because he knew how much institutional and personal pain they would inflict. He agreed with the critics who had seen the massive GM reorganization of 1984 as a failure, and he had no desire to repeat the lesson. With the current cuts, and Reuss's NAVO plan, perhaps it would be wise to hunker down and wait out the storm. "The market will come back and save us" was one of Reuss's favorite aphorisms.

But two factors worked against this wait-and-see fatalism. The first was external and economic. The recession of 1990–92 was unusually pervasive, with a psychological staying power that lingered long after economic indicators should have headed up. People were hesitant to make major capital purchases—like autos. If they did, they were more likely to look at efficient, reliable cars from Japan, Chrysler's minivans, or Ford's Taurus. As if sales were not poor enough, GM had a problem with some of the customers who *were* buying. In 1992, almost three-quarters of a million GM car sales were to fleets, primarily car rental firms. These big buyers had the muscle to drive prices to below cost, but the immediate cash they offered had long proven a tempting lure.

A second problem for Stempel was internal and even more complex than national economics. John Smale and the other outside directors had begun caucusing on their own in the later days of Smith's tenure, and they continued these meetings after Stempel took over. At these chats, the directors valued their legal advisors. Ira Millstein gave them outside counsel on what institutional investors and analysts were saying, and Harry Pearce offered intelligence from the inside. As company losses grew more critical, Pearce and Smale found more people in the GM structure raising alarms over the company's course.

Finance, long the ultimate route to power in GM, had been

shuffled to the back of the room under car guys Stempel and Reuss. The two "saw each other as trustworthy colleagues in an organization where the insufferably arrogant bean counters had long lorded it over the car guys," according to Ingrassia and White.[1] But the bean counters knew how to fight back. Various sources in finance were uncovering truly scary numbers. Long-term debt was 35% of equity by 1991. Given GM's enormous equity, this indicated a huge debt load. The growing cash pinch was forcing the company to trim contributions to its already underfunded pension fund. Robert Stempel lacked the allies in finance that had long helped Roger Smith smooth over such shortfalls.

GM's product planners had their own concerns. Each of the major divisions had a planning staff to keep an eye on strategy, industry, and economic developments. Like finance, it was a stepping-stone post that helped move bright people along in the GM structure (indeed, executive team member Jack Smith had once served as head of worldwide product planning). After Reuss developed his NAVO plan, the various planning staffs took a long look at his "pyramid thing" with its consultant-speak medley of missions, visions, initiatives, and values—and were unimpressed. These planners formed a rump committee headed by GM truck division planner Mark Hogan and did some of their own number crunching. It was quickly apparent that even if the market did return to save GM and bring back its 40% market share, Stempel's efforts to bail out the company were too little too late. Over the summer of 1991 the group shaped a far more comprehensive strategy of reorganizations, plant closings, cost cuts, divestitures, and layoffs and built support among their top divisional executives. In October, the plan was pitched to Reuss, who shot it down none too happily. Aside from being an obvious no-confidence vote for his NAVO, he saw it as an admission of defeat for the grand old General Motors.

Meanwhile, John Smale was taking a deeper interest in GM's troubles. He had retired from his full-time duties as chief of Procter & Gamble in early 1990. Smale sat on only one other outside board, J. P. Morgan, where he served with Morgan CEO Dennis Weatherstone, also a GM director. For an underperforming CEO like Bob Stempel, an outside director with time on his hands could be a

---

1. *Comeback,* Paul Ingrassia and Joseph B. White, Simon & Schuster, 1994, p. 283.

dangerous thing. Shortly after Stempel's succession, Smale had formed the habit of dining with him on Sunday nights before the monthly board meetings, held on Mondays. What had started as pleasant, supportive catching up grew more pointed and serious over 1991 as Smale's concerns increased. Cash reserves were growing more critical—at the end of 1991's third quarter they stood at only half GM's usual cushion. What did Stempel plan to do? Essentially, Stempel told Smale and the other directors that he intended to steer a steady course. "Don't worry, the market will save us."

Indeed, the market did soon bring results, but it was the bond market, not the sales market, and the message was less than pleasing. In November 1991, Standard & Poors, alarmed by GM's deteriorating cash situation, placed the company's bonds on a credit watch. GM had long held an A1 bond rating and seemed almost as safe (and at times more so) than the U.S. government. A downgrade in its bond rating would threaten the ability of General Motors Acceptance Corporation, the financing division, to place cheap "commercial paper" debt. Given the enormous cash flow of a company such as GM, the result could be devastating. Wall Street scented blood, and GM's stock price plunged one and three-eighths in a single day.

The stock hit alone cut shareholder value by over $800 million. Ira Millstein no doubt let the board know how popular this made them with the institutional shareholders, who had long kept GM in their portfolios as a safety nest egg. The outsiders' group of Smale, Marriott, McLaughlin, Weatherstone, and Wyman (which now also included Edmund Pratt, retired chairman of Pfizer) in October met with Millstein to discuss board strategy for coping with the losses. Shareholders, at one time likely to sell their holdings if they lost faith in the company, by the early 1990s were more inclined to hold on—and sue the board for being asleep at the switch. Millstein, Smale, and the other directors chose to launch their own survey of the situation and of Reuss's turnabout strategy. The directors informed Stempel of their move, but he failed to read it as a warning signal.

The bond downgrade threat hastened action on the board study, and Smale increased his digging into the company. By early December 1991, when the group met just before the regular board meeting, they felt they had enough information and cause to act. At the December board session, the outsiders bluntly told Stempel that stronger responses to the crisis were needed. Stempel was supposed to be a change maker, and change was what the directors wanted. Micheline Maynard quotes an anonymous GM manager who met with Stempel after that meeting. "Stempel came back, and he was going nuts. He said we've got to have a plan to mollify the board, and make it look like we're taking decisive action."[2]

Despite such dubious commitment, Stempel soon delivered. On December 18, he announced huge changes. GM would close 21 factories over the next four years, cut 74,000 workers, and take a $2.8 billion restructuring charge. GM's North American capacity would be cut by one-fifth.

The move bought Stempel some time with his directors but also stirred fresh concerns. Stempel had hastily rushed ahead with the cuts, not informing the board until the night before the announcement. Worse, he had avoided actually naming any of the plants to be closed. Though he later said that he didn't want to announce specific plant closings just days before Christmas, his hesitation only worsened the anxiety. Now workers at *all* GM plants could spend the holidays worrying about whether the Grinch would soon strike. And some of the plants to be closed would no doubt be the very high-tech showcases Roger Smith had built at great expense a few years earlier.

And where was Smith during this upheaval? Though retired, he was still a member of the GM board. In most other corporations, the emeritus chair would hold a position of power on the board, often able to act as the lead director. This informal dean, liaison, and power center on the board acts as a counterbalance to the CEO/chair. But Roger Smith had burned up most of his boardroom goodwill even before he retired. As it became clear that saving the corporation would sweep away much of his legacy, Smith grew increasingly isolated among the outside directors. This left a vacuum in the boardroom for an informal leader. Someone who had CEO experience, was widely respected in the business world, and, given GM's straits, had time for a hands-on commitment. Someone like John Smale.

In December, the outside directors, led by Tom Wyman and counseled by Ira Millstein, began lobbying Smale to undertake a more formal fact-finding mission within the company. If his earlier

---

2. *Collision Course,* Micheline Maynard, Birch Lane, 1995, p. 112.

poking about had been a gentle nudge to Robert Stempel, this was intended to be a shot across the bow. A conference call of outside directors was held in January 1992, just before the regular board meeting. Wyman feared that the figures the board received were so untrustworthy, and GM's situation so dire, that the board should deputize Smale to conduct a formal corporate review. In the same call, Millstein noted that such a review was a vital part of the board's fiduciary duties. Smale, though concerned over events, was also a former CEO. He hesitated to make such a move upon Stempel's turf without unanimous support of the board. Wyman and Millstein soon gained this support, and the GM board suddenly shifted from watchers to doers.

4

John Smale Wants Answers

The January 1992 meeting of GM's full board was noteworthy for two reasons. First, the chairman/CEO was absent. Robert Stempel had joined (or as he saw it, was dragooned into) President George Bush's trade mission to Japan. Stempel and the other chiefs of the big three automakers were in Japan to encourage the locals to buy more U.S. cars. The locals asked why the U.S. automakers put their steering wheels on the wrong side and why their CEOs earned so much. President Bush, suffering from the flu, highlighted a state dinner by vomiting on the Japanese prime minister.

Things were going little better at home. The second noteworthy aspect of the GM board meeting was that a crucial resolution was passed by the board. The outside directors, with Ira Millstein present, voted to deputize John Smale to act as the board's agent in dealing with the chairman and to compile information on the state of the company. Upon Stempel's return to the United States, Ira Millstein met him at the Detroit Metro Airport to brief the CEO on what had transpired. Stempel seemed to listen carefully to the lawyer's report, but at its conclusion, he asked Millstein what the directors were really seeking. Millstein says he was stunned by this question and told Stempel as diplomatically as any attorney could that the directors sought a radical shake-up. Stempel seemed impassive, an ominous sign all around.

In February 1992, Stempel's management team dropped the other shoe on the plant closings, announcing which factories would be shuttered. Stempel also revealed a plan to consolidate North American auto production into an omnibus North American Operations system. At any other time, such a move would have been hailed as a major breakthrough, but governance events at GM were taking on a life of their own. John Smale had begun his fact-finding in earnest and was shocked to find the differences between what the board was hearing and reality. North American losses for 1991 came to over $12 billion, bloodletting that even the world's biggest company could not long bear. Smale was studying analysts' reports, studies on quality and finances, and projections, and he was interviewing top people. In a round of discussions with the company's upper executives, he soon found they could be divided into two groups: Stempel's guys and everyone else.

Stempel's loyalists, who were also loyalists to Reuss, talked up the NAVO plan, counseled patience, and put a smiley face on the future. Smale found their adherence to the official line so uniformly well practiced as to be predictable. The "everyone else" segment of top management was far more disturbing. Many of the executives seemed almost eager to spill their troubles to someone, and a few even wanted to know why the board hadn't acted earlier. Their criticisms were specific, particularly regarding Reuss and financial figures, and were very consistent. Finally, these insiders were strikingly gloomy. Smale polled them on the likelihood that GM would face a financial crisis within the next year. He hoped to hear that such an emergency was unlikely. Instead, he was hearing that the chances were better than even.

Shaken, Smale presented his findings to the board on March 22. The outside directors convened at the GM building in New York—at Ira Millstein's offices five floors above their usual teakwood retreat. Events would prove the location a fitting one.

Smale offered the board factual support for many of the criticisms he had heard for months. GM was measurably the least efficient automaker in the United States. Its production capability far outstripped current demand or any realistic future demand. GM was the slowest in the market at developing new products. There was little confidence in Bob Stempel's reorganization plan—and great concern that a fiscal collapse would occur before the end of 1992. The directors could no doubt imagine investors and the media asking, "Where was the board?"

The outside directors delegated Smale to meet with Stempel as soon as possible to share their findings and to solicit his response. Smale asked Stempel to meet him in the offices Smale retained at Procter & Gamble in Cincinnati, perhaps a psychological move to take the chairman off his familiar turf. On March 25, Smale offered Stempel the board's blunt assessment of current turnaround efforts: "We've concluded it won't work."[1] The board wanted major changes from Stempel in a hurry, starting with the replacement of Lloyd Reuss. Stempel was given three days to digest the board findings and frame a response. He would meet with the board on the 28th in Chicago to state his case. Smale was still trying to buck up the chairman, frankly warning him that the meeting would be tough, but would also be his chance to prove himself the change maker the company needed. Unspoken, and likely unperceived, was the threat that it would be his last chance.

The meeting was held at the Chicago O'Hare Marriott (standard procedure, since the Marriott chairman was also a GM director). It included all the board's outside members, as well as the ubiquitous Ira Millstein. Millstein had given the directors a sort of governance boot camp over the past few months. He was opening them up to the new demands on boards, alternately supporting them and scaring them to take a firmer hand. But at the March 28 meeting, he let the directors run the show. Smale again gave the report of his findings. Stempel then offered his response.

If the directors expected Robert Stempel to suddenly get religion, they were disappointed. He responded with most of the same points he had been making for months. The recession was a toughie. The turnaround plan was in place. The board must be patient and allow him and his team to do their work.

The core of active outside directors, especially Smale and Wyman, were frustrated. Even some of the fence-sitters, such as the Reverend Leon Sullivan, the board's social conscience since he was named a director in 1971, now lost faith in Stempel. The directors convened to review their options and then gave Stempel their decision. Lloyd Reuss was out as president, to be replaced by Jack Smith. Robert O'Connell, Stempel's finance chief, was also out, blamed for many of the bad numbers. Also to be reassigned were EDS Vice Chairman Robert Schultz and Executive Vice President F. Alan Smith. And, in the most shocking change of all, the directors wanted Stempel to step down as chairman of the GM board's executive committee, essentially the management/board nerve center

---

1. *Comeback,* Paul Ingrassia and Joseph B. White, Simon & Schuster, 1994, p. 295.

and nexus. John Smale would take over as chairman, serving as "lead director," a position long discussed by governance thinkers such as Millstein and academic writer Jay Lorsch. The decisions would be announced at their next formal board meeting, at EDS headquarters in Dallas, on April 6.

Stempel fought a rearguard action after returning to Detroit, trying to save the jobs of his crew, particularly Reuss. He leaked word to his management committee of what the board was planning and complained of the board's panic and unreasonableness. On April 5, the night before the board meeting, Stempel, Millstein, and the outside directors met over dinner, and Stempel pleaded for the jobs of Reuss and O'Connell. Perhaps the board was having second thoughts over their resolution; perhaps Stempel made some valid points. At any rate, in a final session that evening between Stempel, Smale, Millstein, Weatherstone, and Pratt, the board made a concession. Reuss would not be fired but would lose his board seat, and Jack Smith would still become president, as well as COO, the title denied Reuss two years earlier.

The next day, April 6, was a sad anticlimax for those in the know, especially for Reuss, Schultz and O'Connell. Ira Millstein didn't even stay in town for the conclusion but took an early flight back to New York. It was the board's job now. For the business world, however, the GM board coup was epochal, on par with the turmoil of recent years in the Soviet Union. "This is nothing short of a revolution," said auto writer and analyst Maryann Keller.[2] "After the stunning board coup on April 6, nothing will be the same again," enthused Alex Taylor III in *Fortune*.[3] Suddenly Jack Smith, an anonymous member of the GM team, was a business star, and the dour-looking Robert Stempel seemed a character of Shakespearean tragedy.

The GM Board of Directors, meanwhile, was finding it had gained celebrity status, and the board did not care for the honor. Ross Perot's "pet rocks" had overnight become the uneasy symbol for boardroom revolution. "The kind of directorial power over a company exhibited by Smale and his allies could become to business

---

2. "An Outside Director's Coup inside GM," Maryann Keller, *Washington Post*, April 12 1992, p. H1.

3. "The Road Ahead at General Motors," Alex Taylor III, *Fortune*, May 4, 1992, p. 94.

in the 1990s what hostile takeovers were in the 1980s," observed the *Washington Post*.[4] The board either didn't foresee the revolution they had launched or didn't want to see it. "The directors really didn't view this as that big of a deal at the time; they just thought they were doing their jobs," says a top GM executive.[5]

The outside directors, particularly Smale, were also anxious to avoid the appearance of any imperial ambitions. Almost immediately after the changes were announced, Smale hurried out a follow-up press release making clear that neither he nor any of the other directors sought a day-to-day role in running the company. Director Ann McLaughlin was quoted as saying the move wasn't "a one-two punch," with removing Stempel as the next step.[6] Unless, of course, that step became necessary.

---

4. "Outside Director's Coup," *Washington Post*, p. H1.
5. Author interview, November 1995.
6. *Comeback*, Ingrassia and White, p. 300.

5

"There Is No Worst-Case Plan. . . ."

Certainly the spring of 1992 brought signs of hope. The radical restructuring scheme suggested by GM's planners (the one rejected by Lloyd Reuss) was welcomed by Jack Smith and put into place with great speed. The separate divisional engineering groups were merged, over 10,000 central office workers were cut, and a Jack Smith protégé from Europe, Jose Ignacio Lopez, was brought in to cut $4 billion from GM purchasing contracts. In May, GM sold an offering of $2.2 billion in common stock, easing the cash crunch.

John Smale, despite his hands-off image, threw himself into his new role as head of the board's executive committee. He took control of the board's agenda and set up regular reporting schedules for Robert Stempel. Despite the obvious power shifts, Stempel remained the board's chairman and the GM CEO, so his involvement was crucial for a turnaround. But the events of April actually seemed to make him more passive and uninvolved. As the spring and summer passed, Smale reported to the board that Jack Smith was making great progress. Stempel, however, was withdrawn and unresponsive. The outside directors were again growing angry at him, feeling that he had squandered the shock effect of the April turmoil. Possibly Stempel had been right in pleading for his subordinates' jobs, viewing himself and them as a package deal. By stripping Reuss and O'Connell of their jobs, the board may not have liberated Robert Stempel as much as broken his legs.

Smale needed Stempel as his liaison to management but found him increasingly intractable. For inside work, Smale made more use of Legal Department Chief Harry Pearce. Pearce's star was rising rapidly in the GM structure. He had taken over operation of the EDS division from Robert Schultz in April. Soon, he would become, in the words of Micheline Maynard, "the insider who is the link to GM's outside directors. . . . Pearce reports to Smith, but in reality he functions as Smale's man in GM's upper ranks."[1]

Smale would need a tough insider in the months ahead. The early signs of a turnaround were soon washed away by a fresh flood of bad news. Leaders of United Automobile Workers, still angry about Stempel's handling of the plant closing schedule, triggered a September strike at the Lordstown, Ohio, stamping plant. Parts from Lordstown were needed throughout the GM system, so the effect quickly rippled through other plants. Negotiators soon settled with the local but gave costly concessions on keeping the plant open. Stempel was responsible for labor negotiations, and the board read his actions as a message to the UAW that strikes were an effective tool to sabotage plant closings.

And financial market woes were again at the door. GM was still burning cash away too fast, and the Lordstown settlement told the markets that GM's biggest fixed cost, labor, was going to stay high. Less than a year after the last bond-rating crisis, a new one flared up, with Moody's Investors Service threatening to downgrade the status of GM debt. Future pension fund liabilities also looked scarier than Roger Smith's once rosy presumptions. GM's treasurer, Harrison Golden, prepared a report for management on the looming financial threats facing the corporation. Before Stempel could see it, though, someone leaked the report to the board's outside directors.

If the board was still capable of shock after the past year, it was shocked now. Smale especially must have been irked to find that, with all the dirt he had uncovered, there were still major surprises such as these hidden away. The items were discussed at an October 4 executive committee meeting, with Stempel absent. Labor costs, bond downgrades, pension liabilities. . . . The chill wind of possible bankruptcy swept through the room. Harry Pearce was dispatched to brief Stempel on the report, who then joined the meeting to give his reactions. What, Smale wanted to know, were Stempel's worst-

---

1. *Collision Course,* Micheline Maynard, Birch Lane, 1995, pp. 281–282.

case plans, should all these financial forebodings come to pass? According to Stempel, the directors were panicking again. He had no worst-case plan because one was not needed. It wasn't going to happen. "In that moment," wrote Ingrassia and White, "Bob Stempel sealed his fate."[2]

2. *Comeback*, Paul Ingrassia and Joseph B. White, Simon & Schuster, 1994, p. 308.

6

A CEO Coup

The next two weeks were busy ones. Smale commissioned outside director Dennis Weatherstone, CEO of GM investment banker J. P. Morgan, to work with Wyman and Anne Armstrong to develop a detailed internal financial analysis of GM. Ira Millstein's office also came back into action, working with Smale to contact and consult with the outside directors. Millstein's office helped draft changes in GM bylaws that would permit an outside director to serve as chair of the company. Smale and the board worked their inside contacts to build support, check loyalties, and find out the current status of key data and employees. By late 1992, the GM directors had a strong handle on the company's infrastructure. People committed to change were in key positions in finance, legal, planning, and production.

About this time, mid-October, rumors began appearing in the media. The *Washington Post*'s October 13 front-page headline read, "GM Board to Chairman: Stand Up to the UAW." The board was rankled with the way Stempel had folded on the Lordstown strike and wanted him to take a tougher stand "or risk losing his job."[1] Board discussions had been leaked by a source obviously on or near the board. If that weren't enough to bring down the beleaguered chairman, Stempel suffered a minor coronary attack while at a meeting in Washington and was hospitalized for two days. The board kept its counsel while Stempel received tests, and, improved, he left the hospital on October 15 and returned to Detroit.

---

1. "GM Board to Chairman: Stand Up to the UAW," *Washington Post*, October 13, 1992, p. A1.

On the front page of the *Washington Post* for October 21, the lead story was a piece on the 1992 presidential campaign, then at the endgame. It discussed how George Bush's re-election bid was entering terminal gloom. There was another bit of despair on the front page, however. "GM Chief Pressured to Resign," said the headline. Board sources were quoted as sending signals to Stempel that it was time to depart. The outside directors "want Chairman Robert C. Stempel to step down within the next month."[2]

Stempel, ill, alone, and isolated in his 14th-floor office in Detroit, made one last effort to assert control. He met with GM public relations aide Jim Crellin about drafting a statement for John Smale to release, a statement expressing the board's full support for its chairman. The next day the statement had been drafted and was about to be sent to Smale when the board's lead director again beat Stempel to the punch.

Smale was all too aware of the media speculation, but he was also aware of the board's responsibility. He worked with Ira Millstein to draft a media statement of his own, a masterpiece of lawyerly language that, although saying nothing in particular, managed to say everything. It was faxed to Stempel and then released to the media. In essence, it said that the board had taken no action on management changes at General Motors but would continue to reflect on how to best meet the company's leadership needs. "I'm not an English major," Stempel would later reflect, "but you could be a second grader and read that one."[3] After all the months of missed signals, lost opportunities, and miscommunications, Bob Stempel had finally gotten the message from his outside directors, loud and clear. On Friday, October 23, Stempel faxed a letter of resignation to John Smale. The following Monday, October 26, it was announced to the world.

The General Motors board had made history, though the board seemed no more comfortable with their status now than they had been in April. The day Stempel's resignation was announced, there was a meeting in New York to determine GM's new management team. The participants offered an interesting snapshot of the new power centers in GM: Smale, Jack Smith, Harry Pearce, and

---

2. "GM Chief Pressured to Resign," *Washington Post,* October 21, 1992, p. A1.
3. *Comeback,* Paul Ingrassia and Joseph B. White, Simon & Schuster, 1994, p. 312.

Ira Millstein. While Jack Smith would move up to the CEO's slot, it was decided to install Smale as outside chairman, a move that had been in the works before Stempel left. This "separate chair" position was another board innovation championed by Millstein and other board thinkers. It looked as if General Motors would become a test bed for governance reforms.

Certainly, Smale and the other directors were reaching for ideas in the wake of the revolution. An unnamed source told the *Washington Post*, "The board has bitten off more than it can chew, and now they're running around trying to get advisers to tell them what to do."[4] But this implies that the directors were amateurish in their actions. Events suggest otherwise. Although the GM board was obviously feeling its way through a new situation (and arguably took too long at it), the directors ultimately launched a coup with precision and purpose that would have done any South American junta proud. Moreover, the GM board had served as a role model to many other corporations facing sluggish results and hapless CEOs. "If GM could do it . . .?" would be a leading question asked in many boardrooms for months to come.

The General Motors board had shown that an American corporate board could act with strength and determination in dealing with management. But a look back at business history suggests that this new board power is not so new after all.

---

4. "GM Board Weighs Company's Future," *Washington Post*, October 31, 1992, p. C1.

7

Corporate Planks and "Lesser Commonwealths"

Certainly no one wants to wade through another history of business with merchant traders, joint-stock companies, and other first-term MBA trivia. But there is one historical anecdote on the corporate board that is simply too endearing to be ignored. In the earliest days of colonial business, the directors and the investors in a corporation were largely the same small group. This group would meet regularly down at the wharf, the countinghouse, or even under a convenient tree, usually without furniture enough for a proper, sit-down meeting. A board would be laid across some barrels to form a crude table, and this "board" came to be the symbol representing the assembled owners of an enterprise. If the business was feeling particularly hale, a few stools might be available for the members, but usually the group could afford only a single comfortable chair. This chair was reserved for the leader of the assembled squires, who had the privilege of sitting his businesslike self in it during meetings. This "chairman" was usually the largest investor and led the meeting.[1]

Thus, the heart of today's corporate governance came about through unwillingness to waste business assets on furniture.

These early, crude intimations of our present corporate form hint at another aspect of the first corporations, their essential rusticity and hands-on directness. The early explorers at the frontier of

---

1. *Corporate Governance,* Robert A. G. Monks and Nell Minow, Blackwell, 1995, p. 180.

Western business were experimenting with something very new, the concept of incorporation. The chartering of corporations traces its American roots to England. Monopoly powers of trade were granted to favored groups, typically for colonial trade or industries perceived as being in the national interest. The Hudson's Bay Company was perhaps the best known and retained a monopoly over fur trade within its territory. Other royal charterings created most of the original colonies. These charters inevitably included monopoly provisions favoring the Crown. For example, they might require that all raw materials be shipped back to England or that certain manufactured goods sold in the colonies be imported exclusively from the mother country. Not only were such restrictions imposed as a monopoly, they could be granted and withdrawn arbitrarily. Abuse by England of such privileges irritated the growing colonies and was a factor prompting the American Revolution. Indeed, the Declaration of Independence cites the Crown's "taking away our Charters" as one of the colonials' grounds for divorce.

The new American nation thus started life with a less than sympathetic attitude toward the concept of incorporation. Corporations were viewed, particularly by the more populist firebrands such as Thomas Paine, as synonymous with monopoly, avarice, and inhumanity. They were damned as artificial devices to extract wealth from a helpless yeomanry, and chartering was condemned as a corrupt devil's bargain between those with power and those with money.

Yet the corporate form, like another business device, usury, was begrudged as a necessary evil. The investments required to build a new nation required vast sums, with attendant risks. Individuals with the requisite bank accounts (not to mention taste for limitless personal liability) were few and far between. Alexander Hamilton was the new nation's earliest and most powerful advocate of the corporate form. In 1791, his proposal for a nationally chartered bank became the first Bank of the United States. In 1792, the fledgling institution helped divert a national financial panic and was viewed by Eastern financial interests as a success. But the bank's tight fiscal policies made it unpopular with Western interests, and its charter was allowed to expire in 1811.

Also in 1791, the busy Hamilton formed what author John Chamberlain cites as "probably the first true corporation in the

United States,"[2] the Society for Establishing Useful Manufactures. SUM, as it was called, was envisioned as a sort of new industrial city (indeed, it formed the nucleus of what would later be Paterson, New Jersey). It was also to have been something of an eighteenth-century conglomerate, manufacturing a bit of everything, from paper products to fabric to metal goods. The management structure of SUM was likewise progressive with control vested in the hands of a panel of 13 corporate directors, which is in fact the average size of a 1990s corporate board. Hamilton and his partners raised some $625,000 in capital and conducted some modest manufacture. But lack of skilled managers and needed technology doomed the project, which failed in 1796. Hamilton's earlier corporate dream, the Bank of the United States, was rechartered in 1816, partly to help deal with public debt from the War of 1812. This second bank did well under the guidance of financier Nicholas Biddle. However, it ultimately came to grief after raising the ire of President Andrew Jackson, and again the national bank was allowed to lapse in 1836.

Hence, the first half century of our republic saw a cycle of large corporate ventures that failed, both the victims and the affirmation of populist fears. States became the only practical source for issuing corporate charters. However, the word "practical" is relative. States would charter a corporation only through a vote of the total state legislature, and only after strenuous debate. In most cases, charters were also granted only for specific projects and limited amounts of time. Even within these limits, incorporation could face further arbitrary blows. In the early 1800s, New Jersey declared that it had a right to assume state ownership of corporate properties, and several states banned banking corporations outright. This was seen as a wise populist defense against greedy capitalists until well into the nineteenth century, and some modern observers, such as authors Richard L. Grossman and Frank T. Adams, still view this as having been a golden age for citizen control of the corporate form.[3]

The reality was somewhat less rosy. Legislative attempts to hobble incorporation was an issue of power sharing. The corporation, with its distinct legal presence, certain shields from personal liability, institutional immortality, and power to raise funds, is es-

---

2. *The Enterprising Americans,* John Chamberlain, Harper & Row, 1962, p. 41.
3. *Taking Care of Business,* Richard L. Grossman and Frank T. Adams, Charter Ink, 1993.

sentially a little government of its own. As far back as 1651, Thomas Hobbes observed that corporations were like "many lesser commonwealths in the bowel of a greater."[4] Elected officials are notoriously averse to sharing power, especially when it comes to granting some of their more unique privileges. This made the concept of private incorporation in the United States an endless flash point for many of our more libertarian thinkers, who have been of two distinct minds on the concept. Some viewed the corporation as a valuable check on the powers of government, while others, as noted above, saw capitalist usurpation. The result was a business form that, despite its obvious potential, was for most of the century after the Revolution caught in an ideological tug-of-war.

But there were more prosaic reasons for state governments to keep incorporation tightly stoppered. Early nineteenth-century investors seeking to dig a canal, build a turnpike, or launch a bank had in each case to convince their state legislatures to pass a chartering law. This process was no easier or less time-consuming two centuries ago than today. It is no wonder that by 1800, only about 200 for-profit corporate charters had been granted nationwide.[5] The harsh, arbitrary limits on incorporation mirrored the very monopoly charters the Americans had rebelled against—and invited similar abuses.

Rather than assuring eloquent debate and close examination of each project, the Herculean effort of incorporation instead prompted generous use of bribes and sweetheart deals for those in power. The process of assuring close citizen oversight, in itself, "invited bribery and corruption," according to author Harvey H. Segal.[6] Indeed, there may have been motivation within government to limit the number of corporate charters precisely because of the value such an artificial ceiling would have on the market for palm greasing.

Such corruption of the chartering process inevitably made approvals dependent less on merit than on payoffs. Whether the corporation was sought for a useful, socially valuable project or a wasteful private enrichment scheme, legislators would lend their support

---

4. *Leviathan,* Thomas Hobbes, 1651, p. 218.
5. *Taking Care of Business,* Grossman and Adams.
6. *Corporate Makeover: The Reshaping of the American Economy,* Harvey H. Segal, Viking, 1989, pp. 5–6.

(and move bills along) when offered a suitably remunerative piece of the deal. Early incorporation rules resulted in something oddly like prohibition—criminalizing the entire process, lowering the standards for final products, and driving money underground (and out of state tax coffers).

In the years leading up to the Civil War, pressure to broaden the incorporation process rose. Aside from the less savory aspects of legislative chartering, it became apparent that allowing general incorporation would bring more fees and taxes into state treasuries. Connecticut passed the first general incorporation law in 1837, allowing incorporation "for any lawful purpose." More states followed suit, but the process of simplification was a lengthy one, with New York not allowing general incorporation until 1875 and Delaware not until 1899.

8

Exit the Owners, Enter the Managers

Largely forgotten in this shaping of the corporate form, right up to current scholarship, has been the role of the corporate board. Back under their prerevolutionary tree, sitting uncomfortably around their corporate plank, we found directors who could make the best possible claim to representing investors—they *were* the investors. At least some of those directors would have been the day-to-day managers of the concern as well. In Adam Smith's hypothetical pin factory, the owners would undoubtedly have been able to sit down and handle any stage of manufacturing as well as the laborers. As late as the 1840s, corporations were few and small, and they involved daily contact between owners, directors, and managers. Indeed, these titles usually all applied to the same handful of partners. "Owners managed and managers owned their enterprises," observes Alfred D. Chandler Jr.[1] Even in corporations with relatively dispersed ownership, investors comprised no more than a handful of people, most of whom lived within walking distance of the others. Shareholder meetings could then be the ultimate in direct democracy, the business equivalent of a New England town meeting. Those eighteenth-century gents sitting around their corporate plank would likely still have recognized their directorship roles a century later.

This is not to say that the role of the corporate director had become stagnant. Industrial growth and complexity, particularly in such fields as railroading and consumer goods, were changing the

---

1. *The Visible Hand: The Managerial Revolution in American Business,* Alfred D. Chandler Jr., Belknap, 1977, p. 37.

demands on boards by the time of the Civil War. As ownership dispersed, as industry became enormously larger and more complex, and as the capital demands of enterprises soared, a new specialization developed. Owners became investors, increasingly divorced from the work their money was performing. Managers became the people who specifically ran the company, from the shop floor all the way up to the executive office.

The railroads, beginning in the 1850s, blazed a path for this fragmentation. Cornelius Vanderbilt, Jay Gould, and Jim Fisk are remembered to this day for their freebooting capitalism in creating railroad industries. But it is unlikely any of these rail barons even knew how to stoke a boiler (indeed, Vanderbilt delayed moving into the railroad industry until he was in his 60s because he so disliked trains). The railroad industry required trained technocrats to invent new standards for engineering, scheduling, logistics, accounting, law, and administration. Further, with thousands of dispersed employees, railroads demanded increasing layers of organization, bringing many specialized levels between the money barons and the brakemen.

Other new industries followed the railroads' lead in the decades after the Civil War. Telegraphy, meatpacking, consumer machinery (sewing machines, reapers, etc.), and mass retailing went national. They called for specialized organization, marketing, and manufacturing skills quite different from those demanded by the local merchants of the past.

At the top of the industrial ladder, finance and ownership were likewise becoming more complex. Despite the stock hijinks of such capitalists as Fisk and Gould, it was difficult for one man or even a small group to float the huge sums needed to build or buy a railroad. This dispersal of ownership brought a boom in the trade of stock and other complex financial instruments. This in turn nurtured the growth of U.S. capital markets through powerful investment bankers, such as J. P. Morgan. Those industries that followed the railroads were able to exploit this growing capital structure. When high finance was combined with the great industrial consolidation and trust movement of the late 1800s, ownership became even more complex. It proved far more profitable to buy, sell, and manipulate company control than to fuss with building a better mousetrap (or sewing machine, or plow, etc.) The business of keeping the trains on time was left in the hands of the increasingly professional managers discussed previously.

The concept of the corporation, which in 1800 had been a limited, vaguely disreputable business form with only a handful of applications, had by 1900 become the premier type of business. The census that year found 40,743 corporations nationwide. Although this was less than 8% of all businesses in the United States in 1900, corporations produced 59.5% of the gross national product. The ability to raise large amounts of capital, to limit liabilities, and to shape a business entity with a life beyond a single owner had proven enormously versatile, an engine for infinite expansion.

And the board of directors became . . . Well, no one was quite sure where the board fit in. Perhaps this is the reason why the shelf of literature on corporate boards is so bare—directorship served as little more than an occasional legal title for those who owned the firm anyway. U.S. business history until well into this century treats the corporate board as an invisible topic, using the terms "director," "manager," and "owner" interchangeably. The turn-of-the-century corporate board more closely resembled modern Japanese or German boards, with their blend of inside employee directors and outside financial interests. Bankers, financiers, trust partners, and the top managers of the corporation would, when necessary for legal or strategic purposes, switch hats from these tasks to become directors of the firm. Their corporate roles had grown separate, but like "the boys down at the lodge," they could put on their funny hats once a month and work together. The board was a legal device for legitimizing actions already in the works, existing largely on paper to fill paperwork needs.

At first glance, this would suggest board impotence during this era. But, given such estimable membership, the nineteenth- and early-twentieth-century arrangement gave directors real muscle. The trusts and mergers of the era, prompted by the need to shape more efficient national markets, often left financiers or their proxies on the board in the role of arbiters. In 1902, Judge Elbert Gary, representing Morgan interests on the board of U.S. Steel, prodded rival farm implement firms McCormick and Deering to merge into the new International Harvester company. This matchmaking was not altruistic; it was done to assure continued trade with two major U.S. Steel customers. And in 1906, George W. Perkins, chairman of the new company but also a Morgan partner, compelled even tighter consolidation of the still-fractious firm.[2]

This money connection indicates the strength of the era's corporate boards, but also their weakness. Their powers were in large part derivative. While the modern outside director certainly derives legal power from the shareholders, the power of those who represented the financiers came about in the reverse manner. Modern directors, at least in theory, are elected to the board to represent the shareholders. But a century ago, the financier proxies would be on the scene to represent J. P. Moneybags et al. no matter what. Their membership on the board was only a device for legitimizing this oversight.

However, the continued rise of managerial power in the years leading to World War I eroded this board connection to owners and led to a slow shift in board composition. The founding families and financiers of such new giants as DuPont, Armour, Standard Oil, and General Electric were a vital boardroom presence in these companies' early years. But, at varying rates depending on the industry, the director/owner representatives drew in their horns, becoming less and less a boardroom force. John D. Rockefeller still held his seat on the Standard Oil board, but his personal involvement flagged with time. The executive committee of the board of General Electric included J. P. Morgan and Charles H. Coster, but both were heavily committed to deal making on other fronts and offered little personal involvement. Even I. E. DuPont de Nemours, which in the early years of this century was solidly owned, managed, and governed by the founding family, saw the number of DuPonts on its board slip to a minority by the 1930s.

Taking the place of these noted capitalists on the board, both in function and increasingly in number, were the professional managers. Berle and Means, in *The Modern Corporation and Private Property*, discuss how control of the corporation slowly, inevitably slips from the hands of owners in a model now called the "Berle/Means corporation."[3] Through such devices as proxy voting, set terms of office for directors, changes in dividend policy, and board authority to change the company's capital structure, power was fi-

---

2. Ibid., p. 409.
3. *The Modern Corporation and Private Property*, Adolf A. Berle and Gardiner Means, Harcourt, Brace, & World, 1932, 1968 (rev.).

nessed from the owners and centralized in the boardroom. Since the managers increasingly sat on the board, or dictated who did, management gained de facto control of the helm. Once again, the board was indeed a power center, but it was powerful as a tool, not as a distinct entity.

Berle and Means saw the above process as inevitable given our capitalist system. But the growth of very different board/management/owner structures in other Western democracies has caused some to have doubts. In his insightful work on corporate governance, *Strong Managers, Weak Owners,* Mark J. Roe details a perhaps unintentional government/business "conspiracy" to limit outside influence on U.S. corporate boards. As Roe notes, banks, insurers, mutual funds, and pension funds are the major boardroom players in countries such as Germany and Japan, and their U.S. counterparts likewise hold huge amounts of equity in the United States. In 1993, banks held assets of $4.9 trillion, insurers held $2.3 trillion, mutual funds held $1.2 trillion, and pension funds (public and private) held $3.4 trillion.

Such chunks of equity would seem to guarantee obeisance from the board, at the least, and more likely board seats for these 900-pound gorilla holders. Indeed, each of these entities has, at some point in our present century, either been in a position to exert serious corporate control or made a run at such power. However, in a process extending from the turn of the century up to the present, each of these owners has been stymied. Government regulation, infighting, or public concern has risen to hobble their boardroom powers. As Roe summarizes:

> Banks, the institution with the most money, have been barred from owning stock or operating nationally. Mutual funds generally cannot own control blocks. Insurers can put only a fragment of their investment portfolios into any one company's stock, and for most of this century, the big insurers were banned from owning any stock at all. Pension funds are less restricted, but they are fragmented; securities rules have made it hard for them to operate jointly to assert influence. Private pension funds are under management control; they are not yet ready for a palace revolution.[4]

---

4. *Strong Managers, Weak Owners,* Mark J. Roe, Princeton University Press, 1994, p. 21.

Finally, the populist forces that over the years have risen to keep these "big money" interests from influencing the boardroom would be even more inimical to a direct government presence on the board. Thus, every time an outside power has arisen with the strength to be a boardroom kingmaker, it has been in its turn knocked down. This leaves a vacuum in providing the board with a realistic outside source of clout, but it is a vacuum that management has proven quite willing to fill.

The 1929 stock market crash and the subsequent prolonged depression of the 1930s increased this insularity of corporate governance. The major sources of capital and ownership mentioned above faced, along with severe financial turmoil, new regulatory and legal restraints. Banks and insurers, in particular, were under a New Deal odium. Besides, they had more urgent problems than trying to gain seats on corporate boards. The major reform laws of the time, the Securities Act of 1933 and the Securities Exchange Act of 1934, placed their most serious restraints on sources of finance, and among the stated aims of these laws was to encourage broad, yet unintrusive equity ownership.

The Roosevelt administration brought its reform efforts into the boardroom as well. The 1933 and 1934 acts ended some of the more high-flying stock escapades but also brought stability and confidence back to the financial markets. National Recovery Administration mandates and efforts to boost organized labor were more divisive, however. Business groups and the administration fought to a draw on the more radical provisions of the NRA, but union power rose greatly by the end of the 1930s and became a new factor in governance.

Otherwise, corporations were largely left to govern themselves during the difficult depression years. Managers were forced to become more productive and innovative for basic business survival. They pushed and expanded the concepts of scientific management, created modern marketing techniques, and launched new industries, such as chemicals, electronics, broadcasting, and aviation.

The Second World War imposed a number of turbulent factors on corporate governance, but most were outside the power of the board. Massive conversion to military production plus shortages and directives affecting all aspects of the business were day-to-day management headaches. Boards could offer some longer-range perspectives though. Board insight was useful on such topics as implementing postwar reconversion, protection of public brand images when civilian products were in short supply, and government relations.

The war effort allowed the Roosevelt administration to reach more deeply into corporate America than the New Dealers could have dreamt possible during the NRA days. However, the administration had learned a few lessons on working with big business during the NRA battles, the foremost being that it was wiser to co-opt business than to fight with it. This, combined with distracting intragovernment squabbles between the military and Roosevelt's New Dealers, left business to take a leading role in the war production effort. General Electric President Charles E. Wilson took a leave of absence to administer the War Production Board, and many other top executives followed his lead. The speed and scope of wartime change exposed the state that corporate governance had fallen into by the midcentury mark—the board existed to approve what management was already doing.

9

The Walnut-Paneled Wonderland

The modern era of corporate governance truly came into its own in the years after 1945. Most of the planet was either trying to rebuild from the ashes of war or was still struggling out of colonial or third-world status. The United States, unbombed, suddenly rich, and confident, offered a corporate model that seemed unbeatable. The postwar corporate board likewise seemed a paradigm for success, even if it did remain a subsidiary of management. Certainly the members who had achieved board membership felt assured of their status as members of the elite. "Board meetings have a pomp and circumstance appropriate to the occasion and the class. The walnut-paneled rooms, the gray flannel suits, the boned-and-polished shoes, the good cigars, the deep rugs, murmurous acolytes and courtiers . . ." Earl Latham observed in 1959.[1]

This walnut-paneled aristocracy remained a fairly stable world from the end of the war until well into the 1970s—and an insular world, too. Loading up on inside directors was accepted practice for most of the postwar era. According to Stanley Vance, over 60% of large industrials had a majority of inside directors in 1950. This proportion was virtually unchanged 13 years later at slightly over 59%.[2] However, Conference Board surveys of the era found the percentage of insiders somewhat lower, with a steadily increasing level of outside representation. Still, half of the directors on top corporate boards were commonly either current or former employ-

---

1. *The Corporation in Modern Society,* Earl Latham (contrib.), Harvard University Press, 1960, pp. 224–225.
2. *Boards of Directors,* Stanley C. Vance, University of Oregon Press, 1964, p. 19.

ees until the early 1960s. Typically these insiders were the CEO/ president, the COO, the treasurer, executive vice presidents, divisional vice presidents, and perhaps some general managers. Although there was mild debate on the wisdom of majority inside boards, Vance could write as late as 1964 that evidence supporting the value of outsiders on corporate boards was "fragmentary, or even completely lacking."[3] Indeed, Standard Oil of New Jersey (later Exxon) would not add its first true outside director until 1966.

The symbolic status of board membership, both for insiders and outsiders, was such that board compensation was considered a trifling matter for decades. From the late 1800s until well into the 1900s, outside investors considered their board service a matter of looking after their assets. Such basic housekeeping was thought no more deserving of remuneration than balancing one's own checkbook. Still, there was a tradition of lightly compensating directors, particularly outsiders, for their time. National City Bank, precursor of today's CitiBank, placed a $20 gold piece at each director's spot around the board table (directors in attendance divvied up any coins left by no-shows). By 1961, the average meeting fee was still only $200.[4] Payment of annual retainers for board service remained uncommon until the 1930s, and as late as 1950 retainers were offered at only about 20% of major corporations.[5] Board benefits for outside directors were unheard of until the 1960s. As today, there was scholarly debate about director compensation, but the issue was whether board pay was too *low* to attract quality people.

In the 1966 book *The Corporate Director* (coauthored by later quality guru Joseph Juran), a chapter on board recruitment could be safely titled "Searching for the Man" without fear of gender conflicts.[6] Boards definitely sought only qualified *males* to fill outside director slots, and white males at that. The number of women and minorities on postwar corporate boards was so minute that statistics on their presence were not even noted until the mid-1970s.

---

3. Ibid., p. 7.

4. *Corporate Directorship Practices,* National Industrial Conference Board, Study #103, 1962, p. 31.

5. *The Corporate Director,* J. M. Juran and J. Keith Louden, American Management Association, 1966, p. 225.

6. Ibid., p. 204.

In 1975, Johnson Publishing Company founder John H. Johnson reflected that "ten years ago . . . there were no blacks on the boards of directors among the Fortune 500 U.S. corporations" (and in the year he wrote, there were still fewer than 100).[7] Also in 1975, the Conference Board pondered that "there appears to be some ambiguity about the role of these new directorial types."[8] For decades, that walnut-paneled, white male boardroom remained sacrosanct.

But even within these diversity constraints, deciding who would join the board of a major postwar corporation was no simple matter. The naming of inside directors to the board was most often a functional or career step. As a rule, the head of an acquired firm would join the board as part of the deal. More common was the naming of top employees, with board election a mark of having arrived within the company; "just one more way of providing a distinguishing symbol—like a key to the washroom," Myles Mace quoted an anonymous corporate president.[9] Director status was an internal reward and morale builder, as well as a method of noting those who were on the inside track toward the CEO's chair. It also connoted membership on the CEO's team—and CEOs found it soothing to meet with their inside director team before the general board meeting to assure that no one would spring any surprises.

Such surprises would not be good form at the board meeting, where a smooth flow of scheduled agenda items was highly valued. After a good luncheon, the meeting would begin with a review of the last meeting's minutes, followed by an operational review, divisional reports, presentations by company staff, financial reviews, and approval of new capital projects. While the board may have been free to doze, the staff presentations were high-pressure, make-or-break opportunities for executives. They were worthy of great investments of man-hours, dollars, and personal lives. One such board presentation, by Ford Motor Company Whiz Kid Jack Reith in 1955, was considered an all-time corporate tour de force. Reith gave the Ford Board of Directors (which included only two outsiders at

---

7. *The Corporate Director: New Roles, New Responsibilities,* John H. Johnson (contrib.), Cahners Books, 1975, p. 25.
8. *Corporate Directorship Practices,* Jeremy Bacon and James K. Brown, Conference Board, 1975, p. 43.
9. *Directors: Myth and Reality,* Myles L. Mace, Harvard Business School, 1971, p. 113.

the time) a powerful several-hour presentation to pitch a major restructuring plan. The spectacle included brilliant, well-rehearsed rhetoric, 50 hand-lettered display charts, and exhaustively researched figures, all proving the logic, indeed, the urgency, of the plan. The board was sold and unanimously approved the restructuring, which would launch a whole new company nameplate—Edsel.[10]

"Typically, few if any questions are asked by outside directors, and rarely are questions asked by insiders," recalls Mace.[11] Outside directors were unlikely to spring any such questions, especially after their good luncheon, because some of them may well have been dozing. In 1950, a study of the outside directors of 75 large corporations found 57% were over 60 years old,[12] and until the late 1950s, age limits for outside directors were rare. By 1961, the Conference Board found only 23% of its manufacturing company respondents had any form of board retirement policy (although adoption of such policies increased rapidly over the following decade).[13] Directors in their 80s and even 90s were accepted boardroom fixtures (though presumably they were regularly dusted). General Motors for many years retained its founders on the board with faithfulness such as the Chinese Communist Party shows to surviving "Long Marchers." Charles S. Mott served on the GM board for almost 60 years, and Alfred Sloan, who started running GM in 1923, was still a director in the mid-1960s. Board terms typically ran one year, but re-election of the entire board slate was as certain as the sunrise. Barring major career changes or legal improprieties, outside director tenure lasted until death or until the director chose to retire.

From the 1940s until the 1970s, such eternal board election could not seriously harm the value of the board because value was measured less by the director's contribution than by his status. Even international corporations tended to stick with prominent names from their hometown area, although with New York City still the headquarters for many corporations, star names within this range

10. *The Whiz Kids,* John A. Byrne, Doubleday, 1993, p. 226.
11. *Directors: Myth and Reality,* Mace, p. 12.
12. *The Scientific Appraisal of Management,* Jackson Martindell, Harper, 1950, p. 11f.
13. *Corporate Directorship Practices,* Bacon and Brown, p. 49.

could be quite extensive. Then as now, active CEOs of other firms were the most prized board candidates, especially if they brought the proper social connections, family lineage, or school backgrounds. Prestige was sought among director candidates both to present a "trophy board" to the world and to assure that the director would gain the respect of his fellows. When the youth of the 1960s rebelled against the Establishment, they could find its best personification on corporate boards. "Regionally, each area has its elite," a director of the era told Mace. "Sometimes many will in fact be members of the same golf or social club."[14] This intimacy also helped in cases where CEOs sat on each other's boards, encouraging a gentleman's agreement not to raise unpleasant issues.

As final assurance that director candidates would be both "our kind of people" and compatible with the executive team, board nominations almost always came from the CEO. Mace quoted two CEOs who *started* their descriptions of the board search process with, "I select the new board members . . ." and "Once I have decided on the man who should be our new board member . . ."[15] When the nomination process began with the CEO telling the board who he wanted, there was little more to do than vote "aye" and welcome the new man to the team. The idea of a board nominating committee to handle searches was largely unknown until the 1960s.

Status, connections, CEO experience, unwillingness to ask awkward questions—directors until the 1970s required these qualities for their portfolios. This should not imply that these directors were uniformly clueless nonentities. No doubt most of these postwar directors were indeed savvy, well-connected people, intelligent and perceptive enough to have attained substantial positions in the business world. However, the busy careers of many outside directors meant that they were unlikely to pry deeply into the workings of the company—or in some cases, even to open their meeting envelopes. Aside from the board meetings, they spent little time on company business. Committees of the board, beyond an executive committee, were uncommon until the 1960s. Such committees that did exist were often either narrowly focused (executive compensation

---

14. *Directors: Myth and Reality*, Mace, p. 89.
15. Ibid., p. 95.

and stock committees) or ill-defined ("policy" or "appropriations" committees).

Board pay was small enough to prevent director dependence on board service, but by the same token, gave them little investment in the company, either psychological or financial. Virtually no company required that directors own any of the firm's stock, and board pay in shares was unthinkable. However, a mid-1960s board writer granted that "it is traditional that a director purchase at least a few shares as a means of displaying interest in the company."[16] Noblesse oblige.

Orientation or education programs for directors were likewise haphazard. Formal outside training programs for board members at the business school or professional association level were virtually nil. Orientation could consist of little more than giving novice directors the past few years' annual reports. The status of board membership did not translate into any attention or study among business schools and major consulting firms. Especially among more progressive business thinkers, U.S. corporate boards were sniffed at as a symptom of everything wrong with corporations. As late as 1973, *Economics* by Paul A. Samuelson, the bible of most postwar business graduates, made only a single mention of corporate boards in all of its authoritative bulk. And this was a less-than-hearty endorsement that "it would be going too far to say that most boards of directors act simply as rubber stamps."[17] Students thus graduated and entered the business world knowing little about how governance worked, and being even less impressed. In a 1994 interview in the *Corporate Board* magazine, management guru Tom Peters was uncharacteristically at a loss for words on the subject of board excellence, finally confessing that during his graduate years, "I doubt we spent three seconds studying boards."[18]

Inside the boardroom, scholarship and standards were likewise unexamined. Beyond the basic legal duties of care and loyalty (both of which courts of the era interpreted broadly), directors were on their own. These ad hoc aspects of governance resulted in wide variations in board practice—and board quality. Boards were not

---

16. *The Board of Directors and Effective Management*, Harold Koontz, McGraw-Hill, 1967, p. 145.

17. *Economics* (9th ed.), Paul A. Samuelson, McGraw-Hill, 1973, p. 114.

18. Peters interview, *Corporate Board*, September/October 1994, p. 32.

expected to regularly evaluate themselves, and as for evaluating the CEO, well . . .

There remained a few checks on the boardroom power of management and specifically the CEO. The combined CEO/chair position, the norm in modern corporations, was less common in the immediate postwar years. Indeed, there was a good deal of flux between what constituted a "chair," a "CEO," and a "president" (the latter two have tended to merge into a single CEO title over the decades). However, a 1962 study found that of 206 corporations, only 22% combined the title of CEO and board chair in one position.[19] This would suggest that CEOs often had a watchful eye from the board monitoring their performance. However, this division falls apart on closer inspection. The combined position was much more common at large corporations, which have tended to be trendsetters in management techniques. Further, the idea of even *naming* a distinct, permanent chair was not that widely observed—the same study found that only 39% of board charters required election of a chair at all. Finally, when a formal, separate chair existed, he would often be the former CEO emeritus, on his way "up and out." In these cases, the person elected to serve as a board check on management power was a lame duck manager himself.

Despite all the factors that tended to soothe the CEO's boardroom nerves, occasional ringers or "irrational" directors might still sneak in. In 1966, Juran and Louden offered advice for the CEO having to deal with "interference" by a director engaged in "discussion of operations without the prior knowledge or the prior arrangement of the CEO." By "go[ing] around the CEO for bootleg information," this boardroom "culprit" is at best "an irritation to the CEO." Steps up to and including a board policy resolution are suggested for dealing with the "irrational, or nosy, or irritating" director.[20]

The postwar U.S. corporate board in many ways mirrored postwar U.S. business management. Both stood at the helm during a time of phenomenal growth and prosperity. Between the years 1950 and 1970, the U.S. Gross National Product more than tripled, soaring from $285 billion to $977 billion, and by the next year

---

19. *The Board of Directors,* Koontz, p. 185.
20. *The Corporate Director,* Juran and Louden, pp. 294–297.

topped the trillion-dollar mark.[21] While much of this growth is credited to the old-line corporations, the postwar period also saw great entrepreneurial success. Such companies as IBM, Litton, Hewlett-Packard, Xerox, and Texas Instruments either were founded or came into their own after the war. However, as their growth soared, they tended to pass within years through the same entrepreneurial to managerial-based boardroom evolution that had taken the old giants decades. In 1960, Xerox President Joe Wilson persuaded his board to plunge into a risky stock offering to support the huge expenses of building and launching the 914 Copier, the first practical photocopier. Only 16 years later, Xerox had an opportunity to launch what could have been the first true personal computer, but the company rejected the idea because it was expensive, risky, and had nothing to do with photocopiers.[22]

But prosperity tends to affirm itself. From 1945 to 1969, the United States experienced only the mildest of recessions. Our economic system and its managers seemed unstoppable. And a corporate board that served only as a thin buffer between anonymous, quiet shareholders and the managers who ran the show seemed ideal.

---

21. *The World Almanac,* 1974 ed., p. 85.
22. *Fumbling the Future,* Douglas K. Smith and Robert C. Alexander, William Morrow, 1988.

10

The Return of Massive Shareholders

In a sense, the power of U.S. corporate boards had always followed the money trail. Board power rested in the financiers and founding families early in this century. Later, as U.S. managers rode a wave of breathtaking postwar prosperity, they consolidated their hold on the boardroom. True, these managers were not owners (indeed, most owned little equity in their corporations), but they were making the money, and truckloads of it. U.S. pretax corporate profits hit almost $85 billion in 1969. The managers and the boardrooms they operated were firmly in command.

However, by the late 1960s, money was also starting to pop up in some odd new venues. Stock ownership, like election to a board of directors, had for decades been limited to a fairly small circle of intimates. In the old days, as noted, equity in corporations had been held by a limited number of major financiers. Stock ownership boomed to a broader group of investors in the teens and twenties, a factor in weakening the boardroom grip of the "money men." But the 1929 stock market crash had brought this expansion of ownership to a tumbling halt, and the days when every bellboy and secretary owned a few shares passed as well. Those who still had a taste for finance usually stuck with bonds and other forms of debt, leaving the stock exchanges incredibly quiet by modern standards. In 1941, total New York Stock Exchange trading volume for the *year* was only 125 million shares.[1] (In early 1995, five times that volume traded in a single day.) From the depression until well after World War II, equity ownership was limited to a golden median.

---

1. *The New Game on Wall Street*, Robert Sobel, John Wiley & Sons, 1987, p. 56.

Enough people held stock to keep big concentrations out of the boardroom, but distribution was not wide enough to make corporate governance everybody's business.

The sluggish volume and light trading of the time also suggest another pacifying factor for corporations—low volatility. The market reforms of the New Deal era, plus the general skittishness of the stockholding population, meant that people and institutions held their stocks for the long term. The dowager who for decades made her regular trip down to the bank safety deposit box to clip bond coupons might well have had her stock certificates gathering dust there also. Low interest rates, low inflation, and lingering preference for stable returns over quick profits made most investors *investors*, not speculators. The book *Barbarians at the Gate*, in tracing the history of R. J. Reynolds Tobacco Company, notes how founder R. J. Reynolds launched an early employee stock ownership program. Though resisted at first by Reynolds workers, the rich dividends made employees eager holders, and the stock was handed down from generation to generation. "Don't you ever sell that Reynolds stock!" was a popular admonition down in Winston-Salem.[2]

But even in the golden age of white-shoe corporate boards, forces were underway to shake up ownership. In the immediate postwar years, the need for increased capital investment prompted campaigns to broaden stock ownership. NYSE President Keith Funston in 1950 launched a publicity crusade urging the middle class to "Buy a Share of America." This was helpful, at least as far as most pretentious-sounding publicity campaigns go, but the real explosion of ownership came through less direct means. Federal policies of the same era began encouraging investment in pension programs by allowing the federal tax deduction of pension payments and expenses and granting tax deferral of the eventual plan receipts to the retirement years, when there are many tax advantages.

Another link in the chain was forged in the United Auto Workers' 1950 contract with General Motors. UAW pension holdings, previously kept safely in bonds and similar debt instruments, could now be invested in stock. The idea caught fire and, given how unionized the U.S. workforce was at the time, rapidly turned Joe

---

2. *Barbarians at the Gate,* Bryan Burrough and John Helyar, Harper & Row, 1990, p. 48.

Lunchbucket into Joe Investor. Pension fund holdings rose from less than $15 billion in 1951 to $150 billion in 1971[3] (and increased another tenfold to $1.5 trillion by 1993). A growing share of this money found its way into the stock market. Indeed, the enormous holdings of pension funds and other institutional investors led to the rise of block trading on the stock exchanges. Stock, traditionally traded in 100-share lots, was suddenly being bought and sold by the thousands and ten thousands. Although the size of their holdings made pension funds a bit unwieldy, they soon became an investor force impossible for boards to ignore.

Another indirect source for increased shareholding was the rise of mutual funds. Mutuals were small and limited in the prewar era, with only 68 funds holding assets of $400 million in 1940. But in the postwar world, mutual funds were seen as another good tool to ease the proletariat into stockholding. Through aggressive marketing, funds had amassed holdings of $1.2 trillion by 1993. Beyond the size of their holdings, mutual funds represent a constantly changing stock mix, a volatile, huge portfolio of fund managers in search of ever better yields. Moreover, like the pension funds, their firepower makes them a market leader. If a key fund loses faith in a stock, it can fulfill this opinion by sending a thumbs-down signal to other investors.

The wider world was also shaking up the boardroom by the 1970s. By the late 1960s, inflation had become troublesome, approaching 7% annually by 1970. Although the Nixon administration's wage and price controls suppressed inflation a bit in the early 1970s, by the middle of the decade it came roaring back, reaching an annual rate of 12.3% by 1974. Such inflation made many traditional investments seem like pikers and increased the value of returns in today's money as opposed to waiting for less valuable dollars down the road. Interest rates became likewise turbulent. Steady economic growth, viewed as a postwar American right, began to stagnate after 1973—helped in part by the shock of higher energy prices, the first of which occurred that year. The energy crisis in turn aggravated a rising U.S. trade deficit, particularly with Japan. The 1970s word "stagflation" was coined to term the combination of low economic growth, interest rates that touched 20%, and annual inflation of more than 10%. It brought the undoing of both the

---

3. *The New Game*, Sobel, p. 59.

Ford presidency in 1976 and the Carter administration four years later, and it proved just as intractable for business.

Investors and financial markets were thus ready for faster movement and more risk as the 1970s moved into the 1980s. The financial community delivered. The market for options expanded and diversified greatly; bonds, long considered the most ho-hum of investments, were rediscovered in new, fast-moving variable-interest forms. Even high-risk junk bonds became respectable. New York Stock Exchange commissions, firmly fixed since the dawn of time (or so it seemed), became negotiable in 1975. Electronic trading and information systems created a global village for financial trans-actions, warped such moves along at the speed of light, and caused avalanche effects through computer program trading.

The 1970s brought cynicism for most of our major institu-tions, and after the military and the presidency, business suffered in its turn. Business despoiled the environment, was racially insensitive, and had been asleep at the switch while the Japanese ate our lunch. And a few voices were also starting to question the role of corporate governance.

11

Clearing Out Deadwood on the Board

As the 1980s dawned, corporate boards found themselves in a business world that offered opportunities and dangers in equal measure. Corporate America was ripe for restructuring. Stock prices, despite all the new technical innovations, had been sluggish throughout the 1970s, a lingering effect of inflation and a second energy price shock in 1978–79. Tepid productivity increases approached their tenth anniversary, and the U.S. trade deficit continued to climb. From 1980 to 1982, the Big Three U.S. automakers lost a combined $8 billion,[1] with Chrysler spending the years 1978 to 1982 in a more or less continuous near-death experience. Tight money policies, begun late in the Carter administration, were slow in ending stagflation but did cause a recession in 1980.

Although there was no lack of explanations for the ongoing economic funk, U.S. management's co-opting and silencing of boards was a little-noted factor. Why did governance make a difference? Many of the ills business faced at the beginning of the 1980s were painfully caused by lack of management interest in shareholder value, the very province of the board. Diversification policies, going back to the 1950s, had long been very popular with top management. By shaping huge conglomerates, corporations could diversify, spread risk, and seek synergies among very different market segments. At least that was the thinking.

Tex Thornton's Litton company was the trendsetter in conglomerates. Thornton founded the company in 1953 by talking in-

---

1. *Power and Accountability,* Robert A. G. Monks and Nell Minow, Harper Business, 1991, p. 125.

ventor Charles Litton into selling his magnetron tube company to
Thornton rather than ITT because Tex had bigger plans for it. Indeed, he calmly predicted that he would build the new firm, with
$3 million in sales in 1953, into a $100 million company within five
years. By assembling a team of sharp managers, Thornton sent Litton on a flurry of growth through acquisition funded with company
stock and reached his $100 million goal in only four years. Litton
was perhaps the first conglomerate to intentionally shape itself as
such from inception. Though he started buying up small high-tech
electronics firms, Thornton reached ever further afield to office machines to shipyards to microwave ovens to frozen foods. In 1967
Litton stock was trading at $120 per share, almost 50 times earn-
ings.[2] Such a premium seemed justified because the continually
growing company was setting the standard for synergy, combining
dissimilar industries and making them more valuable than they
would be separately. The market for microwave ovens and frozen
food, for example, would surely grow hand in hand.

Litton had plenty of company in the postwar diversification
boom. Indeed, at times it seemed that corporations were competing
to see who could devour the most dissimilar companies. Well-en-
trenched CEOs, with little effective check from their boards, could
expand their empires, justify higher salaries, and show shareholders
impressive, fast growth, at least on paper. Shareholders were slow
to complain that such expansions offered few economies of scale,
took the company outside its area of expertise, and created little real
value. ITT, Gulf & Western, LTV, Textron, Beatrice, and other conglomerates grew into monuments to their CEO's hubris, outstrip-
ping the powers of management to profitably operate. Litton reported a sharp decline in profits for 1967, and in 1968 its stock
tanked. The 1970s were spent slimming down and rationalizing
Litton as well as other conglomerates, a word which rapidly came
to signify an unmanageable sprawl of industries.

By the beginning of the 1980s, the still swollen remains of
conglomerates continued to be a factor in the U.S. business scene.
Less splashy but much more common was a near cousin, the overreaching, hard-to-digest acquisition. Major corporations, while not
necessarily seeking conglomerate status, made large acquisitions that
in later years seemed hard to explain. Xerox bought Scientific Data

2. *The Whiz Kids,* John Byrne, Doubleday, 1993, p. 484.

Systems for $1 billion in 1969 then sold it for one-tenth the price six years later. In the 1970s, oil companies bursting with cash bought everything in sight, Mobil grabbing Montgomery Ward, Exxon purchasing Reliance. Then, in the 1980s, oil prices (and oil stocks) dropped. The overall slowing of economic growth and sharper foreign competition were among the factors leaving the United States with too much capacity in too many industries.

Inside the corporate boardroom, directors were also dealing with accumulated deadwood, with results that would prove just as dramatic. By the early 1980s, stirrings of independence were detectable on many boards. The economic downslide of the 1970s had caused a few spectacular business failures and near failures. Penn Central Railroad collapsed in 1970 in a very spectacular manner, almost causing a national financial crisis. Later investigation by the Securities and Exchange Commission and the U.S. House Banking Committee showed the Penn Central board to have been dismally out of the loop on the impending failure, which required a government bailout of $125 million. An SEC report on Penn Central noted that "throughout the entire Penn Central debacle, including the loss of many hundreds of millions of dollars by shareholders, the board had done nothing."[3] One of these sadder-but-wiser board members, Cabot Corporation Chairman Louis Cabot, later observed that a director "must be prepared to pass judgment on men who may be his personal friends."[4] By 1980, Lockheed, Rolls-Royce, Chrysler, and International Harvester had also found themselves among this unhappy elect of spectacular business basket cases. Penn Central, however, was precedent setting because a number of derivative lawsuits were filed against the board, and the SEC also sued several outside directors for damages in 1974.

This was an uncommon action at the time but part of a growing trend toward greater legal responsibility for directors. Certainly corporate directors had been found liable in the past for abuse of inside information or blatant dishonesty. Although most state codes spoke solemnly (if vaguely) about the director's fiduciary duty of care, duty of loyalty, and "prudent man" standards, case law gave directors wide latitude. As of the 1960s, the California code said no more than that directors "shall exercise their powers in good faith,

---

3. *The Fallen Colossus,* Robert Sobel, Weybright & Taley, 1977, p. 313.
4. *Managing the Managers,* Edward McSweeney, Harper & Row, 1978, p. 12.

with a view to the interests of the corporation," which could mean very much or very little and usually tended toward the latter. In an era when boards were considered impotent, this seemed reasonable. Courts had traditionally given boards the benefit of the doubt, even if their decisions (or indecisions) later proved disastrous, as long as no criminal or fraudulent intent could be proven.

But suddenly, boards were being sued for neglecting their duty of care—failing to ask questions of management, not keeping shareholders informed, and more specifically, letting the stock price crash. Activist courts and increasingly restive shareholders had begun raising the bar at the start of the 1970s. In a 1969 case, shareholders seemed to have a strong complaint against BarChris construction company, contending that the firm, which had suddenly declared bankruptcy several years earlier, had made false statements in its stock registration. A district court in New York delivered a shock by finding the company *and its directors* liable, concluding the board had failed to apply due diligence in reviewing financial statements. Decisions through the 1970s confirmed and expanded such standards. In the 1972 *Gould v. American Hawaiian Steamship Co.* case, a Delaware court found that negligent behavior by outside directors created liability. When Delaware courts speak, corporations listen.

The result of this liability shift was felt early. Directors' and officers' liability insurance claims rose 900% between 1966 and 1970 according to one insurer,[5] and such liability growth continued exponentially through the 1970s and into the 1980s. By the mid-1980s, there was a brief liability insurance crisis, with some corporations unable to buy coverage for their boards at any price or finding that their new policies were riddled with exemptions. Although actual money judgments against directors remained rare, the boardroom grapevine and the growing insurance pinch stoked board fears of liability out of proportion to the real danger. Directors of the early 1980s were increasingly concerned that they would be sued if they failed to do their jobs well.

Aside from the courts, other branches of government also sought to put their fingerprints on the board by the 1980s. Beside the corporate pratfalls noted above, there were splashy cases of bribery, illegal campaign contributions, and payoffs to foreign govern-

---

5. *Board Life*, Robert K. Mueller, AMACOM, 1974, p. 33.

ments in the 1970s. Government officials expressed their concern about corporate America all over the front pages, and new laws cracked down on foreign corrupt practices and campaign funding. In several key cases, government settlements reached directly into the boardroom in surprisingly blunt ways. Lockheed and Northrup, to settle charges of corporate bribery, agreed to set outside director quotas for their boards and assure all outsider membership for key committees. Such precedent-setting moves were a "federal usurpation of the rights of stockholders" to choose their own representatives, according to Stanley C. Vance.[6] In the 1974 *SEC v. Mattel* case, the toy maker was likewise ordered to make major changes in its board structure, including the addition of outsiders. The SEC further insisted that these new Mattel outside directors have no ties to the company—with the SEC defining what constituted "ties." Such court-mandated restructurings of boards were not isolated examples in the 1970s; Phillips Petroleum, McDonnell Douglas, Kaiser Steel and Playboy Enterprises were among dozens of corporations that reshaped their boards under the gavel. Not only were corporate decisions coming under legal fire—directors themselves were being carted out of the boardroom.

During the Carter administration in the late 1970s, such governmental rethinking of corporate boards was being carried to its next logical step. Perhaps it was too reactive for the government to wait until a company committed mischief before saying who should and should not serve on the board. Why not be proactive and have the federal government mandate board composition *before* trouble strikes? In the current deregulated age, this idea would seem like a Rush Limbaugh horror story, but two federal bills were introduced in 1980 that would have brought exactly such a federal takeover of corporate boards. The Protection of Shareholders' Rights Act was sponsored by Sen. Howard Metzenbaum (D-Ohio). It was prompted in part by the 1977 Senate hearings Metzenbaum had chaired on the role of shareholders in corporate governance. The Metzenbaum bill, which would apply to all corporations with more than $1 billion in assets, would have required a majority of outside directors on the board and mandated audit and nominating committees composed exclusively of outsiders. Direct shareholder nom-

---

6. *Corporate Leadership*, Stanley C. Vance, McGraw-Hill, 1983, p. 125.

ination of directors and cumulative voting would also have been compelled.

A 1980 House bill on governance, the Corporate Democracy Act, sought even more radical goals. It included six subsections to remake, in the words of the bill, "the internal structure of our large corporations." As in the Metzenbaum bill, boards would have to include a majority of outside directors, as well as independent audit and nomination committees. But the House bill, sponsored by Rep. Benjamin Rosenthal (D-New York), would have gone much further, limiting outside directors to seats on only two boards, setting up criminal penalties for failure to meet director duties of care and loyalty, and requiring "just cause" for the discharge of any employee. Corporations affected by the act would be federally chartered, an idea championed at the time by Ralph Nader. Annual report disclosure was to have been drastically expanded to include reviews of employee race and gender mix, pollution standards, and chemicals used in manufacturing processes. Two new board committees would be required, a "supervisory" committee to review governance policy and board pay, and a "public policy" committee to review corporate social policies. Plant closing notification standards were also included (an idea that, years later, would be revived and passed into law).

Both bills died during the 1980 session of Congress and, with Ronald Reagan in the White House, essentially disappeared off the threat board. But it must have been obvious in the boardrooms of major companies that there remained deep dissatisfaction with corporate governance among regulators and advocacy groups. The ideas packaged in these bills still had strong supporters within government, the sort who do not simply give up and invent new mischief. Corporate directors would have to make at least a few of these concerns for stricter governance standards their own.

Other issues were arising in boardrooms at the start of the roaring 1980s and were often expressed by new voices. A shift in boardroom composition had started in the 1970s, with the most obvious aspect that women and minorities were finally being named to board seats. The first case of a major company naming an African-American to its board occurred in 1965 when retailer W. T. Grant elected Asa T. Spaulding. The real breakthrough, however, came in 1971 when General Motors named the Reverend Leon Sullivan, a black civil rights leader, to its board. Sullivan proved an effective spark plug both for black board representation and for civil rights. During his tenure at GM he drafted the Sullivan Principles for corporate dealings with South Africa, and this code was widely adopted by other major companies. With GM leading the way, the paradigm quickly shifted, and the lily-white boardroom went from being the norm to being an embarrassment. By 1973, 9% of major corporations had at least one minority board member, and by 1982, this percentage had climbed to 23%.[7]

Women had never been entirely absent from the boardroom, but the handful who held seats before the 1970s were invariably the spouse, mother, or daughter of founders or major holders. Although this kept them rare, such status put them in a position to occasionally exert real power. In 1945, Clara Ford, wife of founder Henry Ford, held a good chunk of stock in their namesake company and a position on the board. She bluntly told her aging husband that unless their grandson, Henry Ford II, was named to head the company, she would dump her shares on the market, bringing a loss of corporate control the old man simply couldn't bear. He relented, naming "Hank the Deuce" president that September.

The status of women on corporate boards progressed steadily through the 1970s and, indeed, showed better penetration than that of minorities. The share of major boards with female directors increased from only 11% in 1973 to 27% in 1982.[8] These results sound impressive, but board progress by women and minority members was most common at the largest of Fortune 500 firms, with companies further down the scale lagging. Also, the above results show only the percentage of boards with *at least* one woman or minority member. The single token female and minority director has been common for so long as to become an issue itself in recent years. Women had a bit more luck at gaining multiple seats on a company's board (AT&T, Dow Jones, and Textron were examples by 1983[9]), but until recently, the typical boardroom formula remained, as executive pay gadfly Graef Crystal tartly observed, "ten friends of management, a woman and a black."[10]

---

7. "Board Composition and Governance: 1973–1982," Lester B. Korn, *Corporate Director (Board)*, March/April 1983, p. 17.
8. Ibid.
9. *Corporate Leadership,* Vance, p. 106.
10. Quoted in *Power and Accountability,* Monks and Minow, p. 77.

Despite their quantitative problems, women and minorities were becoming a *qualitative* factor in the boardroom by the early 1980s. A board with even one black or female director will have a slightly different focus and agenda than a board with none. And these breakthrough directors tended to be strong individuals who had already fought their way to prominence in the world despite discrimination—unlikely yes-men (or yes-women) for any CEO.

Less noted than this shift in complexion and gender, but ultimately more important, was the changing balance of inside and outside directors. Although actual practice varied widely (General Electric traditionally had an outsider-dominated board and Standard Oil exclusively insiders), the postwar norm on most major corporate boards was a majority of inside employee directors. From the 1920s to the 1960s, the average big-league corporate board consisted of slightly more than half insiders.[11] There was (and is to this day) endless debate over precisely how to define an insider versus an outsider. But, if the company's retired CEOs and other top executives are included with the "home team," as of the early 1960s, directors in some way tied into management still held sway. Yet 20 years later, a real demographic change had occurred. Even academic Stanley Vance, a strong advocate of inside directors, would admit that on the typical Fortune 1000 company board, 60% of directors by the early 1980s were outsiders.[12] What caused this major shift?

Even in the days when fretting over board value seemed as useful as debating the reality of Santa Claus, the high ratio of insiders drew pointed, specific criticism. Myles Mace, as diplomatic as he was, wrote in 1971 that most reasons given by CEOs for having insiders on their boards "are essentially fallacious and specious."[13] In 1967 Harold Koontz wrote that the debate on inside/outside board composition was "perhaps the most contentious issue"[14] facing boards. Although Vance had led a strong counteroffensive supporting inside directors since the early 1960s, more powerful forces in both the government and business world were demanding more

---

11. *Boards of Directors,* Stanley C. Vance, University of Oregon Press, 1964, p. 19.
12. *Corporate Leadership,* Vance, p. 106.
13. *Directors: Myth and Reality,* Myles Mace, Harvard Business School, 1971, p. 127.
14. *The Board of Directors and Effective Management,* Harold Koontz, McGraw-Hill, 1967, p. 122.

outsiders on boards. In the late 1960s, the New York Stock Exchange decreed that all listed companies must have at least two outside directors. Various business groups, such as the American Institute of Management, came out in favor of outsider-majority boards. In 1978, Harold M. Williams, at the time chairman of the SEC, supported a total ban on inside directors. The idea created such an uproar that Williams dropped the idea. But as with the radical board restructuring bills of the same era, the message to boards was clear: make a few changes on the inside, or face a lot of changes from the outside.

The final spur for outsider-majority boards was indirect, but conclusive—the rise of committees. The value of forming a separate audit committee of the board had been recognized since before World War II. However, the full use of such a committee, to say nothing of one headed by outside directors, remained uncommon. The business crime scandals of the 1970s returned the topic to urgency, however, and the SEC, the American Institute of CPAs, and investor groups pushed the concept with growing vigor. In 1978, the New York Stock Exchange followed up its outside director mandate of a decade earlier by requiring that all listed companies have an audit committee with a majority of outside directors. The NYSE move confirmed an already growing trend. A Conference Board study found that the use of audit committees among manufacturing companies had soared from 19% in 1966 to 45% just six years later.[15] By 1982, 98.2% of all corporations surveyed by Korn/Ferry (and not just NYSE companies) had independent audit committees.[16]

The use of committees could help clear up another mystery of board structure—nominations. The process of filling vacancies on corporate boards had always been quite obscure to those outside the company. Precisely what value a new director brought to the board could be very hard to dope out, aside from the fact that he belonged to the same college frat as a current director and, of course, the CEO liked the cut of his jib. Specific talents often seemed incidental. This did not mean that people of ability were banned from the board. Rather, there seemed to be no objective criteria at all, much less tactical recruitment for distinct board needs.

---

15. *The Conference Board: Corporate Directorship Practices,* Jeremy Bacon and James K. Brown, Conference Board, 1975, p. 99.
16. "Board Composition," Korn, p. 17.

Instead of a step-by-step headhunting process, the nomination of directors had long resembled the murky, subjective "tapping" of initiates for a college secret society, like Yale's Skull and Bones.

So, consensus formed that if a committee was good for audit, it was good for nominations, too. Nominating committees formed at a rapid clip during the 1970s and, like audit, required a majority of outsiders for legitimacy. Once again, the strongest outside push for the committee came from the SEC. Beginning in 1977, staff and commissioners began dropping broad hints that the best way to improve the talent and independence of directors was to improve the machinery for nominating them. In that year Enforcement Division head Stanley Sporkin called for reform within boards to take the nomination process out of the hands of management. The next year, the busy Harold Williams cited nominating committees controlled by independent outsiders as a board necessity, though he stopped short of mandating their use.

Instead, the commission approached nomination reform obliquely. New board composition disclosure was proposed in 1978 and included specifics on how directors were sought, whether there was a nominating committee, and how independent the committee members were. Although some of the definitions of "independence" were loosened in the comment phase, the message had been received by corporate America. When the Business Roundtable endorsed the idea of independent-majority nominating committees in 1978, the rush was on. Between 1973 and 1982, Korn/Ferry found that corporations with nominating committees boomed from a negligible 2.4% to 56.6%.[17] The greatest growth hit in the late 1970s, with 38% of a survey group forming nominating committees in 1978 alone.[18] By the beginning of the 1980s, corporations had to explain to shareholders what they were doing—or not doing—to select better directors, and most had a formal nomination structure in place.

If audit committees were the top priority and nominating committees second, the bronze medal for third place would have to be the restructured compensation committee. Unlike the other two, comp committees of a sort had long been common. Between 1973

---

17. Ibid.
18. *Corporate Directorship Practices: The Nominating Committee and the Director Selection Process,* Jeremy Bacon, Conference Board, 1981, p. 9.

and 1982, Korn/Ferry found their prevalence had increased only 10%, though at 86.3% they were the second most common committee after audit.[19]

Comp committee change came about internally. Executive pay had, for many years, been a relatively simple matter of salary and bonus, with stock considerations usually a separate affair. As pay packages became more complex (and remunerative), there was a need to consolidate salary, bonus, stock, and benefits into one package—and under the review of one committee. Also, the push for disclosure noted above extended into the realm of executive pay, which started its climb into the stratosphere during the inflationary 1970s. The past procedure of feeling out the CEO for what he wanted, and then hiring a pay consultant to justify it, seemed obscure and untrustworthy. It was thought that stronger comp committees would, if not cap top executive pay, at least tie it more closely to performance, which would in turn lead to better tools for executive evaluation. Through the remainder of the 1980s, as executive pay leapt from generous to mind-boggling, this seemed like a vain hope. But at least the infrastructure for pay reform was in place.

Indeed, "infrastructure" was the buzzword for the great changes in corporate boards that had occurred by the time Ronald Reagan took office. The late 1970s and early 1980s saw a wave of change in how boards were to function, how they were shaped, the answers they were expected to give, and, particularly, who would join them. Many of the changes were synergistic—audit and nominating committees required more skilled outsiders who, once on the board and named to committees, would tend to suggest the names of more outsiders, and so on. The more the board is reformed, the more it will want to reform.

Yet the new, independent board structure would remain only a blueprint for some time to come. Corporate boards, even when they have changed in ways that satisfy their critics, have tended to move very slowly. The growing number of outsiders, the committees, and the new pressure on boards would face a time lag before results would be seen. By the early 1980s, these changes had shaken up the traditional walnut-paneled, management-controlled board, but had left a vacuum in its place. The old board system, despite its flaws, functioned because it was essentially a branch of management.

19. "Board Composition," Korn, p. 17.

Boards were powerful not as an independent body, but because they were one of the hats worn by the top executives, a hat that brought with it certain legal powers. The boardroom reforms were, by the 1980s, creating the "office space" for a truly independent, empowered corporate board, but as of yet no one was able to legitimately use that power. Shareholders were still largely dispersed and quiet. The activist government role, which had jawboned so much of the change of the 1970s, had been put in cold storage as soon as Ronald Reagan took over. Despite some new questions (and questioners) from the boardroom, top managers could, at least for the time being, feel reasonably sure of staying in control of the situation.

But then everyone started trying to take over the damned companies.

12

Raiders Hit the Boardroom: "This Is Not a Drill"

Corporate mergers are no big surprise in U.S. business history. Mergers, takeovers, consolidations—by various names they have crashed through Wall Street in periodic waves for a century. From the merger movement of the 1890s to the stock and trust manipulations of the 1920s to the conglomerates and Wall Street gunslingers of the 1960's corporations would devour each other in regular cycles that usually rode in on bull stock markets. Even the 1970s, raddled with inflation, malaise, and disco, saw an increase in takeovers and buyouts as acquirers took advantage of sluggish stock values.

Each wave saw the development of new techniques and instruments for taking over companies, and by the 1980s there were two exciting new tools. First was a thriving market in high-yield bonds (as they were called by friends; enemies called them junk bonds), and second was the leveraged buyout. LBOs allowed bidders to acquire almost any company with debt. Junk bonds were the easily obtainable debt that made such transactions possible. With leveraged buyouts as the engine and junk bonds the fuel, the 1980s saw corporate ownership change hands on a scale previously unimagined. From 1982 to 1988 over 10,000 ownership transactions were completed in the United States, with another 3,500 international transactions. Total capitalization on these horse trades came to over $1.5 trillion.[1] During the 1980s the Dow-Jones Industrial

---

1. *The Money Wars*, Roy C. Smith, Truman Talley Books, 1990, p. 106.

Average climbed from the 1,000 level that had stymied it for a decade to 3,000, despite a 500-point crash in 1987. Corporations devoured each other whole in transactions friendly or otherwise and swapped divisions at a terrific pace. Managers bought up their own companies, and firms desperately restructured and divested to create as much value as quickly as possible.

The history of the 1980s takeover frenzy is too near to require a detailed telling here, and its effects are still being debated anyway. Less studied, though, has been the impact of the buyout decade on the corporate boards of the United States. Fresh from their recent reforms and still feeling out their new structures, major corporate boards suddenly found themselves squarely in the middle of the biggest financial, legal, and media cross fire imaginable.

Takeover terminology and tactics exploded as a specialty in the 1980s, leaving boards scrambling to catch up. An early defense against board takeovers was to seek shareholder approval for staggered board terms and "fair price" provisions. "Staggering" the board means dropping the traditional policy of electing the entire director slate yearly and extending board terms to three years, with a third of the board up for election yearly. Raiders who obtained majority control would thus still require several years to dump the entire board. "Fair price" provisions were designed to thwart two-tier offers, in which a raider would buy stock at a premium up to the point of control, but offer less desirable terms to remaining holders. A fair price rule essentially mandated the highest price for everyone, making takeovers that much more costly. Between December 1982 and June 1984, nearly 300 corporate boards proposed some combination of these measures, and 94% were approved.[2]

The staggered board provision was a novel concept in takeover tactics. Not only was the board raising a defense to takeovers, the board *itself* was the defense. Although the tactical value of a staggered board plan was undeniable, it was, and still is, controversial. Many shareholder advocates argued that staggered boards deny holders the power to change their representatives at will. The board becomes entrenched—but then also helps entrench management. A staggered board allows the CEO to use the board as a human shield against takeovers. A final, if unwitting, side effect of stagger-

---

2. *Board Games,* Arthur Fleischer Jr., Geoffrey C. Hazard Jr., and Miriam Z. Klipper, Little, Brown, 1988, p. 75.

ing was that it extended the tenure of directors. All of the steps taken a few years earlier to increase the number of outsiders and minorities now ran into a procedure that delayed the already slow process of board rotation.

As the takeover decade progressed, boards faced a daunting arms race. New takeover tools prompted clever new defenses, which then faced renewed takeover innovations. Greenmail, poison pills, white knights, bear hugs, crown jewels, the Pac Man defense— terms that sounded like Mafia wise-guy euphemisms would be invented and then rushed to the top of board agendas almost simultaneously. The complicated terms of many takeover defenses made it difficult for directors to judge precisely how various shareholder groups would be affected. Indeed, the complexities and vagaries of some defenses were intentional, concocted to create uncertainty for the raider as to their impact. When Household International was in play in 1985, the poison pill approved by the board was 48 pages long, with its stated intent to create "complicated situations that may be difficult for a potential raider to evaluate."[3] If such plans created uncertainty in the minds of buyers, they must have given the directors who had to defend them pause as well.

The players involved in takeovers also shifted regularly, sometimes within the same deal. The typical image of a hostile takeover involved an outside raider making a run at the company, with the CEO/chair resisting and the board backing the CEO. Aside from the question of what was really being defended—the company or management—the interests involved seemed fairly straightforward. But what happens when management *itself* is launching the buyout? What if a member of the board is one of the raiders (as occurred in the 1985 run on Household International)? What if the CEO urges the board to accept an exploding offer in a hurry? What if competing offers reach stratospheric heights, yet remain roughly comparable (the 11th-hour situation in the 1988 RJR-Nabisco takeover)? To say that the board must then make a judgment call was damned weak advice when the dollar amounts reached the billions; the media, investors, and regulators watched with a cynical eye; and it was a sure bet that someone would end up suing no matter what the choice.

But the takeover wars also went to the very heart of what a

---

3. Ibid., p. 82.

corporate board is supposed to do, probably more than any other business issue of the past. Company boards, often with little notice, were thrust into deciding the very essentials of corporate ownership and shareholder value. The usual domain of the board—profitability, strategy, expansions, finance—were vital issues, but still matters that could be handled monthly after their good lunch. Takeovers were panic, "this is not a drill" affairs that required emergency board sessions, 25-hour days, and strong stomachs. "The defenses were really there to give us time to think, to reflect on an offer," recalls veteran director Raymond Troubh.[4]

All takeover responses, tactics, and decisions not only made their way into the boardroom, but hinged on the board for action. Poison pill defenses, which evolved from the fair price provisions, grew popular in part because, unlike fair price policies, they could be activated by the board without shareholder consent. Crown jewel defenses, in which a valued corporate asset would automatically be sold in a hostile takeover, came directly under the board's purview—a bad choice could leave the company crippled. The Pac Man defense, in which a target company would respond with a counter-bid for the raiding company, required the board to make a massive leverage gamble.

Although media coverage during the takeover era concentrated on tales of greed and derring-do by F. Ross Johnson, T. Boone Pickens, Ron Perelman, and other deal makers, a closer reading of the histories show that pitching to the board was key to most takeovers. The 1988 buyout of RJR Nabisco may have required billions of dollars in leverage, but it hinged on Henry Kravis's and George Roberts's salesmanship to the board. "If ever they were to win over the board, this was the time. . . . Each [director] had to be convinced the Kohlberg Kravis [Roberts] bid was safe, secure, and in the best interests of employees and shareholders."[5]

Throughout this pressure, confusion, and media spotlight, boards had to make some very fundamental decisions, often in a hurry. What are the real shareholder interests? Is this price the best price? Is the company being valued correctly on the stock market? How solid is the financing? Could we realize more value by restruc-

---

4. Author interview, February 1996.
5. *Barbarians at the Gate,* Bryan Burroughs and John Helyar, Harper & Row, 1990, p. 477.

turing on the inside? These questions were further complicated by the takeover era's tendency to blur and overturn traditional measures. The company's per-share price could be quite different from its true value, not to mention its breakup price. There were short-term gains versus the long-term health of the company. And if shareholder interests were not enough of a quandary, there were the interests of nonshareholder groups, including employees, suppliers, and local communities. Many states passed stakeholder constituency laws allowing the board to consider noninvestor interests in takeover situations.

But these and other defense tactics also raised an ugly little question about all antitakeover measures, a question that shareholder activists asked with increasing urgency as the 1980s progressed. Were the stakeholders who most concerned boards and CEOs the boards and CEOs themselves? Step back and look at corporate governance as it works in theory, and it seems very hard to justify most antitakeover measures. Aside from assuring the best deal for all equity holders and prohibiting coercive pressure to sell (concerns that were addressed early in the takeover era), why should boards do *anything* to avoid takeovers? The board exists to assure the maximum value for shareholders, and management holds its position solely as a means to that end. If the raider is offering $60 per share for stock that is trading at $30, directors should have a better reason for saying no than vague allusions to "the long-term interests of shareholders." Anything less suggests that management is well entrenched, holding all the strings, and fighting exclusively for its own interests. The board seemed at best to be overly identified with management, and at worst safely in the CEO's pocket.

Too many of the big buyouts of the 1980s left directors in this compromising position. At Freuhauf company, a hostile buyout offer from the outside was countered by an inside management bid headed by the CEO. How unbiased was the Freuhauf board in weighing these two offers? The board allocated $100 million in corporate funds to support the management group's bid and agreed to pay its breakup fees and the fees of its investment bankers. It signed a no-shop agreement with the management group and refused to consider counteroffers from the outside suitor, even though the suitor was willing to top management's offer. Although a U.S. District Court compelled the board to rescind some of its sweeteners to management, the CEO's group ultimately won out with a $1.1 billion, $49 per share offer.[6] No one even attempted to suggest that the board had maintained a level playing field.

In 1988, Shamrock Holdings made a pass at Polaroid. After many delays on the part of Polaroid CEO I. MacAllister Booth, a negotiation meeting with Shamrock was set for July 13. On July 12, Booth convened an emergency board meeting to empower a previously discussed Employee Stock Ownership Program (ESOP) to buy up a controlling 14% of company stock. Three outside directors were unable to attend the hastily called meeting, and those attending received no written details of the ESOP in advance. Still, the plan, costing $300 million, was approved, along with a management-proposed restructuring scheme that included employee pay cuts. Polaroid announced the plan that day, and then thoughtfully canceled the next day's meeting with Shamrock. Stood-up and brokenhearted, Shamrock proceeded with a hostile tender offer at a maximum of $47 per share. It also sued in Delaware court to have the new ESOP struck down, stating that the plan's hasty approval as a takeover defense suggested that the board had breached its duty to shareholders. The court upheld the plan, however, and after appeals, Shamrock gave up on its bid—after negotiating a deal under which Polaroid would pay Shamrock's $20 million in expenses.

---

6. *Board Games,* Fleisher, Hazard, and Klipper, p. 183.

13

Board and CEO Goodies: "Treat Them like Kings"

Such results left critics wondering how boards would have met takeover threats if they *had not* become more independent during the 1970s. The growing core of independent outside directors too often dealt with takeover issues as if their first concern was maintaining the current management team—as well as maintaining their own board status. A reason for this could have been the growing personal benefits of sitting on the board of a Fortune 500 corporation. The cozy postwar boardroom of the CEO reigning over peaceable insiders and buddies was, no doubt, shifting to a more independent board of estimable outsiders. Still, smart CEOs found a few tricks up their sleeves for keeping the board on their side, and most of these techniques had dollar signs attached.

Although the $20 gold piece days were long past, most director compensation as late as the 1970s was still stuck at the gratuity stage. In 1975, a survey found that directors of the largest corporations were paid meeting fees ranging from $200 to $2,500. When combined with an annual retainer, the average director was earning only around $11,500 yearly.[1] A few years later, though, the numbers started to climb, averaging $15,660 in 1981 and $16,990 in 1982, according to a Korn/Ferry study.[2] Board pay really spiked in 1985, rising almost $5,000 that year alone.[3] But cash compensation tells

1. *Managing the Managers,* Edward McSweeney, Harper & Row, 1978, p. 96.
2. "Board Composition and Governance: 1973–82," Lester B. Korn, *Corporate Director (Board)*, March/April 1983, p. 18.
3. "Board Composition and Governance: 1983–92," Richard M. Ferry, *Corporate Board,* September/October, 1993, p. 17.

only part of the story. The real boom in making directors comfortable came in perks and fringes. In 1978, Edward McSweeney could still write that directors were "forgotten men when it comes to special perks and benefits."[4] But by the late 1980s, this was changing fast, with director pension programs, use of company cars and air travel, charitable donations, and insurance coverage easing the director's burden. Stock options and grants for outside directors also started to catch on in the 1980s, ostensibly to align directors' interests more closely with those of shareholders, but more often as a risk-free added source of income. Directors might also be hired as consultants by the corporation, providing services wholly outside their board duties, and paid at the rates large corporations typically pay top consulting talent. And with takeovers becoming a concern, directors started being fitted with their own golden parachutes for potential changes in control, packages similar to, if less munificent than, those provided for management.

That parallel with management hints at both the genesis of coddling the board and its rationale. If board pay and perks shot up during the 1980s, CEO pay was bursting at the seams. Stories about Time-Warner Chairman Steve Ross arranging seven different long-term incentive plans (the total theoretical payoff could have hit $236 million) and UAL Chairman Steven Wolf pocketing $18.3 million from his ailing airline were staples of the greed decade.

Closer inspection showed that many such budget busters existed only on paper and would require the exercise of all long-term stock options or best-case company results for the ideal payoff. Still, behind the headlines, CEO pay was waxing large. Between 1981 and 1988, a sample of "total pay opportunity" for CEOs of $2 billion corporations more than doubled, from $613,000 to $1.4 million.[5] Starting around 1980, CEO pay increased at a rate more than double the rise in the consumer price index through the remainder of the decade.[6] On a more directly populist note, by the end of the 1980s, executive pay researcher Graef Crystal estimated that average U.S. CEO pay was 160 times that of a typical worker

---

4. *Managing the Managers*, McSweeney, p. 97.
5. "Trends and Challenges for the Compensation Committee," Gary C. Hourihan, *Corporate Board*, November/December 1990, p. 15.
6. "Executive Pay: Out of Control?" Carl Levin, *Corporate Board*, January/February 1992, p. 3.

and several times that of top CEOs in other major industrial countries.[7] As the tide of public concern over massive takeovers and mergers crested, it was in turn overwhelmed by a larger wave of anger (tinged with envy) over "obscene" executive pay.

The board of directors was ultimately responsible for these pay trends, though the impetus came from CEOs. Despite the rise of compensation committees on the board, and increased use of professional outside pay consultants, the CEO remained the key source for most comp proposals. As late as 1991, a survey by the Hay Group found that 85% of compensation committee chairs got most of their CEO pay ideas from . . . the CEO.[8] While "this is what I want, take it or leave it" cases were unlikely, a shrewd CEO could send the message that executive pay and perks at the company should not be allowed to lag behind the Joneses. The board would be more amenable to such raises if the CEO had first assured that the *directors* were receiving their due. A board that is made comfortable will be more likely to make the CEO comfortable, and vice versa.

There were more than simple material drivers for such an executive strategy. During much of the postwar period, the CEO could typically depend upon a board of inside management directors sprinkled with a few distracted outsiders. With the evolution of boards, however, directors became increasingly independent outsiders. Though management still held most of the cards, particularly in generating the numbers and data on the company, the CEO's direct power over the board was weakening. How does the CEO/chair keep such a board agreeable and supportive of his or her policies?

F. Ross Johnson, for one, knew the answer. During his tenure as chairman of Standard Brands, Nabisco, and then of RJR Nabisco, he made the wooing of directors a specialty. The bestseller *Barbarians at the Gate* offered many insights on what had been the biggest, messiest takeover in U.S. history, but hidden among its pages, it also offers a primer on how to co-opt and cultivate a board of directors. In the world according to Ross, "one of the most important jobs a CEO has is the care and feeding of the directors."[9]

---

7. *In Search of Excess*, Graef Crystal, W. W. Norton, 1991, p. 205.
8. "In Review," *Corporate Board*, May/June 1991, p. 25.
9. *Barbarians at the Gate*, Bryan Burrough and John Helyar, Harper & Row, 1990, p. 26.

- Make friends with the board. Ross Johnson's first big break came at Standard Brands where, as president, he was a palsy, outgoing contrast to then-Chairman Henry Weigl's dour, prickly ways. When an internal crisis erupted over Johnson's expense accounts, Johnson was able to turn the tables on Weigl, threaten to quit—and end up being named by the board as new CEO. Johnson did not forget the favor and "treated the directors like kings,"[10] adding perks and introducing them to his sport and showbiz buddies, such as Frank Gifford. Compensation committee chair Andrew Sage received special bridge-building treatment, which paid off handsomely for Johnson. CEO pay, which for Weigl had been $200,000 yearly, promptly jumped to $480,000.

- Be a board mentor. Opening up the boardroom meant that many people who would have been unlikely candidates in earlier years, such as academics and civic leaders, were now eligible to join the elite. The leap from academic penury to the rich world of directorship could be quite dazzling, especially if a masterful CEO made himself or herself conduit for the goodies.

  This was a lesson Johnson and other bosses learned from R. J. Reynolds CEO Paul Sticht. Juanita Kreps is today one of America's elite corporate directors, having served on the boards of Chrysler, J. C. Penney, and other major corporations, and serving as secretary of commerce under Jimmy Carter. However, she was just a rising academic at Duke University when Sticht named her to the R. J. Reynolds board. He also proposed her to the Chrysler board (where Sticht was likewise a member), endowed several major chairs and fellowships at Duke, and made a number of impressive donations to the Duke University Endowment. When Nabisco and Reynolds merged, Ross Johnson made sure Kreps stayed on the new board, and likewise cultivated her favor.

- Give the board more than it wants. And before it wants it, especially if trouble is brewing. Not only can the board be pampered into a positive frame of mind, but the CEO can subtly limit or threaten perks to express disfavor. As CEO

---

10. Ibid.

of RJR Nabisco, Johnson cut the number of board meetings but increased director meeting fees to $50,000. The large fleet of corporate aircraft Johnson accumulated (so extensive it was dubbed the RJR Air Force) was placed at the directors' use for travel anywhere, at no cost to the board. Johnson may have grumbled to intimates about the time involved in acting as the board's travel agent, "but I know if I'm there for them, they'll be there for me."[11] In due course, they were. When Johnson sought to squeeze out Paul Sticht, who had been named emeritus chairman after the RJR Nabisco merger, the board readily acquiesced. The first sign that Sticht was on his way out: Johnson decreed that he must personally authorize Sticht's use of company aircraft.

Johnson also made good use of board pensions. When his team announced their management buyout (MBO) bid for RJR Nabisco, one of the board's first concerns was how the move would affect their ten-year, $50,000 yearly board pensions. At a comp committee meeting the day after the bid was announced, a proposal to extend the pensions to *lifetime* status was to have been discussed. The committee decided (despite some hurt feelings) to table the idea because it might at that point seem improper.[12]

- Consult with your directors. Or at least *pay* them to consult with you. One of the great CEO discoveries of the 1980s (expanded upon in the 1990s) has been the "soft money" influence of director consulting contracts. Along with their regular board and committee duties, directors can be paid handsome amounts to perform sometimes ill-defined consulting work for the corporation. While pay and perks serve as broad feel-good tools for the entire board, consulting contracts allow the CEO to put money in the pockets of specific directors—and serious money at that.

At American Express corporation, CEO Jim Robinson showed early mastery in the uses of board consulting. Henry Kissinger joined the AmEx board in 1984 and was immediately signed to

---

11. Ibid., p. 97.
12. Ibid., pp. 184–185.

perform consulting services for the firm as well. His consulting fees ran in the range of $350,000 to $500,000 yearly, dwarfing Kissinger's standard board pay. Former President and AmEx Director Gerald Ford received around $100,000 yearly for consulting with the company. Other directors who were on the payroll over the years have included Richard M. Furlaud, former AmEx CEO Howard L. Clark, and AmEx insider Aldo Papone. When a CEO succession battle erupted in 1992, a majority of the board supported Robinson. Rawleigh Warner, an AmEx director and leader of the anti-Robinson forces, spoke for many governance observers when he commented that "it's quite obvious that most of the American Express directors were under Jimmy Robinson's thumb."[13]

At RJR Nabisco, Ross Johnson (who himself would later join the AmEx board), spent the 1980s perfecting the art of board consultancy. Director Robert Schaeberle received a six-year consulting contract worth $180,000, and Andrew Sage was paid $250,000 yearly for financial work. Johnson proposed director and Combustion Engineering CEO Charles Hugel for the post of nonexecutive chairman of RJR Nabisco—and paid him $150,000 for his services. During the run-up to the battle for RJR Nabisco, Johnson went one better with Hugel, who chaired the special board committee charged with deciding who would win the company. Johnson allegedly asked Hugel to stay on as a director if the management group won the auction, offering an impressive piece of the MBO action in the bargain. This last move was finally too much and struck Hugel as a potential bribe.[14]

Indeed, in the end, F. Ross Johnson did seem to go too far with his board. Turned off by the "corporate greed" uproar surrounding the sale of RJR Nabisco, they ultimately lost faith in Johnson and accepted the competing bid from Kohlberg Kravis Roberts. Still, by the time of the takeover battle in 1988, Johnson seemed to have let his board pampering duties slide, with only one board meeting between May and October of 1988. Perhaps F. Ross Johnson had simply lost his golden touch with directors. Or perhaps there were other forces at work.

---

13. Rawleigh Warner, speech to conference on "CEO and Board Relationships: Toward Common Ground," April 28–29, 1993; quoted in *Corporate Governance*, Robert A. G. Monks and Nell Minow, Blackwell, 1995, p. 380.
14. *Barbarians at the Gate,* Burrough and Helyar, p. 177.

14

Bill Van Gorkom Goes to a Party

The relationships between U.S. CEO/chairs and U.S. corporate boards, and within the boards themselves, have always been quite personal ones. From the largest to smallest corporations, hints, impressions, and chemistry have been measures of the CEO's success as fully as stock price and price/earnings ratios. Even when boards would finally rouse themselves to can the CEO (and General Motors in 1992 was by no means the first instance), the motivators usually came from within the company or within the boardroom. The current concept of a "lead" director, who acts as liaison for the board, acknowledges this informal board hierarchy.

Even the new outside directors who made their way onto boards in the 1970s and 1980s were adopted into (if not co-opted into) the family. As within a family, the process of decision making may seem murky to an outsider. There is an unspoken collection of motivations, relationships, agendas, pecking orders, and temporary ententes. There would likely be a sound business rationale for a major board decision, especially one as freighted with danger as selling the company. But behind it would be the framework of feuds, prerogatives, and goals that actually led the board to choose Plan A over B or C or any other letter of the alphabet.

At the start of the 1980s, how the board made its decisions was still largely the board's business, and the corporate veil protecting directors from liability remained mostly intact. What the board decided, free of criminal bad faith, government would not rend asunder. But by the mid-1980s, this murky, yet unchallenged world of decision making was being painfully second-guessed. The courts were looking more closely and often did not like what they

found. Boards were being held liable for poor decisions, and directors' and officers' liability insurance was growing more dear.

The legal system in Delaware, state of incorporation to most
major U.S. corporations, had long served as the foremost arbiter of
board prerogatives. One estimate finds that 20% of the state budget
is generated by incorporation fees and taxes,[1] though few companies
actually have a physical presence there. As a result, the Delaware
courts have a uniquely powerful influence on U.S. corporate law,
for example, forming the nation's only chancery court exclusively
to adjudicate corporate matters. Some view this as positive, allowing
one of our states to act as the canary in the coal mine by being the
first to sniff out problems in corporate law. "One of the reasons
Delaware keeps its leadership is because our courts see [business]
pathologies first," observes Lewis S. Black Jr., a noted Delaware
attorney and specialist in corporation law.[2] Others are less generous,
seeing a state government and judiciary hopelessly in the pocket of
corporate interests. In a 1990 *Esquire* article (cheerily titled "Delaware Puts Out"), Joseph Nocera slashed at the state's courts: "If
states have become whores in the modern age, giving away their
favors to any corporation that so much as casts them a flirtatious
glance, then Delaware is the Mayflower Madam."[3] Between these
two views, there is consensus that, for good or ill, Delaware courts
have a powerful influence on U.S. corporate law.

Thus, a 1985 series of decisions by the Delaware Supreme
Court regarding how boards make their decisions sent a resounding
shock wave through the corporate world. The first of these decisions,
cited as *Smith v. Van Gorkom,* has been one of the most discussed
and influential in the history of U.S. corporate law. Every conference
and publication on the role and liability of boards still gives it prominent mention. The aftershocks were both immediate and long last-
ing. Yet the decision itself was a narrow one, and the specific trail it
blazed in legal precedent has seen little subsequent traffic.

The case had its beginnings in 1980, with board and management discussion of how to manage a company that literally had too
much of a good thing. Trans Union Corporation, headquartered in
Chicago (though, of course, incorporated in Delaware) was a bil-

---

1. "Delaware Puts Out," Joseph Nocera, *Esquire,* February 1990, p. 47.
2. Author interview, December 1995.
3. "Delaware Puts Out," Nocera, p. 47.

lion-dollar conglomerate, with such diverse holdings as the Union Tank Car Company, lease operations, and manufacturing. Under Chairman and CEO William Van Gorkom, the company had proven successful and projected a 20% annual income growth into the 1980s. Besides the chairman, there were nine men on Trans Union's board, five of them outside directors. The outsiders were an estimable group, including William Johnson, chairman of IC Industries, Robert Reneker, former chairman of Esmark, and W. Allen Wallis, chancellor of the University of Rochester. The quality of these outsiders, plus the board's top executives who served as inside directors, resulted in a near textbook example of board soundness and talent. Chairman Van Gorkom and his board were, in the words of one authority, among "Chicago's best and brightest business leaders."[4]

In short, this was the sort of business and leadership one would expect to face the pleasant problem of too much of a good thing. The "good thing" in question was tax credit resulting from the purchase of new equipment. As a heavy user of large capital equipment, Trans Union accumulated many such Investment Tax Credits (ITCs) but was not profitable enough to fully use these credits, which added up to a substantial sum. With a continued surplus of ITCs on the horizon, plus a projected cash surplus, Trans Union was, by 1980, a company in the mood for change. The board discussed such alternatives as acquisitions or a stock buyback, but Van Gorkom, in discussions with his management team, raised the notion of selling Trans Union to a company that could use the tax credits. The group also discussed an LBO led by management. Some numbers in the $50 to $60 per share range were tossed around, with Van Gorkom indicating that he would be willing to sell the 60,000 shares he personally held at $55 per share. Van Gorkom dropped the MBO idea due to potential conflicts of interest, but the $55 share price would stick in his mind.

The idea of selling the company also stayed on his mind, and in September 1980, he approached Chicago friend Jay Pritzker to discuss a deal. Pritzker, chairman of the Marmon Group, had by 1980 built a reputation as one of the Midwest's foremost deal makers. With some new figures based on the $55 per share price, Van

---

4. *Board Games,* Arthur Fleisher Jr., Geoffrey C. Hazard Jr., and Miriam Z. Klipper, Little, Brown, 1988, p. 17.

Gorkom proposed a deal to Pritzker who, within days, accepted. Pritzker made a few stipulations regarding preliminary purchases of Trans Union stock, and one kicker—the offer was an exploding one, and unless the Trans Union board approved within three days, the deal was off. Over the next 48 hours, William Van Gorkom was a busy man. He met with his management team on the deal, negotiated with Trans Union's bank about forming a syndicate to finance the buyout, and consulted an outside attorney on details of the transaction.

There were, however, some folks who he never got around to see during those busy two days: the Trans Union board. At a board meeting on September 20, 1980, Van Gorkom finally outlined his case to the directors but did not tell them that he was the original source of the $55 per share price. He did not try to pitch the price as the best obtainable (although it was roughly a 50% premium over the market).[5] He only maintained that the price was a fair one. And he pointed out that the deal would expire the next day. Copies of the agreement were available at the board meeting, but none of the directors had a chance to see it in advance.

The board did not stampede into the sale. There were a couple of hours of discussion on whether the board could be sued for failing to take advantage of the offer before it went boom and of what would happen if the company were put in play. But in due course, the board approved the agreement, subject to a 90-day window when Trans Union could accept (but would not solicit) competing offers. The deal would then be recommended to shareholders for approval. Van Gorkom signed the final agreement that evening— at a party. The Delaware court later found that neither he nor any of the directors had actually read the final wording.[6]

During the following weeks, other offers were discussed (including an abortive $60 per share offer from Kohlberg Kravis Roberts), but the Pritzker offer did a good job of locking out other deals. Essentially, once Pritzker's Marmon Group had its financing lined up (and it did by early October), only a superbid could have dislodged it. Despite growing concerns that Trans Union may have been lowballed, the board on January 26, 1981, reiterated its sup-

---

5. *The Money Wars*, Roy C. Smith, Truman Talley Books, 1990, p. 149.
6. *Corporate Governance*, Robert A. G. Monks and Nell Minow, Blackwell, 1995, p. 210.

port for the Pritzker bid, and in February it was approved by share-holders. The merger of Trans Union into a unit of the Pritzker empire was formalized immediately after.

But the end of the merger brought the start of legal challenges. A Trans Union shareholder group led by one Burks Alden Smith sued William Van Gorkom, the Trans Union board, and the Pritz-kers, alleging damages from an inadequate sale price and inadequate care by the directors. The case wound its way through the Delaware courts and in July 1982 was decided in favor of the Trans Union board. Smith's group appealed to the Delaware Supreme Court.

It was this court that in January 1985 fired the shot heard round the boardrooms of the world. In a 3–2 decision, the majority reversed the lower court, finding that Trans Union's board had failed to adequately investigate the value of the price offered, to ask Van Gorkom how the price came about, and to fully examine the details of the Pritzker offer. Not only did the court find the board negligent in its duties, it found them "grossly" negligent. This made them *personally* liable for financial damages. With damages defined as the spread between the purchase price and an estimate of what the company could have brought, liabilities would total in the millions.

The Trans Union directors had made a number of strong arguments in defense of their actions. The final price of $55 per share was a substantial premium of almost 45% over the then market price of $38 per share. By the time the board learned of the offer, it was set to explode in less than a day, so speed in deciding was essential. They had not simply rolled over for the CEO—the directors mandated a market test period for the bid and improved the terms under which other offers could be made. The board's collective résumé of experience was an impressive one. While this may sound a bit arrogant outside the courtroom, it is powerful legal evidence that if these men thought the deal smelled good, it indeed was good. And in what should have been the clincher, the shareholders had overwhelmingly approved the transaction on the terms offered. *Vox Populi, Vox Dei.*

The Delaware Supreme Court was not buying. No one disputed that the $55 per share bid was a premium over the trading price. However, there was no evidence of proper analysis to show whether it was the best premium, the lowest, or just middling. Indeed, most evidence showed that Van Gorkom had become stuck on the price early in the process and that subsequent research served only to back it up. As to the deadline, the court seemed to dismiss it by saying that "haste makes waste." The board's collective savvy did not include investment banking experience. Without an independent valuation of the company and the bid, the directors, estimable though they may be, were frankly feeling their way in the dark. The market test was found to be too loaded in favor of the Pritzker bid, and as for the shareholder vote, if the process up to that point had been flawed, the owners were approving an unsubstantiated offer with inadequate facts at their disposal.

In summary, the Van Gorkom decision was breathtaking in its implications by simply holding up the mirror of logic to precedent on board duty of care. This precedent for many years held that the final *outcome* of a board's decision was not the issue but that the board's decision *process* was. If the board maintains proper loyalty and care in its decision making, the ultimate result may still be a cropper, but the courts will grant the board a safe harbor for its decision and not try to substitute their own judgment. In *Van Gorkom,* the court raised the level of decision-making required by turning the results test inside out. The ultimate result of the board's decision may be good for shareholders. It may also be bad. But that result is not the issue. If the board decision making process *itself* is flawed, or at least unproven, then the board has failed in its duty, hang the outcome.

The *Van Gorkom* decision was both astounding and controversial. Indeed, two of the five judges on the state supreme court dissented vigorously, finding that the board had acted within its powers. Although the Trans Union board has over the years become a shorthand term for poor board decision making, a closer look at the facts show that their behavior was hardly egregious. While the KKR counteroffer of $60 per share sounds better, it was based on less firm financing. Many unquestioned board decisions have been made on less information over the years, and given the directors' proven background, it is hard to imagine a group better qualified to make such a grave decision on short notice. Some believe that the Delaware judiciary was only trying to send a message to boards to be more attentive and, more specifically, to not let management take control of the takeover process. In the words of Lewis Black, who was a counsel in the case, Trans Union's board was "in the wrong place at the wrong time."[7]

---

7. Author interview, February 1996.

Before the case reached the damages stage in the fall of 1985, the directors and the plaintiff group settled out of court for $5.5 million in damages to the shareholders and $18 million in legal fees (such lopsided arithmetic would prove a hallmark of director liability cases). Only $10 million of this was covered by the directors' D&O insurer, although several sources indicate that Pritzker reimbursed the directors for their out-of-pocket losses.

15

"Omnipresent Specters" and "Revlon Duties"

The year 1985 would bring another precedent-setting director liability case from Delaware, and in some ways it was a sequel to Trans Union. Both dealt with takeovers, both shook up how boards actually shaped their decisions, and both made it clear that the days of dozing through board meetings had irrevocably passed.

In the early 1980s, T. Boone Pickens had proven the adage (if it isn't already an adage, I'll invent it) that you don't necessarily need to win to be a winner. From the base of his Mesa Petroleum Company, Pickens had become a feared oil field raider. His runs at Gulf, Phillips Petroleum and others in Big Oil had not brought him control, but had instead earned him millions in greenmail. Pickens's failed takeover attempts would either prompt the target company to buy back his shares or put the company in play, raising the ultimate price of the equity he held. In either case, Boone made lots more money than he ever could have pumped out of the ground. He turned his attentions toward Unocal Corporation in 1985, where he encountered an immovable object in long-term Chairman Fred Hartley. Hartley, oil-patch tough and savvy, had formed the present Unocal by masterminding a 1965 merger of his Union Oil company with Pure Oil. That $900 million deal was the biggest merger in history to that time.[1] Hartley thus knew a few things about takeovers, as well as how to fight them. Unocal's 14-member

---

1. *Board Games,* Arthur Fleisher Jr., Geoffrey C. Hazard Jr., Miriam Z. Klipper, Little, Brown, 1988, p. 93.

board was evenly split between insiders and outsiders and included National Medical Enterprises Chairman Richard Eamer and J. L. Kellogg Graduate School Dean Donald Jacobs.

Pickens, after increasing his holdings in Unocal during early 1985 (to about 13% of outstanding shares), in April launched a two-tier, front-end-loaded tender offer. The first half of the offer involved a cash bid for 64 million shares, which combined with his present holdings would give Pickens control. The second tier would offer junk bonds in exchange for the remainder of shares outstanding. As with all such offers, the goal was to encourage holders to tender quickly to take advantage of the cash offered for the first tier. Pickens claimed that his goal in this takeover was control of the company, not greenmail, which by 1985 faced growing hostility from shareholder groups and regulators.

The Pickens offer, which was $5 to $6 above the current market price, did not set well with Hartley and the Unocal board, which immediately met to form a response. As opposed to the Trans Union takeover, the Unocal board had solid financial and evaluation counsel, including Goldman Sachs and several prominent legal firms. After discussion of alternatives, the outside directors met in caucus and chose an innovative defense strategy. The board would launch a self-tender, buying back its own shares at a price of $72, a substantial premium over the Pickens offer. As a final touch, the offer would not extend to shares held by Pickens. There would be no greenmail this time.

Pickens immediately filed suit in Delaware, claiming that the Unocal board's limit on the self-tender was discriminatory and a betrayal of the board's fiduciary duty. Unocal countered that the move would protect shareholders who might be left on the short end of Pickens's two-tier offer. A Delaware trial judge granted Pickens a temporary restraining order on the Unocal offer but expedited an appeal to the state supreme court. On May 17, 1985, the Delaware Supreme Court found in favor of Unocal, stating that the board was within its duties to buy back its stock as a defensive measure. The two-tier, front-loaded aspect of the outside offer was distasteful to the court, as was Pickens's well-established reputation as a greenmailer.[2] The court also allowed the exclusion of shares held

---

2. *The Battle for Corporate Control,* Stuart L. Shapiro (contrib.), Business One Irwin, 1991, p. 90.

by a raider, but its reasoning set a new precedent for the board's burden in deciding takeovers.

Boards, the Delaware court held, face a two-part test in determining how far they can go with takeover defenses. The first is the long-established business judgment doctrine. The board must thoroughly, objectively examine the bid and judge whether it will really harm the shareholders' long-term interests. If so, then the board is allowed to oppose it. Indeed, it is the board's duty to oppose it. However, the Unocal decision added a second act to this drama. By erecting antitakeover defenses, the board is inevitably defending itself and management from loss of corporate control (as well as unemployment). This raises (in a masterpiece of legal coinage) the "omnipresent specter" that the board may be acting in its own self-interest. Therefore, when shaping takeover defenses, boards will also face an enhanced duty to show that the threat faced truly warrants the defenses imposed. The first part of the test places the burden of proof where it has traditionally rested, on the plaintiff. But the new test would swing the burden over to the board. The *board* must now prove that its takeover fortifications are reasonable. Otherwise, at least in Delaware, the courts will consider board and management to be building their own Chinese wall.

In the matter at hand, then, the Unocal case was a bit of an anticlimax. The company proceeded with its self-tender, incurring a hefty debt load. T. Boone Pickens negotiated to sell back most of his stock to the company but ended up doing so at a loss (gleeful Pickens critics called this "reverse greenmail"). As in many major legal decisions, the greatest effect would be felt as precedent for cases to come. If the Trans Union case established that the board could not sleepwalk its way through a takeover, Unocal made it clear that even the most basic takeover decisions could now be second-guessed. Now there could be "virtually automatic litigation in every bidding case . . . to remove a defender's poison pill and other defenses."[3]

The year 1985 ended with further turmoil, upsetting not just how boards decide, but what role the board plays during a takeover. In the fall of that year, financier Ronald Perelman used one of his corporate entities to launch a takeover of the Revlon corporation starting at $43 per share. The Revlon board enacted a poison pill,

---

3. *The Money Wars,* Roy C. Smith, Truman Talley Books, 1990, p. 152.

then launched its own management-led tender offer at $47 per share. Revlon also negotiated with the LBO firm of Forstmann Little to act as a White Knight. Revlon agreed to sell some of the firm's most valuable assets to Forstmann if a hostile raider should acquire 40%, a crown jewels defense that also served as a lockup for the Forstmann bid. Perelman's group quickly responded with bids rising to $50 per share and then $53 per share. A bidding war erupted between the management group and Perelman, which soared as high as $58 per share on Perelman's part. The Revlon board still favored the management/Forstmann bid, though, and seemed ready to accept it when the Perelman group sought a restraining order. Their claim: the board was favoring management's bid over the more remunerative outside offer, a favoritism that hurt shareholders.

The Delaware Supreme Court agreed. Most of the board's initial defensive tactics were accepted by the court, indeed even endorsed, as prompting the Perelman group to raise its price, which data indicated had been quite low. However, the court held that once the bidding war took off and once the management group involved Forstmann, the board's job was no longer plotting a defense, but running an auction. The sale of the company to someone, either Perelman or management, had become inevitable. Time then for the board to run up the white flag and seek the best deal for shareholders. And when the board must shift roles to that of auctioneer, it can hardly obtain the best bid by favoring one of the bidders. Perelman gained control of Revlon, and corporate boards gained a further headache in dealing with takeovers. Now they faced a "Revlon duty" from the moment (subjectively decided) when sale of the company became inevitable. Going into 1985, the role and actions of the corporate board had seemed fairly well established. But by the end of that year, nothing seemed certain anymore.

16

The 1980s Board Liability Panic

B usiness history is rich with tales of unusual panics, runs, and stampedes. In the 1700s British speculation in the South Sea Company created one of the greatest speculative bubbles of all time and helped taint the idea of incorporation for a century. In the United States, 1920s speculation on real estate in Florida drove state land prices to levels unimagined even in our age of Disney World and bankrupted many. Panic can work the other way as well, triggering a bear market. Financial panics, such as those of 1837, 1873, and 1893, were triggered by a combination of fundamental causes and business mob psychology.

It may be overstating matters to say that the Trans Union and Unocal cases triggered a legal panic for corporate boards. However, the specter of being sued as a director went from the status of a concern to a near certainty. "Many large corporations were terrified"[1] by the Trans Union decision, according to Abbass Al-khafaji, and if the operative mode was "not panic," according to Lewis Black, "boards and lawyers sure got the message."[2]

Directors' and officers' liability insurance rates soared, and exclusions and limitations on policies broadened and became more common. In 1986, some D&O policies had as many as 40 exclusion endorsements attached,[3] essentially gutting coverage. A 1986 *Wall*

---

1. *Restructuring American Corporations,* Abbass F. Alkhafaji, Quorum, 1990, p. 91.
2. Author interview, February 1996.
3. "Bargaining on D&O Coverage," Corbette S. Doyle, *Corporate Board Special Report on Directors' Liability,* July/August 1991, p. 16.

Street Journal front-page article noted that D&O insurance rates, historically low, had multiplied threefold to as much as tenfold within the past year. Unocal may have won its takeover war, but it had lost its battle for D&O insurance: the moment Pickens announced his takeover plans, Unocal's insurer, Continental Corporation, canceled its coverage.[4] The *New York Times* found that the amount of coverage available had fallen sharply, from $50 to $150 million in 1985 to $10 million to $35 million in 1986. "Companies are paying so much for insurance . . . that they worry they are wasting corporate assets."[5]

In some cases, coverage could not be obtained at all. Liability concerns for the first time became a real factor in candidates turning down board invitations and even resigning from boards. Armada Corporation lost eight of its ten directors when the firm's insurance was canceled. Armada drew up an agreement to reimburse directors who lost personal assets in suits and set about recruiting new ones—specifying that recruits not have much in the way of assets. "It's tough to keep the good directors on the board," observed Ira Millstein. "Even if they stay, the lack of insurance has got to have an impact on them as they make their decisions. Just at the moment when they might need some risk-taking, they're going to go for safety."[6]

The oddest aspect of this liability scare was that most of the anxiety was misplaced. Some have speculated that the Delaware director cases may have been an excuse for D&O insurers to cut back and jump their rates in a market that had grown unprofitable due to competition. "The insurance companies cried wolf," opines Eugene Anderson, an insurance law partner with Anderson, Kill, Olick, & Oshinsky.[7]

The cases that prompted the panic likewise looked less scary on closer inspection. Trans Union, the case that started the deep-pocket fears, had been a very close call. The lower court approved the board's action, and the Delaware Supreme Court split 3-2. Indeed, part of the reason that the Trans Union decision delivered

---

4. "Liability Insurance Is Difficult to Find Now for Directors, Officers," *Wall Street Journal,* July 10, 1985, p. A1.
5. "Director Insurance Drying Up," *New York Times,* March 7, 1986, p. D1.
6. Ibid.
7. Author interview, December 1995.

such a shock to the corporate world was because state supreme court dismissal of the whole matter had been assumed as a foregone judicial no-brainer. Further, the Trans Union board's behavior may have looked egregious in the courtroom, but so would many daily decisions if closely examined by hostile attorneys. Without a shareholder suit, the Trans Union case could have been a simple matter of selling the company for a substantial premium over market price, an item buried in the middle of the *Wall Street Journal*. Whether the Trans Union directors are viewed as bumbling board potatoes or the martyred Wilmington Nine, it is clear that the decision could easily have favored them if they had only secured a bit more documentation.

The Unocal case is even more perplexing. In this case, the board won, yet the decision evolved into a major incursion on board decision making. Ruminations on the "omnipresent specter" of self-interest and "reasonableness" began to litter all the writings and judicial decisions on board duties during a takeover. Yet by their very nature the terms remained ill-defined until a court, long after the fact, resolved that they had been violated. The defense tactic used by the Unocal board—excluding the raider from an offer—became moot a year later when the SEC banned such moves. From the greenmailer's side, growing public criticism (and harsher tax treatment) made greenmail less attractive after the mid-1980s. The key aspects that marked the Unocal case were already on their way out of takeover battles.

But the Revlon case added uncertainty to board liability, a crucial ingredient for panics. At some point in a takeover war, the board was supposed to stop defending and start taking offers. But when? Although Revlon had fully validated poison pills, it also suggested that in some variants, such as the crown jewel lockup, they were a trigger in taking the defense outside the board's control. In effect, the defense *itself* could mean that the company was in play, triggering what came to be known as the board's "Revlon duties."

These court decisions, in themselves limited and ambiguous, triggered the uncertainty that led to a near panic in boardrooms. The process of dealing with a takeover bid, which was already a white-knuckle experience, became even more tense. The board decision-making process, with its long record of informality, subtext, and inscrutability, would suddenly have to be rationalized and then justified in court. Nothing could be quite so lethal to a cozy old boys' network as the knowledge that the whole world is watching. However, this microscope also weakens the value of a board. Outside directors, who at one time may have felt safe dozing through their board sinecures, now went to the opposite extreme of assuming board service was too hazardous and bailing out. Directors may at one time have been indecisive due to passiveness, but the threat of personal liabilities could make them indecisive due to fretfulness. Note that in each of the three key cases discussed above, the board got into trouble because it *did* something. The action may have been wrong, or unjust, or haphazard, but at least it was an action. Suing the board because it *didn't* do something, because it in essence fiddled while Rome burned, was much less likely.

Not that directors simply came to board meetings and stoppered their ears. Procedures for handling takeover situations became more professional, with strongly enforced checklists of valuations, legal opinions, and documentation for every aspect. This fit in well with the increasingly expensive arms race that takeovers had become by the late 1980s. As takeover defenses became more sophisticated and unbreachable, raiders in turn became more sophisticated in countering them. Corporations then required even better defenses. Both sides had growing cadres of investment bankers, lawyers, and counselors to arm them, at ever higher cost. By the end of the 1980s, corporate boards, as embattled and shell-shocked as they were, had learned a thing or two about takeovers.

17

Delaware Gives the Board a Break

One of the things that boards learned was that, historically, merger movements go in cycles. By the end of the decade, the 1980s hostile takeover rage was winding down. The stock market crash of 1987 had dented the junk bond market, and further declines in 1989, plus the fall of such key players as Drexel, Burnham Lambert, brought a money pinch for raiders and a drying up of the market. The number of mergers and acquisitions valued at over $1 million dropped from 4,471 in 1986 to 3,663 in 1990. Contested transactions, that is, hostile takeovers, fell 110% in a single year, from 1988 to 1989.[1]

Corporations were also learning the value of beating raiders to the punch—by restructuring the company from the inside. A 1990 study of 16 takeovers found that the mergers had doubled the original value of the companies, generating $6.5 billion in added value. However, only 16% came from added leverage and tax benefits. Raiders squeezed out the remaining 84% increase in value through operating changes such as streamlined operations, better market focus, and cuts in overhead—in short, restructuring. These were "all actions that could have been taken by existing managements" wrote McKinsey & Company partner Jack Murrin.[2] If a big part of the raider's pitch was to liberate the values hidden within the corporation, why shouldn't current management be the hero and do the

1. Harvey L. Pitt, partner, Fried, Frank, Harris, Shriver, & Jacobson, remarks to the Utility Women's Conference, September 1991.
2. "Winning against the Raider," Jack Murrin, *Corporate Board,* July/August 1990, p. 11.

job itself? With increasingly assertive boards watching over their shoulders, managers could, and did, start a restructuring drive that continues to this day.

Boards also gained some support on the legal front. The tumult stirred by the 1985 Delaware decisions, especially Trans Union, plus the following D&O insurance panic, prompted much discussion in business circles. One aspect was some quiet muttering among corporate legal advisors that Delaware was no longer the friendly corporate haven it had once been. Citing the growing problems in retaining good directors (and, cynics thought, the state's need to give corporations what they want), the Delaware legislature in 1986 passed Section 102 (b) (7), a major overhaul of its liability law. The law allows the shareholders of Delaware corporations to shield directors from liability to the company or shareholders for duty of care violations. Duty of loyalty torts would still be banned. One legal commentator observed that the directors of corporations in the state would be free from monetary liability "even in the context of gross negligence."[3] Had this law been in effect at the time of the Trans Union takeover, it is unlikely that the board would have owed a dime.

Also, public and media opposition to takeovers spread, and other states did their part to limit raids on local corporations. Between 1985 and 1990, 23 states passed some form of antitakeover legislation, most to help a specific state firm fight a specific takeover battle.[4] Many of these proposals were derided by shareholder groups as rewriting the laws to protect home-state companies. In 1990, Pennsylvania passed Public Act 36, which broadly expanded the "stakeholder" interests to be considered in weighing a bid. An editorial in the *Wall Street Journal* summed up PA 36 as "an awful piece of legislation."[5] The law proved so controversial that a third of all state corporations exercised their right to opt out of its protection. In 1987 the U.S. Supreme Court approved an Indiana control share statute, passed to aid the state-based Cummins Corporation in battling a takeover threat. Such laws severely limit the voting power of stock secured for a takeover bid. In 1990, the court

---

3. *The Battle for Corporate Control*, Michael Bradley and Cindy A. Schpani (contrib.), Business One Irwin, 1991, p. 116.
4. "In Review," *Corporate Board*, March/April 1990, p. 25.
5. *Wall Street Journal*, April 3, 1990, p. 20.

upheld an even stronger Wisconsin control share law, which essentially gave management veto power over unwanted takeovers. The state of Washington passed an antitakeover law to protect Boeing from a run by T. Boone Pickens, even though Boeing was not incorporated in Washington, but in Delaware. The law was instead carefully crafted to protect companies with a strong employment presence in the state, so that according to Robert Monks and Nell Minow, "the only company it applied to was Boeing."[6]

From the judicial front, the news also seemed a bit more heartening. The takeover of Macmillan, a large information services company, took over a year and involved three different bidders plus a very hard-fighting management team under Macmillan CEO Edward P. Evans. This prolonged, bloody, four-way battle was highly entertaining to corporate spectators. However, it was also enlightening on how Delaware courts viewed the dos and don'ts of takeover tactics. With such pros as Kohlberg Kravis Roberts, Robert M. Bass, and Robert Maxwell involved, the siege of Macmillan involved almost every takeover and defensive strategy then known: ESOPs, management restructuring plans, a variety of competing lockups and no-shop agreements, poison pills, an incredibly byzantine auction process, and generous golden parachutes and breakup fees. In November 1988, the Delaware Supreme Court, asked to rule on a management lockup agreement (and to, in effect, sort the whole mess out), awarded the auction to Maxwell, as well as scolding management for its conduct. In the process of stating its case, the Delaware court addressed (and judged) most of the plays involved in the battle, offering a valuable primer of "thou shalls" and "thou shall nots" for takeovers. Particularly galling to the court was its finding that management had led the board around by the nose, supplying information to them that was "inaccurate, incomplete and misleading."[7]

If the Macmillan takeover was valuable for showing boards where the land mines were on the takeover battlefield, the Time-Warner case helped by clearing out a few of those mines. The 1989 attempt by Time to merge with Warner Communications while

---

6. *Power and Accountability,* Robert A. G. Monks and Nell Minow, Harper Business, 1991, p. 139.
7. *The Battle for Corporate Control,* Jesse Finkelstein, Kevin Abrams, and David Finger (contrib.), Business One Irwin, 1991, p. 242.

evading a bid by Paramount was "the perfect way to end the Eighties," according to Joseph Nocera.[8] More harshly, Robert Monks terms it "probably the greatest incursion in United States history into the rights of shareholders."[9] In 1989, Time and Warner announced a friendly, stock-for-stock merger. Although supposedly a merger of equals, the terms announced by Warner CEO Steve Ross suggested that Time was the weaker of the two companies and hence more vulnerable. Paramount Communications, sensing this vulnerability, launched its own offer for Time. Paramount CEO Martin Davis contended that the terms of the Time-Warner deal made the deal a sale, not a merger, and hence allowed another bidder to sit at the table. Time and Warner hastily restructured their transaction to legally merge Warner into Time. This merger would avoid the sale aspect but weigh the company down with whopping debt, up to $14 billion dollars. This switch-about was performed not only to keep Paramount from knocking at the door but to avoid a shareholder vote on choosing between the two proposals. Paramount's bid would look quite attractive to many investors—too many, the Time and Warner team thought. Paramount sued in Delaware court, alleging that Time's board was failing its fiduciary duty to shareholders. Time's board countered that it was pursuing a long-term strategy that would be supported by a merger with Warner and that it frankly knew what was better for its shareholders than the shareholders.

What a difference four years makes. The 1989-model Delaware Supreme Court found in favor of Time. The company had presented convincing proof that it had a viable long-term strategy for combining with Warner and that the stock market was not recognizing the value of this strategy in the share price. And since Time was technically buying Warner, Time was not facing a change in control, so the board's Revlon duties to conduct a fair auction were not triggered. This meant that the basic Unocal obligation to properly meet duties of care remained the standard. Time directors were able to present impressive documentation of their every move, showing that independent experts and outside directors had made a sound review of their actions. Many shareholder activists were apoplectic

8. "Delaware Puts Out," Joseph Nocera, *Esquire,* February 1990, p. 47.
9. *Corporate Governance,* Robert A. G. Monks and Nell Minow, Blackwell, 1995, p. 385.

over the Time-Warner decision, but the court's finding showed that boards were getting the hang of handling takeovers by the new rules—or exploiting those rules, in the judgment of some.

By 1990, with the collapse of junk bonds, a porcupine-like set of defenses in effect at most companies, internal restructuring, and legislative and judicial support, the age of big-time hostile takeovers had sputtered to an exhausted truce. The liability scare had progressed beyond the pandemic stage and, though it still claimed directors as victims, was becoming a known factor in judging board service. Takeovers and their lesser known but more common cousins, internal restructurings, had become the acknowledged province of the board. The takeover decade and its liability fallout had shown boards that their decision-making processes must be lined up in a row and active. Also, the board must be, if not divorced from management, at least able to show independent judgment. Directors had been toughened by the 1980s but, by the dawn of the century's last decade, had learned valuable skills.

It was about then that a certain shareholder giant snorted in its sleep.

18

A Sleeping Giant Is Still a Giant

By 1990 much of the framework for the activist board of directors had been shaped. Starting almost 20 years earlier, boards had experienced a flowering of diversity in membership. Women and minorities had established beachheads in the boardroom. Though still too often stuck in token status, their fresh views and homeopathic effect shifted outlooks within the board as a whole. More substantial was the influx of outside directors and the solidification of a strong committee structure. By 1990, the average board had reached its current makeup of nine outside directors and three insiders, an impressive three-to-one ratio. Committees were well established, with compensation, audit, and nominating panels on the job, and taking more of the workload. The new boards may still have been uncertain of their duties, too much under the control of management, and receiving enough pay goodies to make them suspect, but members were slowly gaining confidence in their decisions.

Also empowering corporate boards by 1990 was the influence of a decade of takeover battles and courtroom decisions. Note that most of the cases discussed earlier hinged on the quality and fairness of the board's decision making. The assumption was that the board *had* made a decision and that even *not* deciding was to decide. This meant that boards may be thumped on the head occasionally by the court, but that the court was empowering the board through every decision, telling the board to use its powers or pay the price. Even the crowning Time-Warner case, which upset so many shareholder groups, did not fault the rationale of the board's decision but rather upheld the quality of the decision-making process.

The result was a tougher, more powerful, more independent board structure than ever imagined possible. With the 1970s, boards had gained the structure needed to exercise independent power. And in the 1980s, they had gained the toughening, professional standards and legal mandate to act.

Yet one final piece was still missing. Recall that from its earliest incarnation as frock-coated squires sitting around a plank, the corporate board had been powerful. It possessed, however, only a secondary power, derived from the immediate ownership held by those directors. As hands-on owner/directors gave way to financiers, the board's composition changed, but it retained great power. If you represented J. P. Morgan's interests on a corporate board, you had little problem in making your voice heard. When the entrepreneurs, capitalists, and titans of the boardroom made way for the managerial directors, the board's source of clout never even left the building. It had only to migrate down the hall from the CEO's office to the boardroom once a month. The top brass in the executive suites were the top brass on the board. This made the board formidable, but again, only as a legal mask for the executives who held power anyway.

The new, improved boards of the 1990s had divorced themselves from these puppet shows. The outside independent directors were now empowered CEOs, academics, and civic leaders. Despite the advantages seen in these new outside directors, they had one serious disadvantage compared to their predecessors. They lacked a mandate. No doubt that, by the start of the 1990s, the courts and liability lawyers had made it abundantly clear that boards had a *responsibility* for performing their fiduciary job. But who did the board really represent? When last we saw the shareholders of the United States, they had dispersed themselves into a quiet Berle-Means haze of impotence. Their holdings were small, transitory, passive, and often held by a distant trustee. This shareholding base was both as vast and yet as immaterial as a cloud. But, little remarked until the late 1980s, the billions of shares out there, scattered so long to the wind, were rapidly recoalescing into a power base that could potentially back directors up in a boardroom revolution.

Almost all writings about the power of institutional shareholders sooner or later use the term "sleeping giant." The implied metaphor is that all other aspects of corporate endeavor, boards, management, other equity holders, corporations themselves, even government regulators, are squabbling Lilliputians shocked to attention when the slumbering mass of Gulliver lets out a grunt and rolls over.

The figures would surely seem to support this image. The holdings of corporate pension funds; public funds, such as the California Public Employees Retirement System (CalPERS) and TIAA-CREF, the national educators' fund; insurance companies; foundations; and mutual funds have indeed become impressive. Pension fund holdings grew at an annual rate of 14.6% during the 1980s, hitting over $2 trillion by 1987.[1] The equity holdings of private pension funds alone topped $666 billion in 1989,[2] and by the beginning of the 1990s, the holdings of institutional investors in the largest 1,000 corporations approached 50%.[3] Descriptions of institutional investor holdings, and particularly those of pension funds, always seem to edge into the galactic. "If all of the equity held by TIAA-CREF was stacked up in dollar bills, it would reach to Jupiter"—that sort of thing. Holdings in specific companies are also quite eye-popping. As of 1990, the New York State and Local Retirement System was the tenth largest institutional holder of General Motors stock, as well as the tenth largest holder of Ford stock. When the New York holdings were combined with those of CalPERS, the two funds were respectively the fifth largest holder in GM and the fourth largest in Ford.[4]

Such market strength made institutions mighty, even if it did limit their flexibility. Like Gulliver, it was difficult for them to even scratch an itch without causing great repercussions. Further, it became increasingly popular for them to index their holdings, spreading them throughout broad, semipermanent investments. This was especially true for pension funds. While this might encourage investment manager fatalism, it also pushes managers to take a more hands-on role in the companies they are married to. If you are on an enormous ship sailing a preset course across the ocean, you can

1. *The Battle for Corporate Control,* Ira M. Millstein (contrib.), Business One Irwin, 1991, p. 70.
2. *Power and Accountability,* Robert A. G. Monks and Nell Minow, Harper Business, 1991, p. 183.
3. *The Brancato Report on Institutional Investment,* 1995.
4. "Institutional Shareholders: Con," Donald G. Margotta, *Corporate Board,* September/October 1990, p. 18.

shut yourself in your stateroom and hope for the best. More likely, though, you'll keep a damn close watch on the captain.

With such enormous, concentrated holdings in major companies, it is easy to see why, by the mid-1980s, institutions appeared the likeliest source of firepower for a true board uprising. Boards' improved structures and growing savvy and independence formed an ideal conduit for the greatest chunk of focused ownership seen in decades. Institutions needed a voice, and the board needed backup. What could be more natural? Yet despite this obvious symmetry, the influence of the big investors in the boardroom proved limited, uncertain, and at times contradictory.

Pension funds and mutual funds started their rise to prominence in the 1950s, and by the 1970s, their equity holdings had grown so large as to displace individuals as the major source of stock ownership. Mutual funds developed as a tool to encourage broad stock investment in the United States and proved highly successful, with $1.2 billion in assets by 1993, half of it in stock.[5] The potential influence of mutual funds on governance was recognized as far back as the 1930s, even before they actually were an influence. The federal Investment Company Act of 1940 nipped most mutual fund governance tinkering in the bud by limiting the control of mutual funds over company holdings and mandating diversification. Unable to own controlling blocks and with their need for great liquidity and jackrabbit changes in position, mutuals made little effort over the years to resist such restrictions on activism. However, the enormous growth of mutual funds had by the early 1990s made some degree of sway over governance inevitable. John Neff, senior manager of the Vanguard group, sent notes to Chrysler directors when he felt they were waffling on setting a successor for Lee Iacocca (and in 1996 Neff was named to Chrysler's board). More representative, though, was Fidelity Magellan fund's Peter Lynch who, before joining the board of W. R. Grace in 1989, sold the fund's stock in Grace.

Pension funds are another, more complex story. Among the institutions, pension funds alone own almost one-third of the market.[6] They represent two distinct segments, private funds and public

---

5. *Strong Managers, Weak Owners,* Mark J. Roe, Princeton University Press, 1994, p. 102.
6. Ibid., p. 124.

employee funds, with private fund holdings roughly double those of public funds.

Private pension funds, the single most massive piece of the institutional pie, have had a checkered history. Although the term "pension fund" today evokes images of a massive, fiduciary investor, 50 years ago the words would suggest something much darker. Between unfunded pensions leaving hapless retirees in the lurch and union looting of member savings, pension fund was a buzz term for chicanery and dirty dealing. In the Doonesbury comic strip, the ever-larcenous Uncle Duke best signaled his talent for venality by pleading, "But the pension fund was just sitting there!"

After World War II, federal laws both encouraged pension funds to grow through deductibility and made an attempt at reform by forbidding unions exclusive control of their pension monies. Increasingly, private company pension funds were managed by trustees named by the companies themselves. While money in these funds, and its subsequent investment, grew steadily in the postwar era, their organization and aims kept them from exerting any serious influence on corporate governance. With private sector unions cut off from guiding their own funds, labor was stymied.

The corporations had their own reasons to assure that their pension fund managers kept hands off the governance of portfolio firms. General Motors, which in many ways set the trends in corporate pension investment, had plenty of antitrust worries as it was in the postwar era without its pension funds buying controlling chunks of other companies. Indeed, GM fund managers were specifically instructed "not to meddle in corporate governance," according to Mark Roe. The managers were ordered to acquire no more than .0075% of any company's stock.[7] GM and other corporations had other reasons to keep holdings dispersed and their roles inactive. Future political winds might change, allowing unions to gain control of the pensions. Fragmented holdings improved liquidity. And of course, broad—if weak—ownership lessened risk, indicating prudent fiduciary trusteeship.

The importance of acting as a wise trustee became even more vital with passage of the federal Employee Retirement Income Security Act (ERISA) in 1974. The growth in pension plans had revealed flaws in the system, chiefly underfunded plans and vesting

---

7. Ibid., p. 130.

irregularities that left some employees with nothing to show for years of contributions. ERISA mandated better funding for private pensions, formed a federal insurance fund, and set tight new rules for fiduciary responsibility. A company acts as sponsor for a plan, which designates a fiduciary to manage it. Most often this is handled by a committee of the board of directors. This, by the way, gives boards a strong interest in corporate pension funds, but from the inside rather than the outside. The board committee typically designates an investment manager who has ultimate responsibility for the plan.

This trustee has legal liability for sound investment of the pension funds. With the federal government involved through ERISA, "liability" is a word not used lightly. ERISA "put the fear of God into trustees of private [pension] systems," according to Robert Monks,[8] by laying out carefully defined processes for fiduciary duty. For private pensions, that meant following the drill in investment decisions, not straying from conventional trustee wisdom, and avoiding entanglements in nonbusiness matters, such as the quality of a firm's governance. ERISA responsibilities make terms like "innovation" and "concentrated ownership" dangerous to the pension managers, who are encouraged to keep their heads down and follow the herd. Although ERISA applied only to private pension plans, most public plans have kept a de facto adherence to its rules as well, making it the standard for pension fund oversight—and timidity.

If ERISA duties were not enough to keep private pension managers on the straight and narrow, their bosses back at the company were also watching closely. Management has not hesitated to make it clear to pension fund managers that what is good for the company is good for them. Indeed, the CEO of Corporation A has been willing to contact the CEO of Corporation B and suggest that he or she chat with B's pension managers on how they plan to vote their A shares on a ticklish proxy resolution. This reached new heights in 1987, when GTE Chairman Theodore Brophy mailed a letter to CEOs whose pension funds held stock in GTE. Brophy asked the CEOs to communicate with their money managers to "provide specific voting instructions" to oppose a pending GTE proxy proposal.[9]

---

8. *Corporate Governance*, Robert A. G. Monks and Nell Minow, Blackwell, 1995, p. 145.
9. *Power and Accountability*, Monks and Minow, p. 192.

Public pension funds are a different matter, but with some key similarities. They are largely government or quasi-government institutions staffed by elected or appointed officials, or civil servants. Most are state and local funds, although a Federal Employee Retirement System (FERS) was initiated in 1986 and should eventually grow to enormous size. Usually classed with the public funds, although it is technically an independent trust, is TIAA-CREF, the national pension and insurance program for educators and education staff. Although they must meet fiduciary standards similar to private funds, public pension funds have proven more willing to rattle the cage of corporate governance. Indeed, when shareholder activists mention that slumbering institutional giant, they usually point to the public pensions and ignore everyone else.

Public pension funds made their first serious ventures into corporate governance in the early 1980s. These efforts were an outgrowth of the social investment activism that began a decade earlier. In 1970, a group of public interest lawyers and activists bought just enough stock to submit a series of social resolutions at that year's General Motors annual meeting. These "Campaign GM" initiatives were viewed as a progressive triumph, even though only two made it to the ballot, receiving 2.73% and 2.44% of the vote.[10] Such negligible support was a hallmark of the social initiatives submitted in the 1970s, which addressed such issues as South African disinvestment, the environment, nuclear energy, affirmative action, and military manufacture. Indeed, when a handful of social resolutions broke the 10% support barrier in 1975, it was viewed as a major achievement, although this still meant 90% of holders were opposed.

Most of the early social resolutions "faithfully reflected . . . origins . . . in the political struggles of the 1960s," according to author David Vogel, and were presented by ad hoc issue-oriented groups with small holdings. The names suggest the agendas: Clergymen and Laymen Concerned, the Church Project on U.S. Investments in Southern Africa, the Gulf Angola Project.[11] By the end of the 1970s, groups with better organization and more substantial holdings were making their wishes known at annual meetings. The American Jewish Congress led a campaign against the Arab states'

---

10. *Corporate Governance and Institutionalizing Ethics,* David Vogel (contrib.), Lexington Books, 1984, p. 77.
11. Ibid., p. 79.

boycott of Israel and in 1976 put resolutions on the ballots of 70 corporations. Major religious groups, such as the National Council of Churches, and universities with substantial holdings, such as Vassar, Oberlin, and the University of Minnesota, were submitting resolutions on South Africa.

By the early 1980s, then, public pension funds had dipped their toes into corporate governance matters, establishing precedents for activism. They had also found that success need not be measured in actual proxy support. Even if a vote on cutting ties to South Africa drew only a 10% approval, boards and managers would often hasten to defuse the matter by disinvesting. However, this early muscle building on social issues had its downside as well. Pension fund activism did not mean fighting for good governance, a higher stock price, or better management. Rather, it was associated with liberal causes, social protest, and annual meeting gadflys who droned on until the other shareholders were ready to start throwing their chairs.

In sum, there is no doubt that institutional shareholders were a massive force in the governance equation and could well have proven to be the rocket fuel that the board of directors needed. But their conflicting agendas, fiduciary limitations, internal contradictions, and political games meant that getting them to chart a consistent boardroom course was like trying to herd cats. Nonetheless, by the mid-1980s, the takeover turmoil had reached a point where institutions started to perceive some common threats. Both their political and fiduciary agendas were facing challenges. Maybe the sleeping giant would not rouse himself to action, but he did toss a bit in his sleep.

Takeovers drew concern from big investors on several wavelengths. Many of the takeover defenses adopted by corporations also neatly defended management from the shareholders as a group. Poison pills, if triggered, would severely dilute stock prices. Greenmail could make a raider go away but was essentially a ransom paid by management with company funds. Worse, it meant that one holder, the greenmailer, was being paid more for shares than other holders could ever hope to see. Staggered boards and the elimination of rights to call special shareholder meetings made a joke of shareholder democracy. Crown jewel asset sales sold off the *shareholders'* crown jewels, and often at a bargain price. From the outside, too many defenses seemed merely a defense of the current management team and not of shareholder value. The overall effect of many defense strategies was to drive down share prices and also to keep the shareholders from deciding for themselves which offer, if any, provided them with better value.

The institutions, no matter their background or agenda, could all find something in the takeover craze to disturb them. Indeed, some of their concerns put them on both sides of takeover battles. Successful takeovers tended to result in job losses and economic dislocation, of obvious interest to many union-related groups and state funds. Further, while fund managers fretted over the effect of defense tactics, their bosses might well have other agendas. In 1986 the state of Wisconsin's pension fund was planning to object to General Motors's paying Ross Perot three-quarters of a billion dollars to leave the GM board and go away quietly. But Wisconsin's governor scotched the idea—he was trying to coax GM into building a new assembly plant in his state.[12]

Still, takeover concerns prodded the first serious shareholder activism aimed at governance issues. In 1987, 34 proxy proposals were introduced by institutional holders, most dealing with the issue of poison pills. The support these proposals drew, as much as 30%, far outstripped that for social issues. Such support made it clear to boards and CEOs that a new concern was on the horizon and told institutional investors that they now had a real winning issue on their hands. Over the next several years, more such proposals were made, two of which, concerning poison pills and greenmail, received majority votes from shareholders.

Public pension funds led the charge here, with the New York and New Jersey state funds, plus CalPERS, among the trendsetters. The private pension funds let them. In a 1991 article on shareholder activism, General Mills Chairman H. Brewster Atwater observed that he was "never asked about poison pills by a private pension fund, but I am asked all the time by public pension funds."[13] For that matter, activism among the public funds was uncommon, and remains so. Robert Monks quotes one public fund activist: "There might be talk about all the new, awakened shareholders and institutional investors, but there's really not much more than a dozen

---

12. Ibid., p. 186.
13. "The Governance System Is Sound," H. B. Atwater, *Directors & Boards*, spring 1991, p. 17.

public pension funds involved."[14] Without TIAA-CREF, CalPERS, and the New York state and city funds, governance activism would likely never have gotten off the ground.

In the late 1980s, the pension funds also started to gain some allies on governance issues. Research and advocacy groups such as the Investor Responsibility Research Center (IRRC), Institutional Shareholder Services (ISS), the Council of Institutional Investors (CII), and the United Shareholders Association (USA) were of particular value in compiling research, generating public and investor relations, and bringing collective clout to smaller shareholder groups. Although these groups had a wide variety of agendas, members, and leadership (USA was launched by raider T. Boone Pickens; ISS was founded by establishment stalwart Robert Monks), all helped generate ideology and staying power for shareholder influence on governance.

The government was also adding its two cents worth, usually on the side of shareholders. Many pension fund managers found their proxy voting rights a nuisance, especially when the plan's trustee (the corporate managers or the state governor or whoever), pressured them on how to vote. The best way to deal with competing voices on a proposal was to stand pat and not vote at all. In 1988, though, the U.S. Department of Labor released an opinion letter to the Avon corporation that raised the value of proxy voting rights—and their responsibilities. According to the DOL, the proxy votes of a plan's holdings were an asset of the plan, and "the fiduciary act of managing plan assets . . . would include the voting of proxies."[15] Not to vote the proxies is to waste plan assets, negligence that ERISA rules would frown upon. Further, the Avon letter made it clear that the designated plan manager, not the trustee who designated that manager, retained the power to choose how to vote. "The manager would continue to have full responsibility (and liability) for the exercise of the proxy voting decision."[16] Subsequent DOL opinions in 1989 and 1990 drove home this mandate. Although this independence would continue to prove less than perfect in the field, the new DOL ERISA judgments were a warning signal

---

14. *Corporate Governance,* Monks and Minow, p. 134.
15. Department of Labor letter on Proxy Voting by Plan Fiduciaries, February 29, 1988.
16. Ibid.

that pension funds could no longer just kick back, sit on their proxies, and let the world go by.

Emboldened, institutional investors proceeded with more proxy initiatives, improving their coordination and strategies. A 1989 campaign at Honeywell, which included CalPERS, the Pennsylvania school employees pension fund, and ISS, brought shareholder rejection of two management proposals to stagger the board and limit shareholder meeting rights. As a kicker, the coalition noted that Honeywell's common stock price rose 22% over the course of the initiative, signaling market approval of shareholder activism.[17] Although the rise was also influenced by Honeywell takeover rumblings, the shareholder groups pointed to their campaign as a success for everyone—shareholders had done well by doing good.

By the end of the 1980s, corporate managers and raiders were seeking to harness the rising tide of shareholder activism to their respective causes. In 1990 Carl Icahn, rather than using his holdings in USX to launch a takeover, instead submitted a shareholder proposal calling for restructuring the conglomerate. CEOs, rather than trying to quietly slip antitakeover proposals through at annual meetings, started negotiating with major shareholders in advance to reach a compromise. When Texaco entered bankruptcy in 1989, many of the largest shareholders were institutions. Despite limits on public pension fund involvement in bankruptcy proceedings, institutional holders were able to take a seat at the table in Texaco's reorganization. Indeed, CEO James Kinnear and investor Carl Icahn each made pleas to the Council of Institutional Investors to support their competing reorganization plans. Kinnear gained the group's endorsement, and his management plan ultimately won the day.

Not everyone was thrilled by the growing role of institutions in corporate governance. Did the extremely broad holdings of the institutions encourage them to tinker with a corporation, at low risk to the investor but high risk to the company itself? Were some of the funds, especially mutuals, too willing to grab short-term takeover gains at the expense of long-term value? (The dovetailing of institution and raider interests hinted at this.) Do the interests of the large institutional investor always align with those of other investors in the company? If a fund owns large chunks of several com-

---

17. *Corporate Governance*, Monks and Minow, p. 150.

peting firms, will it face conflicts of interest? Despite the mass of their holdings, do institutional investors bring real commitment to governance or are they boardroom dilettantes? They may be *big* owners, but are they the *real* owners? In 1990, Northeastern University Professor Donald Margotta wrote, "What legitimizes the kind of influence institutional managers are attempting to bring to corporations? . . . While the institutions certainly have a great deal of money invested, the money is not theirs."[18]

Up to the 1990s, the institutions did not do much for improving the prospects of corporate boards either. The pension funds' proxy season bombing raids, if anything, tended to drive the board closer to management. It was as if the directors and the CEO were united in battling raiders on their right flank and shareholder activists on their left. The investors, for their part, still saw directors as filling their traditional role: dozing through meetings and voting "aye" when told to. However, as corporations came to accept the influence of institutional shareholders, the institutions began to appreciate the role of the board. The major investors were spread too thinly to provide continuous oversight of corporations. Their role thus far had been more reactive, usually prompted by a major issue, such as distasteful management actions on takeovers or a takeover itself. The board was supposed to exist to represent the interests of shareholders in supervising management. What if, a few progressive business thinkers wondered, just for once, the way things *were* could be brought into line with the way things were *supposed* to be?

---

18. "Institutional Shareholders," Margotta, p. 19.

19

Gloomy Investors vs. Fat-Cat CEOs

Hangovers are interesting things. The excitement, high living, late hours, and helling around that go into creating "the night before" never seem worth "the morning after." The raucousness of the 1980s likewise led to a spate of queasiness as the 1990s rolled around. Since the last hard recession of 1982, the economy had expanded throughout the decade. The Dow-Jones Industrial Average in 1990 stood at almost three times the level of eight years earlier. But government spending and federal deficits were also increasing that year, and spreading defaults in the savings and loan industry were estimated as costing the U.S. government $300 billion by 1993. The Iraqi invasion of Kuwait in August 1990 sent oil prices soaring and left the United States with an annual inflation rate of 6.1%, the highest since 1981. A 1990 federal budget agreement on cutting the deficit had done little to trim the deficit, but the plan's tax increases surely gave a hit to the economy. By the end of 1990, a recession was officially under way.

In historical values, this recession, which lasted from 1990 until early 1992, was rather mild. The 1982–83 recession had struck much harder in real terms, with unemployment soaring to 9.7% in 1982. Yet the recession of the early 1990s had an odd psychological staying power. George Bush, facing an election year with a dour electorate, grumbled, "I haven't really been able to sort out exactly why there has been this degree of pessimism."[1] This recession had the emotionally draining aspect of being very prolonged, starting in the summer of 1990 and dragging on for over 18 months. Despite

---

1. "Why We're So Gloomy," *Newsweek*, January 13, 1992, p. 34.

its statistical mildness, this made the 1990–92 recession the longest since World War II. By the end of 1991 the economy offered many turnaround signs, including record highs for the stock market, low inflation, and the lowest mortgage rates in almost 20 years (indeed, the Federal Reserve was almost desperately trimming interest rates to spark a recovery). Yet, as *Newsweek* observed in a January 1992 cover story (titled "Why We're So Gloomy"), "U.S. consumers have fallen into their deepest funk in years." A Time/CNN poll found that 84% of respondents felt the country was still in a recession, despite the fact that the downturn was economically over.[2]

There were other factors making the early 1990s recession so significant. The restructuring of the 1980s seemed to grow exponentially each year as we entered the 1990s. Unemployment may have been mild, but the jobs lost were not coming back for the foreseeable future. Worse, the new losses were much more likely to be among white collar professionals. The definition of a "consultant" as a manager who had just been laid off came into currency with a cynical twist. Many Americans for the first time began to believe that American upward mobility had climbed to its top rung. Stagnant wages left many U.S. workers trapped in an intractable economic decline, according to an early 1992 *Business Week* article.[3]

But the same *Business Week* item's headline hinted at deeper reasons for malaise in its title: "If It's a Mild Recession, Why Is It So Painful?" Bureau of Labor Statistics economist Jay Meisenheimer puzzled that "there seems to be an underlying lack of confidence that's not just coming from the recession."[4] The surly gloom of 1990 to 1992 seems to have been another, more telling aspect of our hangover from the 1980s. Media coverage of the perpetual recession turned into mass flagellation for the "excesses" of the 1980s. "The 1980s binge" was financed by massive debt, according to a typical observation in the above *Newsweek* article, and "the reckless borrowing made a reckoning inevitable."[5]

Reckoning. Retribution. Nemesis. The message driven home again and again by the media was that the United States was facing

---

2. Ibid.
3. "If It's a Mild Recession, Why Is It So Painful?," *Business Week*, February 10, 1992, p. 125.
4 Ibid.
5. "Gloomy," *Newsweek*, p. 34.

a spiritual payback for the capitalist sins of the Reagan era. We were paying a national penance for LBOs, Donald Trump, junk bonds, Michael Milken, and, of course, for the Gipper. Greed was no longer good.

The 1980s had produced a handy target for this 1990s populist sullenness. For the first time since the age of railroad capitalists and robber barons, top business owners and CEOs were celebrities. Can anyone name the chairman of Chrysler Corporation *before* Lee Iacocca? The decade's takeover wars were a factor in this identification. Warner Communications *was* Steven Ross. Hamish Maxwell *was* Phillip Morris. And, of course, F. Ross Johnson *was* RJR Nabisco. Restructuring, downsizing, and acquisitions on a grand scale were most common at corporations with a strong personal leader. While such moves may have been justified by the times, they also allowed this leader to carve and shape the corporation into a structure uniquely fitted to his or her goals and personality. No one could believe, for example, that Turner Communications would have developed in the same way it did without the idiosyncratic Captain Ted Turner at the helm.

However, at these and many other corporations, leaders shared an uncertainty about the future with their workers. Despite the lingering '80s glitter of being a CEO, all executives, even those at the top, were increasingly no better than their quarterly results. And the way those results were measured for a CEO of the 1990s added to the worries. Corporate executives of earlier decades were valued by the growth and size of their results and empires. Although such yardsticks remained, especially for the exploding high-tech industries, most CEOs were now being judged by how much they *cut*— cut expenses, cut facilities, cut fat, and, of course, cut employees.

If the takeover decade made corporate leadership as uncertain as the metaphorical fiddler on the roof, the defenses required also encouraged a siege mentality. CEOs dug themselves in and made sure at the very least that they had well-packed golden parachutes at the ready, plus pay befitting their status. But this executive nest feathering proved a bit of incredibly bad timing, not to mention bad public relations. By 1991, the United States was enduring both a recession and major economy-wide corporate restructuring, both of which brought falling corporate profits and major layoffs. At the same moment, though, the pay of those famous CEOs was headed violently upward.

If the compensation of U.S. executives had climbed in the 1980s, by the early 1990s it was literally shocking the world. Usually stolid business periodicals such as *Business Week* and *Forbes* were dedicating cover stories to the rising level of CEO pay outrages, and the issue even broke through into the mainstream media, such as *Newsweek* and *60 Minutes*. A 1991 *Forbes* cover story summed up the attitude: "It Doesn't Make Sense."[6] Even such a normally doughty defender of free enterprise as George Will in September 1991 wrote of executives "ripping off capitalism" with CEO compensation that was "generally disproportionate and often ludicrous."[7] In early 1992, President Bush led a group of top U.S. auto CEOs on a trade-building mission to Japan. As noted earlier, the most memorable event of that trip was a flu-ridden George Bush being sick all over the Japanese prime minister. But the *second* most memorable aspect was the storm of criticism faced by the "overpaid" U.S. auto execs who were pleading their case to the Japanese. The CEOs involved truly could not see what all the fuss was about. A year later, when I interviewed Lee Iacocca on the topic, he was still smarting over his treatment, blaming the Commerce Department for not responding to the criticism and grumbling that "the press has been merciless on compensation."[8]

Executive compensation consultant Graef S. Crystal had studied and written on the subject of CEO pay for years, but his message that pay and results were out of line had been a voice crying out in the wilderness. However, after he published a harsh new book on the theme in 1991 titled *In Search of Excess*, he was suddenly popping up in news articles, interviews, and business journals as an official gadfly. One of Crystal's findings was a link between restricted stock grants for executives and company performance—a negative link. If directors choose to give executives restricted stock grants, it is a sign that the stock price is not headed north anytime soon. This is good news if you plan to short the company's stock—not so good if you are already a shareholder.

Popular outrage makes excellent fodder for political advantage.

---

6. "Incentivize Me, Please," Dana Wechsler Linden, *Forbes,* May 27, 1991, p. 208.
7. Quoted in "Executive Pay: Out of Control?" Sen. Carl Levin, *Corporate Board,* January/February 1992, p. 1.
8. "Iacocca on Governance: An Interview," *Corporate Board,* September/October 1993, p. 3.

In May of 1991, a subcommittee of the U.S. Senate held hearings on executive compensation and tax policy and drew some damning testimony. Nell Minow, who was then president of Institutional Shareholder Services, paraphrased Churchill to note that "never have so few done so little to get so much money." At the same hearings, Linda Quinn, director of the SEC's Division of Corporate Finance, hinted that the commission would move to allow shareholders more say in the setting and monitoring of executive pay. Why not extend the current standard for "ordinary business" to include paysetting decisions?[9]

This drive for more shareholder involvement brought the corporate board, specifically the compensation committee, squarely into the pay issue gun sight. Early in the 1990s, activist shareholders were just feeling comfortable with governance issues when the cause that had drawn them, takeovers, became a moot point. The collapse of the junk bond market in 1989 soon cut hostile takeovers to a trickle. As Robert Monks and Nell Minow wrote, "It took the abuses of the takeover era to wake up the institutional investors, and almost before they got started, the takeover era ended. But by that time, a new issue took over: excessive CEO compensation."[10]

Although the popular media was stirring up rage over the *amount* of CEO pay, activists and shareholders were more narrowly concerned with *how* CEOs and top managers were paid and how well the board tied that pay to performance. A particular CEO's pay could be stratospherically high, but estimates by various media and government offices of just how high would vary widely. That is because a complicated mixture of such ingredients as base pay, bonuses, long-term incentives, options, and stock grants could be very difficult to decipher. Often it seemed as if the confusion was intentional, with pay values and bases buried among pages of footnotes in the annual report. Performance incentives for executives could be so rigged as to be near fail-safe. At General Dynamics, a ten-day uptick in the stock price doubled the annual salaries of top executives.

One result of the Senate hearings was a 1991 package of legislation sponsored by Sen. Carl Levin with the noble-sounding title

9. "In Review," *Corporate Board*, July/August 1991, p. 27.

10. *Corporate Governance*, Robert A. G. Monks and Nell Minow, Blackwell, 1995, p. 238.

of the Corporate Pay Responsibility Act. The bill would have allowed shareholder votes on top executive pay policies, compelled simplified, uniform disclosure of executive and director pay, and demanded calculation of the value of executive stock options. For good measure, it included other shareholder reforms, including shareholder rights to nominate proxies and to access the stockholder list, plus confidential voting. A companion bill was also introduced in the U.S. House.

These were not the only government attempts to close in on the issue of executive pay. In the same year, Rep. Martin Sabo proposed a bill disallowing tax deductions for top manager pay exceeding 25 times that of the company's lowest-paid workers. And in early 1992, a House tax reform package first raised the idea of limiting tax deductibility on executive pay to $1 million. The SEC also busied itself on the subject, with more immediate effect. In February 1992, the commission began requiring corporations to accept nonbinding shareholder resolutions on executive pay. Finally, the Financial Accounting Standards Board, under pressure from the Levin proposals, in April 1992 moved to require that the value of executive stock options be deducted from earnings.

Shareholder activists, backed up by public anger and legislative concern, were quick to name names when it came to the root cause of overpaid CEOs. In testimony at the above 1991 Senate hearings, Ralph Whitworth, president of United Shareholders Association, focused attention on the executive pay issue where it would do the most good. "For all practical purposes, boards are appointed by management. . . . Board members are dependent upon—and thus beholden to—the CEO for their positions, pay and perks."[11] Senator Levin was more direct: "Charges are growing that corporate boards are responsible for runaway executive pay, and are themselves benefiting from the excess."[12] In short, the general issue of overpaid executives, and the more specific concern of pay that did not match results, were both symptoms of a larger problem—boards that were in bed with management.

---

11. "Executive Pay," Levin, p. 2.
12. Ibid.

20

A Flowering in the Boardroom

With the upsets, turmoil, and toughening corporate boards had faced over the past couple of decades, we could assume that they would face the pay issues of the 1990–92 recession by hunkering down and waiting it out. Yet it now appears that the combination of sluggish performance and CEO pay was the final element needed to ignite a board renaissance. In the years preceding this explosion, boards of directors had reshaped their membership, with more estimable independent outsiders. They had restructured, with committees increasingly responsible—in the fullest sense of the word—for the business of good governance. The takeover years and the plague of liability had toughened boards, forcing them to act with urgency, to dot their i's and to take no action they could not justify before the entire world. The takeover era had also brought a small but influential cadre of institutional shareholders and activists out of the woodwork and given them the motivation, tools, and skills to be a governance presence. Federal legislation and the SEC were strengthening this power. Although the goal was supposed to be a battle against "corporate greed," the means to this end was to give more authority to shareholders.

The executive pay issue was pivotal because it proved to be the first effective wedge between the board and management. Past issues, such as takeovers, may have given the board more power, but especially at the target company, they encouraged a "we all hang together, or we all hang separately" attitude. Liability suits would hit the board, management, and usually anyone else the strike suit lawyers could think of. But on the issue of pay and performance, all of the board powers, legal precedents, and regulatory policies converged on a common theme—the board is responsible for management.

There was a resolve in the air in U.S. boardrooms in the early 1990s that reflected this new sense of accountability. "We are in the midst of a fundamental change of thinking in the boardroom," wrote former Avon Chairman Hicks Waldron in 1991.[1] Directors for the first time were discovering themselves as a distinct, potent corporate entity, not as the ghost of some other interest. Professionalism as a director trait no longer consisted of knowing the right people and knowing when to keep one's mouth shut. Roger Kenny, director of board search firm Boardroom Consultants, recalls that "the recession of 1990–92 saw the institutional investors getting more vocal, especially CalPERS. This was the trigger that boards needed. I've had directors tell me that CalPERS and TIAA-CREF were the ones that really gave them the backbone to make changes."[2]

In the midst of national discontent over business in general and corporations in particular, there was a sudden flowering of confidence in the walnut-paneled boardrooms. Even the rigors and pain of corporate restructuring seemed to empower boards. While CEOs hacked away at expenses and organizational charts, they were also weakening their own management empires. And if every corner of the company had to become lean, pull its own weight, and even excel to survive, how could the board justify being the only useless decoration left in the corporate structure?

The skills of directorship, so long an afterthought or adjunct of management, began to receive attention as a discrete profession, with standards of practice and unique training requirements. "We began to see board training take off in the early 1990s," recalls Roger Kenny, "though early programs were a bit elementary, or looked at only bits and pieces of governance."[3] In 1992, the Wharton School's Executive Education Department launched its Director's Institute, one of the first formal board-training programs. Corporate directors attended an intense two-day series of mock board meetings for the fictional "MegaMicro, Inc.," sharpening their skills

---

1. "Boardroom Myths and Facts," Hicks Waldron, *Corporate Board,* July/August 1991, p. 3.
2. Author interview, December 1995.
3. Ibid.

and learning about board issues. The program proved an immediate success. The National Association of Corporate Directors had begun offering seminars on governance as far back as 1977, but the association found enrollment increasing in the early 1990s and expanded its programs. Harvard, Stanford, and a number of other universities also joined the director education trend. Director evaluation, long considered an intrusive waste of time when it was considered at all, suddenly popped up as a topic of polite conversation.

New tools and techniques helped back up this rush to reform. The 1991 government concerns over executive pay led to new policies and laws during 1992. In February the SEC announced that it would allow shareholders to submit resolutions on executive pay for a vote at annual meetings, and investor groups quickly put the ruling to work. Proposals were offered at various companies to cut short-term executive incentives, base management bonuses on specific stock price targets, and end repricing of underwater executive stock options, among many others. Although none passed, a proposal at Black Hills Corporation to end director pension plans drew 44% of the vote. The number of proposals was even higher the next year, as was the average support.

In October 1992 the SEC had a busy month. New rules were announced requiring disclosure of the pay of top executives—and requiring the *board* to show how that pay was related to company performance. The compensation committee was required to list the specific factors and criteria used in relating the pay of CEOs and other top execs to company results. Given that very few companies even *had* such factors and criteria, compensation committees found themselves meeting busily for a few months. Executive pay disclosure, formerly dispersed and uncertain, suddenly had to be objective and able to stand in the naked light of shareholder scrutiny. Options and grants had to be valued. The SEC rules frowned on using general boilerplate standards and required graphic comparisons of company results to peer companies. Though the new rules made compensation consulting a boom industry, they empowered compensation committees as never before.

Also that October, the commission revamped shareholder communication rules. While the pay disclosure changes were largely a matter of internal board work, the shareholder reforms had their impact from the outside, making it easier for investors to launch initiatives. Under the old SEC rules, if a company shareholder sought to communicate with more than ten other holders, he or she had to submit the comments to the SEC for advance approval. The changes eliminated this censorship aspect for investors not seeking a change in control, requiring only that a copy of the comment be filed with the commission. Shareholders also gained more access to proxy lists and found it easier to elect their own directors. In 1992, then-SEC Chairman Richard Breeden told me that the reforms were a response to "criticism that government was making participation in governance difficult. We need more investor input, not less."[4] When the new communication rules were proposed, business comments were sharply critical, and the Business Roundtable even threatened suit. However, the final rules were adopted by the end of the year and led to a rollicking 1993 proxy season.

For the corps of investor activists, these changes were good news. As groups such as CalPERS honed their skills and became more sophisticated at activism, they found that dealing with management could bring mixed results. Perhaps it was smarter to make an end run around the CEO and go straight to the boardroom. In late 1991, CalPERS CEO Dale Hanson queried, "How can we make corporations accountable again? We believe that the answer is to focus on the board."[5] Directors, long a minor factor in investor relations, began building contacts with their companies' IR departments. In some firms, such as Avon and Texaco, directors started taking part in IR meetings with stock analysts. In preparing for the 1993 proxy season, Hanson of CalPERS announced a formal strategy of meeting directly with the board members of underperforming companies.[6]

Hanson also sought to give relations between directors and the shareholders a more permanent structure with the formation of Shareholder Advisory Committees (SACs). The SACs would serve as a go-between body of representatives elected by major investor groups to offer input and feedback to the board. Similar committees were also sought by the New York state pension fund and Institutional Shareholder Services. SACs were viewed as a consultative group, able to give the board a shareholder's take on issues like

4. Breeden interview, *Corporate Board,* September/October 1992, p. 32.
5. "What Does CalPERS Want?" Dale M. Hanson, *Corporate Board,* September/October 1991, p. 2.
6. "In Review," *Corporate Board,* March/April 1993, p. 26.

board nominations, pay, and restructuring. SACs met with resistance along the way (their basic function was to do what the *board* was already supposed to be doing), but CalPERS was able to sell Ryder Systems on setting up such a group.

A more powerful message from investors to the board could be sent through the Just Vote No technique. First proposed by former SEC commissioner and academic Joseph Grundfest in 1990, Just Vote No was an organized investor campaign to withhold votes from the management slate of directors. Such a move could bring no substantive result and, indeed, offered no alternative slate. Instead, it sent a strong, if mute, message to the board and to management that they had lost the confidence of a key group of shareholders. It was boardroom passive resistance, the corporate equivalent of a boycott or sit-down strike, and must have appealed to the '60s veterans who could still be found in many shareholder activists' groups.

The negative vote totals themselves were not very impressive. A 1991 campaign at ITT drew 1%, and the next year such moves at GM and Dial brought only 2%. Other 1992 "no" votes totaled 6% at Sears, Roebuck and a highwater mark of 9% at Champion International. Despite its symbolic, nihilistic nature, a Just Vote No campaign could bring some solid results. Publicity of the vote (and one of the keys to Just Vote No was wide publicity) signaled that there was dissension in the shareholder ranks of the company and encouraged raiders to put the company in play. In 1991, Brewster Atwater, CEO of General Mills and governance spokesman for the Business Roundtable, testified before the U.S. Senate that he knew of "no board that would not be moved dramatically" by a strong Just Vote No initiative.[7]

Publicity was the key to another early 1990s investor activism tool, the CalPERS list. Although CalPERS had been active in governance issues since the mid-1980s, in 1987 it began to compile— and later to publicize—a "top ten" list of "underperforming" companies. These were corporations seen as lagging behind peer firms in shareholder return and amenable to improvement by adopting some of the more popular governance reforms. The 1992 list (which was actually a "top 12"), for example, sought more independent

---

7. Quoted in *Corporate Governance*, Robert A. G. Monks and Nell Minow, Blackwell, 1995, p. 221.

outside directors at Time Warner, executive pay reforms at American Express and IBM, and formation of Shareholder Advisory Committees at Chrysler, Polaroid, and USAir group. As a sign of the growing trendiness granted corporate governance, by 1992 the yearly CalPERS hit list was guaranteed coverage in the *Wall Street Journal, Business Week,* and all the other major business media. CalPERS usually found corporations eager to negotiate if it meant staying out of the headlines as a boardroom malefactor.

And the headlines were, assuredly, a place no corporate director wanted to be. Even at corporations with the highest profile, the board members preferred to go about their work in the quiet, personal-chemistry way that had always proven most effective for good governance. Despite the new pressures, despite the liabilities, despite the spotlight on corporate performance, boards work best when they are noticed least. But the early 1990s focus on the failures of corporate performance and the "Who, me? Yes, you" attention that boards received for those failings finally dragged directors onto center stage. Over the years, an unspoken but universally felt attraction of board service had been the status of the title "member of the board." Sure, achieving the office of CEO meant you had arrived, but being named to a corporate board meant the world had *acknowledged* your arrival.

Still, as with other secret societies, your membership was news only among your fellow elect. Service as the director of a corporation, especially on the board of a Fortune 500 company, was something you mentioned to the world sparingly: in your vitae, at testimonial dinners, or in official biographies. If someone *else* mentioned your membership on a board, it was usually negative: "Where was the board of _____ when this disaster was unfolding?" No longer could a company go bankrupt, face indictment, or be fined, and drag only the CEO's name through the mud. Directors now shared the odium, not only on a legal basis, but personally. If the director was inattentive, failed to act, or allowed management to run wild, his or her good name was at risk. As they say in sports promotions, "This time it's personal."

The science of astronomy tells us about the power of planetary convergences. At specific moments over the years, some of the major planets align themselves in such formations that the combined gravitation can cause notable effects on the earth. Compared to that, what happened in U.S. boardrooms in 1992 was certainly no apocalypse, but the alignment analogy holds true. Board liabilities, talents, structure, demands, regulation, and mindset, along with outside ownership, the spark of recession, and pay, all fell into sequence for a few brief moments. But it was enough—enough to launch a boardroom revolution.

21

"The King Is Dead": The CEO Firings of 1992–93

Suddenly it was the spring of 1992, and the board of General Motors demoted its chairman, firing him altogether six months later. If directors of the biggest industrial enterprise in the world could rouse themselves to fire the chairman when results were lagging, was anything sacred anymore? Apparently not, because the period from Robert Stempel's initial dressing-down in April of 1992 to mid-1993 saw an unprecedented string of CEO sackings by major corporations. As of January 1993, 13 Fortune 500 CEOs had been ejected by their boards in the previous 18 months.[1] Compaq founder and CEO Rod Canion lost his job in October 1991, replaced by Chairman and major investor Ben Rosen. James Ketelsen, CEO of Tenneco, was fired in May 1992. Ken Olsen, who had founded Digital Equipment and led the company since the 1950s, was pressured into retiring by his board. In October, of course, the GM board dropped the other shoe in the dismissal of Robert Stempel.

The last week of January in 1993 was a shocking period for boardroom coups, stars falling from the executive firmament in a virtual meteor shower. On January 26, the IBM board, having lost faith in Chairman John Akers, showed him the gate. The very next day, January 27, Westinghouse Electric made the same move with Chairman Paul Lego. On January 29, 1993, the American Express

---

1. "The King Is Dead," Thomas A. Stewart, *Business Week,* January 11, 1993, p. 35.

board finally won a protracted succession battle with CEO and Chairman James Robinson. And in August of that year, the Eastman Kodak board sacked Chairman and CEO Kay Whitmore.

Even now, only a few years later, it is hard to express the sensation this accelerating series of coups stirred in the business world. In January 1993, *Fortune* offered a cover story titled "The King Is Dead" loaded with anecdotes about guillotines and Shakespearean quotes about treachery. The changes were "large, basic and historic" for CEOs, with "the boards of directors themselves, the king's own court to whom he gave preferment, now demanding his obeisance—if not his head."[2]

Despite all this Elizabethan hyperbole, it should be noted that the idea of the boards of large companies firing their top executives was not entirely new or novel. In an intriguing 1983 *Academy of Management Review* article, Mark S. Mizruchi concludes ten years in advance of the board usurpations that directors were already unafraid to exert their control over management when results faltered. Mizruchi found examples of board CEO oustings "plentiful enough to call into question the managerialist claim of the passive rubber-stamp board." He cited such cases as the 1979 firing of Colgate-Palmolive CEO David Foster and the 1981 canning of AM International Chief Roy Ash.[3] Yet, in most of the cases noted, personal factors also played a part in the firing. It could be that a downturn in profits or a bad acquisition was the excuse for a firing already ordained by lousy boardroom chemistry.

Most of the ejected CEOs from 1992–93, however, had built solid relationships with their boards. Indeed, in some cases, like that of James Robinson at American Express, the deposed boss was a long-time master at pampering directors. Each of the CEO firings from this era differed from the others in the same way each company and each human being is unique. Taken together, though, they offer lessons on how power had drifted from the chair's seat to the rest of the boardroom table.

The Rod Canion case at Compaq, arguably the first of the modern CEO sackings, showed how high-technology companies, despite their talent for innovation, stick closely to the classic board

---

2. Ibid., p. 34.
3. "Who Controls Whom?" Mark S. Mizruchi, *Academy of Management Review,* 1983, p. 429.

models for governance. Compaq Computer, founded in 1983, showed years of solid growth under founder Rod Canion, specializing in premium-priced PC innovation. By the start of the 1990s, however, high fixed costs and nimble competitors were shrinking Compaq's niche. In October 1991, a quarterly loss of $70 million was reported, and the company had not introduced any new models in the previous year. Benjamin Rosen, Compaq's board chairman, was one of the company's first investors and still held a substantial stake. For several months before the October loss announcement, he and the board had pressured Canion to implement a strong recovery strategy for Compaq, but Canion's efforts seemed halfhearted. Investors were losing confidence, and the stock price was falling. In October, Canion literally had to pitch to Rosen and the board to save his job. Apparently his salesmanship was not enough. Canion was bounced, and Compaq President Eckhard Pfeiffer was elevated to the CEO slot to launch a turnaround.

At American Express, the overthrow was messier, more public, and much more prolonged. James Robinson III, AmEx CEO since 1977, had followed an aggressive strategy of acquisitions and joint ventures since his tenure began. Such costly additions, including Shearson, Lehman Brothers, and E. F. Hutton, brought uneven results, led by huge losses at Shearson. Worse, by the beginning of the 1990s, AmEx was doing poorly in its core charge card and traveler's check business. The company boasted one of corporate America's all-star boards, including Henry Kissinger, opera star Beverly Sills, Union Pacific CEO Drew Lewis, and William G. Bowen, president of the Andrew Mellon Foundation. As noted earlier, though, in Robinson's hands the AmEx board was also noted as one of the most cosseted and had long proven amenable to the chairman's strategies.

By mid-1992, a faction led by director and former Mobil Chairman Rawleigh Warner Jr. was growing impatient. Still unwilling to oust Robinson, they pressured him to at least set up a succession plan. Robinson waffled until a September board meeting, when Warner read off a sharply critical list of strategic setbacks AmEx had faced under Robinson. Facing a threatened coup, Robinson agreed to announce his retirement, effective at a future date to be determined. A board committee would choose a successor. The price of AmEx stock rose on the news. But Robinson retained enough clout with the board to gain approval of his choice for CEO, then AmEx President Harvey Golub—and to retain his position as chairman.

The decision, announced after a January 25, 1993 board meeting, led to a storm of criticism for the board, which "made itself a laughingstock by letting [Robinson] stay" according to an article in *Fortune*.[4] Infuriated at Robinson's finessing of the succession issue, Warner and two other directors announced their resignations. The board resignations led to increased investor cynicism about AmEx, triggering a fresh dip in the stock price. New CEO Harvey Golub found stock analysts uninterested in his turnaround plans, instead demanding to know how the AmEx board could have taken such a dive. Within days it was apparent to Robinson that he had won the battle, but lost the war. On January 29, he announced that he was resigning his chairmanship as well. Director Richard Furlaud, who had headed the search committee, was named outside chairman. In July 1993, Furlaud turned the reins of chairmanship over to Golub.

---

4. "The Hunt for Mr. X," *Fortune,* February 22, 1993, p. 68.

22

Big Blues, and How to Keep Your Job

The slow decline of IBM has been, after General Motors, the most studied case of corporate rot in recent history. IBM's reliance on mainframe computer architecture as its cash cow left it vulnerable to the multiplication of cheaper, more flexible personal computer networks. Speaking of PCs, IBM had, of course, been the maker who first developed the open-system, DOS-based platform—which everyone who could install a motherboard had proceeded to copy, stealing the market. For 1992, IBM reported a yearly loss of almost $5 billion.

Despite increasingly desperate restructurings, initiatives, and personnel shifts, the IBM of CEO and Chairman John F. Akers was "a flailing giant unable to extricate itself from the mire of an outdated strategy and culture."[1] IBM's 18-member board included many boardroom superstars, such as Thomas Murphy, chairman of Capital Cities/ABC, former Johnson & Johnson CEO James Burke, and J. Richard Munro, who had recently left Time/Warner as CEO. Though staunchly defending Akers, the board faced growing criticism from investors for wilting stock prices. Worse, Akers seemed hidebound by the world-famous IBM command structure, unable to make mold-breaking moves or name chiefs who were not business-as-usual insiders. James Burke, who acted as the board's unofficial leader, gathered director opinion to force a showdown with Akers. On January 26 the IBM board, impressed by the storm hitting the American Express board for giving in to James Robinson

---

1. "IBM's Board Should Clean Out the Corner Office," Judith H. Dobrzynski, *Business Week*, February 1, 1993, p. 27.

the previous day, met with Akers and made its position clear and firm: Akers had to go. "There is going to be change. This is a tough board. This is not American Express," said director Thomas Frist at a press conference that evening.[2] Burke led a board-based search for a new CEO from the outside. The heavily publicized (some thought too publicized) search settled on then RJR Nabisco CEO Louis Gerstner in April.

However, the IBM board was not off the hook yet. Shareholders seemed less inclined to say "thank you" than to ask, "What the hell took you so long?" "The business did get a little beyond us," confessed Richard Munro.[3] In a famous incident a month after the sacking, several outside directors met with CalPERS officials to reassure them that Big Blue was now in good hands. CalPERS chief Dale Hanson proceeded to ask the directors of the world's biggest computer company how many of them actually knew how to use a PC. Mmmm, well, none. How many of the directors even owned a computer? Uhhhh, well . . . (mass clearing of throats). By mutual agreement with CEO Gerstner, several long-time directors resigned from the board that summer.

If January 25 lit the fuse at American Express and the 26th saw the reformatting at IBM, the 27th brought a switch-about for Westinghouse. The bleeding at Westinghouse had gone on for a long time, mostly caused by unwise acquisitions in place before CEO Paul Lego took over in 1990. Lego, who had worked his way up in the company from the engineering side, led a management team that seemed uncomfortable dealing with the diverse company's holdings in real estate and finance. The Westinghouse stock price had fallen from 36 when Lego took command to 13 in January 1993, and losses were in the multibillion dollar range. This did not keep Lego from earning $2.4 million in 1990 and 1991. Efforts to sell weak divisions during late 1992 dragged, and Westinghouse found itself in such rough waters that bankruptcy was even considered.

Major investors had long considered Westinghouse a basket case and had been unusually active in pushing for reform. A November 1992 *Business Week* article on the firm's shareholder critics

---

2. "The Hunt for Mr. X," *Fortune,* February 22, 1993, p. 68.
3. "These Board Members Aren't IBM-Compatible," *Business Week,* August 2, 1993, p. 23.

reads like a Who's Who of investor activism: CalPERS, Robert Monks and LENS, United Shareholders Association, and the New York City Teachers' Retirement System were all attacking Westinghouse management and its board. Indeed, a United Brotherhood of Carpenters fund spokesman was quoted as saying that they had no plans to hammer Westinghouse yet precisely because everyone else was already doing so.[4] However, when the Westinghouse board met on January 27, it handled its decision to fire Lego in a surprisingly adept manner. The board had learned from the Stempel ousting at GM the previous fall and the unfolding controversy over Robinson at American Express. Directors Richard Morrow, former CEO of Amoco, and Frank Carlucci quietly marshaled board opinion and data, and within the course of a long board meeting, relieved Lego of his title quickly and painlessly. Some might say *too* painlessly: Lego received a two-year consulting contract worth $600,000 per year, a lump-sum severance payment of $800,000, and a lifetime pension of almost a million dollars annually.[5]

At the end of January 1993, the boardroom revolution paused for breath, but boards were still on the prowl, and activist investors were still nipping at their heels. Indeed, the chairs of some sick companies, such as Eastman Kodak's Kay Whitmore, were roused to action by the ongoing boardroom carnage. Kodak, the huge, established first-mover in photography, had watched profits and market share sag for years as its inbred management team showed a depressing talent for ditching technology it should have explored while chasing ideas that led nowhere.

Kodak jumped onto Polaroid's turf of instant photography in the 1970s but infringed key Polaroid patents in the process. The result was a shocking patent settlement that cost Kodak almost a billion dollars. Kodak had considered, and then passed on, the new concept of xerography in the 1950s, letting Xerox create an empire. Kodak came back to the field in the 1970s and 1980s, designing copiers that were better and cheaper than those of Xerox, which had its own problems by this time. But Kodak frittered away its edge while Xerox regrouped, and by the early 1990s Kodak was losing

---

4. "The Rebels Are Banging on Westinghouse's Boardroom Door," *Business Week,* November 16, 1992, p. 48.

5. *Corporate Governance,* Robert A. G. Monks and Nell Minow, Blackwell, 1995, p. 192.

money on its copier division. Similar miscues in the videocassette recorder and photo CD-ROM markets followed. The 1988 purchase of Sterling Drug led the company far from its core expertise, tripled Kodak debt, and left the firm with a dog. Meanwhile, nimble competitors like Fuji were nibbling away at Kodak's core photo film business.

Whitmore, who took office in late 1989, inherited many of these woes and undertook some major restructuring initiatives prompted by Wall Street concerns over sagging share price and poor results. These restructuring moves took on a new urgency in January 1993 (no surprise), and Whitmore named Christopher Steffen as Kodak's new Chief Financial Officer (CFO). Steffen was hard-charging (if you liked him, difficult if you didn't) and a cost cutter who brought experience from Chrysler and Honeywell. He promised to shake up Kodak's insular culture. In a January meeting with Robert Monks of the LENS investment group, Whitmore described a massive restructuring program and major work on the core photo business. As an intriguing sign that shareholder concerns were making progress, Whitmore also announced that Kodak's top 40 executives would be required to purchase company stock worth up to four times their annual salary. Finally, Whitmore announced formation of a board committee of outside directors to evaluate the company's restructuring progress.

These moves bought time for Kodak, and for Whitmore, and brought a jump in stock prices. But the love fest did not last long. On April 28, 1993, Steffen announced his resignation, less than three months after joining Kodak. Hired to launch a major overhaul and cost-cutting program, Steffen had found the Kodak bureaucracy hopelessly counterrevolutionary. Also, it was reported, his push for hard and quick economies had alienated the easier-going Whitmore. Investors, who had only started to regain faith in the firm, quickly lost their religion, and Kodak's share price dropped five dollars in a single day. Whitmore soldiered on with the restructuring, but the board's outside directors, chiefly Coca-Cola Chairman Roberto Goizueta and retired New York Stock Exchange Chairman John Phelan, began to search for fresh leadership. In August 1993, Kay Whitmore joined the ranks of corporate insiders who found themselves suddenly on the outside.

These were the central upheavals that defined the boardroom revolutions of 1992 and 1993. As I've said, they were by no means the first cases where a board rose up against management. The 1989 departure of Ford Chairman Donald Petersen is widely accepted as a case where the board told the boss they wanted him gone but allowed him to call it a resignation. However, Ford was doing well at the time, and the firing was prompted less by leadership failings than Petersen's tin ear in dealing with the Ford family members on his board.

Further, some of the revolutions left the general in command, albeit chastened. At Sears, Roebuck, and Company, Chairman Edward Brennan led another of the ailing corporate giants, rapidly outpaced by rising retailers such as Wal-Mart. Sears's retail outlets tended toward large, money-losing "everything for everybody" locations in declining neighborhoods, and its financial and real estate subsidiaries were uneven performers. Brennan, in charge since 1986, was a third-generation Sears man and held five titles with the company, including CEO, chairman, head of the retailing operation, and chairman of the board's nominating committee. Institutional shareholders, including the ubiquitous CalPERS, sought the sale of lagging assets, formation of a Shareholder Advisory Committee, and restructuring.

In 1991, Robert Monks of the LENS group launched a protracted, ultimately futile effort to join the Sears board, where an ever-rising level of boardroom bulwarks were raised against him. Brennan ultimately bested his critics and held on until his planned retirement in 1995. But Sears's shareholder activists still gained many of their goals. A massive restructuring and sell-off of nonretail units, begun in 1992, paid off in improved profits and share prices. Sears had trimmed three inside director slots during its battle with Monks, but these were later filled by two new respected outside directors, Phillip Morris Chairman Michael Miles and retired Kellogg CEO William LaMothe. And Ed Brennan finally shed a few of his titles, recruiting future successor Arthur Martinez from outside the company and putting him in charge of the retail division. If the James Robinson fiasco at American Express showed how a chairman could salvage his job but still lose, Ed Brennan's turnaround at Sears showed how the chairman could both fight off a challenge and make everyone a winner.

23

How to Launch a Board Revolt

What lessons did the boardroom coups, near coups, and sieges of the early 1990s teach? From General Motors on down, there were a number of shared factors that point to the future role of the board.

Problems were most severe at "cozy" companies.   If a company is successful, we point enviously at its "shared values," its "culture," and its "common mythology." If the company is ailing, though, we cut the Joseph Campbell crap and spot the problem as one of inbred, sluggish, stultifying bureaucracy.

Indeed, the difference between strongly cultural companies that are successful and unsuccessful may depend on which point in their life cycle we look at them. IBM, General Motors, Sears, and Kodak were for many years brilliant titans precisely because of their strong, insider-based value structures. IBM and its famous white-shirted, red-tied management clones were a postwar cliché. The tight, feudal hierarchy of General Motors, a huge serfdom overseen from the 14th floor of the GM building in Detroit, was well described by John DeLorean in his book *On a Clear Day You Can See General Motors.* At Sears, as noted, Ed Brennan was the third generation of his family to work at the tribal retailing giant. And at Kodak, Kay Whitmore's attempts to overhaul the Rock of Rochester were subverted by go-slow entrenched managers. Most of these CEOs were career men with the company, long-term parts of the problem, and unable to be part of any solution, much less radical rethinking. The provincial basis of some of these weary giants was also doubtless a factor. GM in Detroit, Sears in Chicago, Kodak in

Rochester—too often companies found themselves with a global presence, but a provincial mind-set and talent pool.

The boards themselves were often shaped by such inbreeding. Although the major companies may have had world-class directors, too often they were willing to let company tradition outweigh the need for radical change. Another, less-noted sign of the hidebound board was that some of the real giants noted above had governance traditions shaped by powerful, visionary long-lived founders. The Watsons, senior and junior, were the heart of IBM from its founding until well into the 1970s. At GM, Alfred P. Sloan designed the essential GM corporate structure in the 1920s, served as chairman for years, and in his ninth decade was still serving as honorary chairman. Such enormous father figures were the sort to whom boards would leave the big decisions, especially in an era when boards were quiet anyway. Such a board culture lingered long after Big Daddy was gone. As I wrote in a letter to *Fortune,* in 1993, "The patriarch eventually leaves, but the board's culture of acquiescence and faith is set, and persists even when follow-up caretakers lead the firm astray."[1]

Despite having many outside stars on their boards, the older, inbred corporations tended to closely marry the management structure to the board structure. Retired chairs traditionally stayed on the board (strong continuity factors at American Express, Sears, and GM), and the companies were not leaders in paring the number of insiders on their boards. As late as 1985, GM still had six inside directors along with Chairman Roger Smith, including former Chairman Thomas Murphy. Such companies, with inbred management and inward-looking boards, proved inflexible and slow to react.

The CEO was an old softie. Now God knows, you did not claw your way to the 14th floor at GM by being a wimp, but you did not rise well through the bureaucracy of the above companies by making waves, either. Asking impolite questions, pushing bold ideas, and thinking the unthinkable is *not* the sort of attitude we encourage around here, young fella. As *Forbes* magazine observed in eulogizing Kodak's Kay Whitmore, he was "typical of a breed who ran most major U.S. corporations in the 1970s and well into

---

1. Letter from the author, *Fortune,* May 31, 1993.

the 1980s. Men (always men) who rose to the top through affability, by being 'one of us,' good and faithful company men."[2]

At GM, one of the reasons Robert Stempel's leadership was hailed in 1990 was Stempel's reputation as "by far the nicest guy in GM's upper ranks." A longtime aide was quoted as saying, "Bob Stempel is just a big, good old shit."[3] He was a lifelong car guy who remained loyal to his team. He hesitated to cut production and lay off GM workers precisely *because* he knew how much pain he would cause. Despite his willingness to streamline the GM structure, Stempel was like Mikhail Gorbachev, both leaders who sensed a need to reform the system but shrank from destroying it.

At American Express, James Robinson had used his long tenure to almost reverse the Company Man stereotype, reshaping AmEx into a Man Company—in his own image. Though seemingly far from the provincialism of other coup companies, Robinson's AmEx was in fact their mirror image duplicate. If GM had created its own little hothouse nation, Robinson had grafted AmEx onto the greater corporate/government power axis, with himself as "corporate America's Secretary of State."[4] One reason it took so long for his board to accept that Robinson was leading the company astray was his terrific image-building skills. An advisor to presidents, director on some of the U.S.'s most distinguished boards, a smooth politician with his own directors, and a member of the southern gentry, Robinson was a one-man definition of the establishment.

When the ousted CEOs were replaced, boards tended to pick permanent replacements from outside the old CEO's in-group, and often from outside the company altogether. Kodak recruited George Fisher from Motorola. IBM lured Lou Gerstner from RJR Nabisco. At Compaq and GM, the nod went to Eckhard Pfeiffer and Jack Smith, insiders who had made their names running overseas operations. By their actions, the boards were hinting that they had gotten the message. They had figured out that shoving the current number two person into the corner office would not do the trick and would indeed only perpetuate the system that had created

---

2. "The Road Not Taken," *Forbes,* August 30, 1993, p. 41.
3. *Comeback,* Paul Ingrassia and Joseph B. White, Simon & Schuster, 1994, p. 164.
4. *Barbarians at the Gate,* Bryan Burrough and John Helyar, Harper & Row, 1990, p. 186.

the current problems. A strong figure from outside the family was needed to take harsh measures.

There is a lesson here, but one that needs careful delineation. The maxim "Nice guys finish last" does, and should, disquiet us. One likely reason Napoleon and Hitler were so willing to lead their countrymen into huge, murderous military ventures is that they *were not* leading their countrymen. Both were outsiders, Napoleon a Corsican, Hitler an Austrian. This gave them the detachment to view the people under their control as expendable means to an end.

This analogy hardly seeks to compare the replacement CEOs to callous dictators. Had these new CEOs not made the tough decisions to cut hard and cut fast (another common denominator), *all* the companies' employees might have found themselves out of jobs. In retrospect, the men brought in to shake up and cut back took actions that saved their companies. Rather than fault the dumped CEOs as being too nice, we should instead fault them as being inattentive and uncertain, willing to accept small failings for too long until they compounded into rolling disasters.

A "present crisis" was needed to goad the board. If the old CEOs let small problems propagate until drastic measures were needed, what did that say about the board? Who is most at fault for a quality control disaster, the guy on the assembly line or the person supposedly in charge of supervising quality control? In the above CEO firings, operating problems had been apparent for a long time, and in cases such as GM and Kodak, for decades. As a sign of the growing focus on boards, directors received their full share of blame for sitting on their hands for so long. In the AmEx case, an institutional investor was quoted as saying, "Think of how out of touch the company's board really was."[5] At General Motors, Robert Monks observed, "The board deserved as much criticism as either Roger Smith or Robert Stempel. . . . Eventually, finally, tragically late, the board did the right thing."[6] The shareholder value of IBM had fallen for six years by the time John Akers left, and industry analysts had been making it clear for nearly a decade that the future did not

---

5. "House of Cards," *New York*, February 15, 1993, p. 28.
6. *Corporate Governance*, Robert A. G. Monks and Nell Minow, Blackwell, 1995, p. 367.

lie with mainframe computers. Kodak's string of bad bets had extended back to the 1970s.

In none of these cases is there evidence that management lied to the board, much less perpetrated any fraud. Aside from using the CEO's prerogative to put the best spin on financials, directors received a reasonably accurate accounting of the company's downhill slide as it happened. Even if the CEO was schmoozing the board and assuring them that things would turn out fine once the darn recession ended, there were plenty of outside voices predicting doom. Industry analysts, stockwatchers, the business media, annual meeting gadflys, and shareholder activists had in every case been sounding the alarm long before the board finally moved, in some cases for years. Plenty of information on their company's falling share prices, rising debt, weak acquisitions, slumping sales, and lack of new products was no further away than the day's *Wall Street Journal*.

Yet these results were still not enough to prompt the boards to act. In most cases, an imminent crisis was needed as a catalyst, even if it was only the capper to a string of disappointments. At American Express, the trigger that led to Robinson's firing was his sluggishness at setting up succession procedures. At Westinghouse, Paul Lego's ouster came two weeks after the collapse of his attempt to sell the money-losing Westinghouse Credit division to General Electric. On January 19, 1993, IBM posted a 1992 loss of almost $5 billion, the largest in U.S. corporate history and IBM's first-ever operating loss for the previous quarter. One week after this double whammy of infamy, CEO John Akers was history. At GM, Robert Stempel was, by the fall of 1992, down but not quite out. Then in October, GM's worsening finances prompted Moody's Investors Service to consider sharply lowering GM's credit rating, cutting off the world's largest corporation from the commercial paper market. Within a month, Stempel was unemployed.

Given the failures, losses, and declines in market share and stock price these companies had endured, it seems hard to believe that the above events were the straws that broke the camel's back. Certainly at GM, the threatened bond downgrade seemed more like just another rung breaking on Bob Stempel's ladder. Yet, despite the new spirit, activity, and purpose of these boards, old habits lingered. Recall that in the CEO firings of a decade earlier, such as Colgate-Palmolive, evidence suggests that the board decided it did not like the CEO's style long before a dip in results provided an excuse for the ouster. The class of 1992–93 may have faced a similar mechanism, although on a much more serious scale. It is likely these CEOs were already terminal by the time a single, unifying crisis moved the coup to its conclusion. If this was truly the case, boards had grown up a great deal by the early 1990s, but not enough. If they hesitated to move until the present crisis, what were they doing through all of the earlier crises?

A "lead director" took the lead.   Over the past few years, a popular academic concept for board independence has been the lead director. The lead director would be an outsider with a strong executive background, much experience, and a get-tough attitude. He or she would serve informally as the board's dean and a counterweight to the combined CEO/chair. I'll examine this idea in more detail later, but the CEO firings of the 1990s suggest that lead directors already do a fine job of designating themselves, thank you.

Boards do not act through spontaneous combustion. In most cases, the fingerprints of one or two particular outside members are found on CEO sackings, especially the opening moves. At American Express, former Mobil Chairman Rawleigh Warner led the charge. At GM, John Smale, chairman emeritus of Procter & Gamble, not only gathered the evidence against Robert Stempel, but took over as GM chairman for three years. In the Compaq case, venture capitalist Ben Rosen was already chairman, making the ouster of Rod Canion that much simpler. James Burke, retired chairman of Johnson & Johnson, organized the IBM board's move against John Akers, backed up by fellow director and Capital Cities/ABC Chairman Tom Murphy.

These tough old buffaloes had only one thing left to prove in their careers—that the board would not be caught napping on their watch. Most were retired CEOs with long experience at running successful companies. They knew just where an underperforming CEO would not want them snooping, precisely because they had been CEOs themselves. They had ridden out a few up-and-down business cycles and could tell the difference between tough times and weak management. And, though no one had elected them, they ideally fit the definition of a lead director. They were able to gain the respect of other outside directors, had the clout to get questions answered within the company, and had the political skills to organize the board without the CEO's say-so.

While this sounds positive, there is still no doubt that even the best of these governance godfathers, such as John Smale, acted too slowly. Particularly in Smale's case, the board also dragged the proceedings out for far too long, six months between wounding Bob Stempel and finishing him off. While experienced CEO-directors know what incompetence looks like, they have likely been in a few such jams at their own companies, or at least have suffered under an overly meddlesome director. Empathy for the sinking CEO may cause them to keep their hands off for too long.

Finally, the great majority of major companies, particularly the Fortune 500, currently have at least one director who meets the above description. The board nomination habit of seeking elder, name CEOs guarantees this. Yet the attention drawn by the above companies, and the subsequent CEO sackings up to the present, shows how uncommon such coups really are. Certainly this is not caused by a lack of underperforming companies. In too many cases, combinations of a tough boardroom leader and a foundering corporation have existed and continue to exist. While these boardroom deans were one of the strongest factors in the board coups of the '90s, they remain an unreliable watchdog for shareholders.

Noisy shareholder groups kept up the pressure. Indeed, it is doubtful most of these boards would have acted without this pressure. As noted, at Westinghouse the hapless Paul Lego was on the "naughty" list of all the name investor groups. Investors grew increasingly displeased with GM in the years leading up to Stempel's ouster, extending back at least to 1986 when Roger Smith essentially paid Ross Perot greenmail to leave the board. The CalPERS snubbing during the 1990 succession process and GM's subsequent financial meltdown brought unprecedented outcries from major shareholder groups. One of Ira Millstein's roles during the GM crisis was to act as liaison between the board and institutional holders, such as CalPERS. And institutional shareholder outrage was one factor making James Robinson's boardroom countercoup victory so short-lived.

Yet there are limits to the power of the best-known institutions. Robert Monks spent two years in his quixotic quest to gain a seat on the board of Sears, to no avail. CalPERS, for all the noise and info-bits it generated and continues to generate, does not often call for boards to take specific actions—such as canning the CEO. When it has sought specifics, such as splitting the positions of CEO and chair, it usually had little to show. CalPERS may have voiced investor outrage over the AmEx board knuckling under to James Robinson, but not until J. P. Morgan, mutual funds, and top stock analysts made clear their disdain was the die cast. Most of the success achieved by CalPERS has come through its role as a publicizer and negotiator, the trailblazer that draws the attention of the quieter but more volatile holders.

Outside agitators—plus inside agitators—played a role.   In an April 1992 front-page story in the *Wall Street Journal*, attorney Ira Millstein was cited as the *eminence grise,* the "Grey Eminence," behind the GM board's demotion of Robert Stempel. Grey Eminence is a powerful, spooky term, suggestive of palace plots, of secret influences, of powers behind the throne. Certainly Millstein had served as the board's chief counsel for five years, but according to those in the know, he was also the board's chief ideologist in organizing and justifying the coup.[7]

Millstein was a longtime critic and thinker on the role of corporate boards and a powerful supporter of board empowerment. In his writings and consultations with boards, Millstein supported the concept of a "certifying board." A certifying board would be one able to act as the corporation's superego, an accountability mechanism and reality check for the board to the shareholders and for the CEO to the board. In the case of GM, Millstein coaxed the board into fulfilling this certifying role—and decertifying Robert Stempel. As if that were not enough, Millstein also served as outside counsel to the board of Westinghouse, where he helped focus the board's moves against Paul Lego. Ira Millstein was not a name that brought comfort to underperforming CEOs.

However, Millstein was not the only board spark plug that proved crucial to the boardroom uprisings. At Westinghouse, lower-level executives provided valuable data to the directors, whom they saw as seeking positive change. Boards were dependent on outside counsel for legal opinions, shareholder views, internal numbers, in-

7. "Behind Revolt at GM, Lawyer Ira Millstein Helped Call Shots," *Wall Street Journal,* April 13, 1992, p. A1.

dustry norms, and other data to back up their case. By "outside," I mean outside the board itself. The spark plug, or mediator, or mole could be a source separate from the corporation or someone within management. There is speculation that, in the GM case, Ira Millstein was less an instigator than a "beard" used by the board and top corporate staff to shift blame for the revolt outside the company. Perhaps it is less appropriate to call these extraboard forces "spark plugs" than to view them as enablers. Rather than lighting the spark, they nurtured the flame until it burst forth into revolution.

24

Good—and Bad—Lessons Learned

These CEO firings, and the more recent ones, such as the sacking of William Agee at Morrison-Knudsen, offer a few other lessons on governance, some less positive. If the 1980s saw corporate management learn the tools and techniques needed to fight off takeovers, the 1990s may have seen them learn how to fight off board coups, or at least delay them. Note that in some of the later CEO firings, such as that at Kodak, the CEO was more willing to at least go through the motions of shareholder and board reform. Kay Whitmore in early 1993 worked overtime to make nice to shareholders, required managers to buy stock, and formed a board Corporate Directions Committee of outside directors. When Christopher Steffen quit as CFO, Whitmore hastened to assure the activist investors that he was still committed to change and appreciated their efforts. Yet he avoided any of their more fundamental governance recommendations, such as splitting the jobs of CEO and chair, or adding more outsiders to the board. Although Whitmore's tactics ultimately failed in keeping him employed, they seem to have bought him six more months to work for a turnaround.

The Sears case showed how a tough CEO who maintained the support of the board could defeat shareholder challenges and keep his or her job. Ed Brennan fought off Robert Monks's efforts to join the board, defeated 1992 shareholder proposals to split the CEO and chair jobs and end staggered director terms, and added outside directors.

The 1995 firing of Morrison-Knudsen CEO William Agee suggested that shrewd bosses learned survival techniques from the deposed CEOs of a few years earlier. Agee, who had headed the construction and engineering giant since 1988, had in the years leading up to his sacking built a reputation for a glamorous lifestyle and for launching big, expensive projects, such as rail ventures. Losses on the rail projects, plus lowball bids on construction jobs, put the firm deeply in the red, with losses of $310 million in 1994. Problems with Agee's leadership and results had been apparent for years, yet as late as 1993 the MK board rewarded him with a compensation hike to $2.4 million.[1]

By early 1995, though, the board finally took charge, uncovered the straits the company was in, and in February fired Agee. The MK board was an impressive group by any standard and included stock guru Peter Lynch, Peter Ueberroth, and former Carter administration advisor Zbigniew Brzezinski. How did this elite miss the financial sinkhole Agee was leading them into? First, the board had been handpicked by Agee with unusual care, most being close friends before they were tapped as directors. Interlocks were a vital part of the cozy MK board, with an unusual twist: Agee's wife, Mary Cunningham, and the wives of several other board members were all on the board of a major charity known as Nurturing Network. Top management at MK below the CEO level was in constant turmoil (CFOs and presidents rarely stayed more than 18 months), so it was difficult for officers to gain intelligence on what was going wrong with the firm. Also, this fast turnover left directors unable to forge any useful links with staff. This combination of family bonding and executive upheaval kept Agee in office until the company's losses were truly desperate. Even after Agee left, the damage proved so great that in June 1996, Morrison-Knudsen filed for bankruptcy. Years after the lessons of the CEO coups, then, shareholders were still able to ask, "Where was the board?"

For positive lessons on firing the CEO, we should begin at the beginning. Remember when founder Rod Canion was squeezed out at Compaq in 1991? This first of the modern CEO sackings may well have been the best from a governance perspective. First, in line with the rapid pace of the computer industry, losses at Compaq had begun only recently. The board was deeply worried over "a six-month decline in revenues, profits and market share."[2] Such losses

---

1. "The Bad News Board," *Newsweek*, April 3, 1995, p. 46.
2. "Compaq's New Boss Doesn't Even Have Time to Wince," *Business Week*, November 11, 1991, p. 41.

had dragged on for years at GM, Sears, and IBM without directors losing any sleep. Also, Canion was in no position to lead the board astray on these setbacks because he was not leading the board at all. His only positions were CEO and board member. Investor Ben Rosen served as a nonexecutive chairman. When Compaq's troubles became apparent, Rosen swiftly urged Canion to shape a major restructuring and cost-cutting regimen. Canion developed the plan and began to implement it, but Rosen "felt that it just wasn't aggressive enough."[3] In a 14-hour board meeting in October 1991, the Compaq board mulled the future of the company. Though they took their time in making the decision, there was nothing tentative about the final result. Rosen led the board in sacking Canion and replacing him as CEO with Eckhard Pfeiffer. Compaq's board structure gave it "the ability to act when we felt it was necessary to act," according to Rosen. A *Fortune* article examining the overthrow could not help but note, "Rosen maintains that if GM's board had been similarly structured, it would have removed Robert Stempel long ago."[4]

The Compaq coup was fast, certain, and strategic, and brought immediate action. Pfeiffer jumped Compaq's ad budget 60%, cut engineering staff, introduced new models, and slashed prices up to 32%. The results? One year later, the business media were marveling over "The Revolution at Compaq Computer."[5] Third-quarter 1992 sales were up 50%, and earnings had quadrupled, hitting $72 million. Market share rose from 3.5% in 1991 to an estimated 6.5% in 1993. The Compaq scenario became ammunition for those who advocated splitting the CEO and chair jobs, and offered an early— if largely unnoted—example of how to do a board coup right.

Discussion of these boardroom CEO firings, whether they were handled well or poorly and no matter the later turnaround, misses one last, crucial point. Even in the Compaq case, firing the CEO is frankly a sign of failure. The pain, publicity, and turmoil it causes, even today, are factors causing boards to shun CEO firings until things get *really* bad. Such a drastic, nuclear option by its nature is disruptive and wasteful. Worse, it suggests that such rough justice is the only real tool at the board's command. If corporate

---

3. "The Revolution at Compaq Computer," *Fortune*, December 14, 1992, p. 80.
4. Ibid.
5. Ibid.

directors face no choices but to either fire the chief executive or exercise their own "Wall Street walk" from the board, then our corporate governance system itself needs improvement.

How can we move beyond this reactionary, fire alarm board style to make boards a true, systematic player in corporate governance? As we move toward the twenty-first-century corporate board, we can see the outlines of this better system of corporate governance dawning. Improved boards are already taking shape from the ground up, with change in who joins the board, how they will function and be rewarded, and how board responsibility will be redefined. These changes are structural and evolutionary, and rarely headline makers. Though they will add up to a reinvention of how U.S. business governs itself, the differences will seem subtle. The twenty-first-century corporate board will be the same as today's corporate board. Only different.

PART II

Toward the 21st Century Corporate Board

25

Board Revolution: This Time We Mean It

Business story headlines announce the radical reforms hitting U.S. corporate boards. "Change Invades the Boardroom," blares *Fortune*. Liability and shareholder pressures on directors have "frightened them into re-examining their own performance."[1] Another *Fortune* article intones that "The Boardroom Is Becoming a Different Scene." The governance forecast is a stormy one: "Beyond the assaults on individual boards, the entire system is under siege."[2] Both articles foresee radical reinvention of the board as imminent.

It is hard to argue with such an apocalyptic assessment of the corporate board, except for one problem. The first *Fortune* article is dated 1972. The second, 1978. I have found many other "radical change is coming" boardroom predictions extending back 20, even 30 years. For the last quarter of this century, wise business observers have regularly made the following observations:

- Boards are not the cozy enclaves they used to be.
- Boards are getting tough with CEOs today.
- Boards face much greater pressure now from the public, the government, and the shareholders.

1. "Change Invades the Boardroom," Peter Vanderwicken, *Fortune*, May 1972, p. 156.
2. The Boardroom Is Becoming a Different Scene," Lee Smith, *Fortune*, May 8, 1978, p. 150.

- Boards are asking tough questions and demanding answers of management.

Indeed, I find it difficult to write about the twenty-first-century corporate board without a distinct sense that I am shouting, "Wolf! And this time we mean it!" Part of this false-alarm syndrome can be traced to the tremendous growth in the reach and immediacy of our business media. When a business trend is noticed, even if it is slow-moving, erratic, and debatable, some media scribe will promptly flack it as the imminent second coming. When this trend displays the inconsistency and sluggishness that were there all along, the media follows up with "What Happened to the Revolution?" stories. The subject is forgotten for a few years until the change is again noticed by some other bright pundit, at which point the whole cycle repeats itself. In this sense, the "new spirit sweeping our boardrooms" is the business equivalent of the video-telephone, which we have been regularly assured is just around the corner at least since the New York World's Fair of 1939.

Thus, some cynicism on the Boardroom Revolution is justified . . . to a point. While there is much the same about the current crop of jeremiads, there are some fresh indicators that suggest that the governance glacier is finally moving in earnest, that *this time* the change is real.

First, there is no doubt that the *level of news coverage* on board functions has increased dramatically during the 1990s, becoming more insightful and sophisticated. A decade ago, it is doubtful anyone at any level of business could have named an outside director of the General Motors board (aside from Ross Perot, who made headlines for *leaving* the board). The firing of Robert Stempel turned the GM directors into celebrities, whether they wished to be or not. Media coverage of major business stories today may look first at the CEO, but attention quickly turns to what the board is going to do—and how it could have allowed such a mess to happen.

When Archer-Daniels-Midland Company faced explosive antitrust and price-fixing charges last fall, investors and business reporters at once focused on the ADM directors and their weak oversight. "Is ADM's Board Too Big, Cozy and Well-Paid?" asked an October headline in the *Wall Street Journal,* the sort of query a journalist never asks without already knowing the answer. The board's large size (17 members), tightness with Chairman Dwayne

D. Andreas (the board had three other Andreases as members), and high pay (averaging $100,000 yearly, almost three times the national average) were considered relevant business news.[3] As we approach the new century, media coverage of boards no longer consists of occasional, vague backgrounders on how great change is coming to the boardroom. The change is here. Board performance is now being handicapped as closely as the CEO's quarterly results. The board's pay, perks, size, and structure are being studied as carefully as share price for indicators of the company's prospects.

Another clue that the revolution in governance has finally arrived is a negative one: *the busy silence of the major institutions.* Ten years ago such reticence would have been the rule, particularly from private pension funds and mutual funds. With the upheavals of 1992–93, however, the institutional investors seemed to be everywhere at once, going public, compiling figures, meeting with directors, and filing resolutions. Although it was rare for the institutions to overtly demand that a particular CEO be fired, they were busy passing ammunition to the board for the final act.

Since 1994, however, the CEO firings have fallen to an occasional tabloid case, usually related to illegal behavior as much as results. The United Shareholder Association folded its tent in 1993, claiming its task of empowering shareholders had been fulfilled. CalPERS President Dale Hanson left in 1994 and was replaced by the much lower-keyed James Burton. In late 1994, Ralph Nader complained to me in an interview that CalPERS was "going quiescent" (drawing an angry response from CalPERS's general counsel Dick Koppes).[4] As we wind down the decade and the millennium, the institutions seem to have returned to their knitting. Oh, CalPERS still produces its list, and we still see lots of shareholder resolutions being filed, but the investor wave of five years ago seems to have abated.

Not really. Better to say that those who once had to shout to be heard now need only whisper. The CEO firings of the past few years, to paraphrase Doctor Johnson, concentrated the minds of surviving CEOs wonderfully. CEO and even director meetings with representatives of the big investors are now common and tend to

---

3. "Is ADM's Board Too Big, Cozy and Well-Paid?," *Wall Street Journal,* October 17, 1995, p. B1.
4. Nader interview, *Corporate Board,* January/February 1995, p. 32.

bring quiet compromise on contentious issues before any noisy proxy battles develop. Fewer shareholder resolutions on governance issues come to a vote today because the institutions use the resolutions as a bargaining chit in jawboning the CEO into change. Only when an agreement cannot be reached do the investors resort to shareholder votes.

The quality of these resolutions has also changed, becoming at once more technical and less defensible on the corporate side. Ten years ago shareholder governance proposals advanced splashy, controversial topics such as South African disinvestment or shedding nuclear-related industries. Although such resolutions grabbed headlines and stirred passions, there were legitimate arguments against them, and they tended to gain results largely as PR gambits. Today's resolutions are like governance cruise missiles, designed to home in on precise, narrow targets—often where the corporation is most vulnerable. The 1996 resolutions presented by the Investor Rights Association of America were aimed at such technical governance matters as board pensions and benefits, requiring director pay in stock, and classified boards. The shareholder communication reforms of 1992 have made it easier for investor groups to pool strategies on such issues, and organized opposition (outside of management or the board itself) is negligible. IRAA was able to achieve a 35.85% average vote on such proposals in 1995, with a number of the resolutions winning outright majorities.

Investor activism, though quieter, has grown more popular in part because it seems to work. A growing body of evidence suggests that shareholder activism raises share prices, even if a takeover is not in the air. Stephen Nesbitt, in a 1994 *Journal of Applied Corporate Finance* article, offers data that suggest a real, beneficial "CalPERS effect" from institutional input. Studying 42 companies targeted by CalPERS as underperformers, Nesbitt found that in the five years after CalPERS came knocking, "these targeted companies outperform the [Standard & Poor] index by 41%." This study also suggested an intriguing clue on the importance of governance in turnarounds. It found that CalPERS's efforts from 1987–89 were much less successful than those launched after 1990. Why? Before 1990 CalPERS had concentrated on putting out antitakeover fires. But starting with the new decade, their strategy shifted to a greater concentration on building value and share price "through more aggressive pressure on management and board directors."[5]

Such a shift from making noise to gaining results through improved strategy is found with all major institutions. Robert Pozen of Fidelity Investments in 1994 wrote that activism could be an effective technique for raising stock prices, but only if the right tools were used. His research cast particular doubt on what he terms "procedural frills," such as forming shareholder advisory committees and splitting the roles of chair and CEO.[6] These "frills" have indeed become less urgent topics for investor jawboning and resolutions. As investor groups have gained a sharper ability to separate feel-good proposals from the serious value builders, management and boards have grown more willing to view investors as someone other than just another barbarian at the portcullis. At least talking with the institutions can do no harm, and their ideas might just raise the share price. Such relationship investing is a trend for the future. The lions may not yet lie down with the lambs, but at least they are in meetings.

With hard evidence that shareholder activism can bring positive results, the traditional activists are gaining reinforcements. Input from institutional shareholders no longer means that all the heavy lifting is handled by the public pension funds, with private investors merely giving an occasional nod. Major commercial funds are increasingly willing to make their voices heard. Campbell Soup Company, long an innovator on corporate governance matters, in 1993 directed the managers of its pension funds to take an activist role in voting their proxies. Companies with more than three inside directors, or which tried to reprice underwater stock options, would receive "no confidence" votes, and the Campbell fund managers were told to support measures tying executive pay to shareholder value. These moves have been warmly applauded by shareholder activists but have yet to receive much follow-up by other private pension plans.

Still, major private funds today seem more willing to exercise

---

5. "Long-Term Rewards from Shareholder Activism," Stephen Nesbitt, *Journal of Applied Corporate Finance,* Winter 1994, p. 80.
6. "Institutional Investors: The Reluctant Activists," Robert C. Pozen, *Harvard Business Review,* January/February 1994, p. 146.

their traditional supporting role in governance—weighing in at the crucial moment to tip the balance. At Chrysler in 1992, upper managers, board members, outside investors, and analysts all expressed their concern that Lee Iacocca was dragging his feet on naming a successor. However, when portfolio managers from Wellington Management went public with their concerns over the delay, the wheels quickly started turning in Chrysler's boardroom. Within a week, the succession of Robert Eaton as CEO and chairman was announced.

As a third major clue that the new process of board change is for real, consider that all this ferment is occurring *during a time of economic growth*. Look back on the recent history of board change, and you will find that most turmoil coincided with economic slowdowns. The early moves to make boards affirmative action employers and to hold them accountable for corporate lawlessness aligned with the recessions and oil shocks from 1970 to 1975. The SEC, legislative, and stock exchange moves to increase director independence and build the committee framework came with the Carter years and the economic malaise of 1978 to 1980. Takeovers kept boards busy during most of the 1980s, but the great CEO firings of 1991 to 1993 were one outgrowth of the lingering early 1990s recession and its gloomy aftermath that hung on after recovery had begun.

Since that time, however, the United States has enjoyed economic growth and remarkably low inflation. Unemployment is also low, as are interest rates. The stock market soared during the first half of the decade, the Dow-Jones Industrial Average bursting through the 5,000 mark late in 1995 and up 33% through the course of the year. Yet despite this market happiness, shareholders keep applying their sub-rosa pressure on boards and CEOs, boards continue to can the occasional CEO, and we keep raising the bar on good governance procedure. Indeed, one downside to a rising stock market is that any company with a sluggish stock draws investor attention like a Wall Street sore thumb. The rising tide does not lift all boats, and modern shareholders, and increasingly boards, demand to know why. Even at top performing companies, investors want to know if all the value possible is being realized. And despite rising profits, the investors still do not like the way management and the board pay themselves.

Boards now have the expertise, motivation, and courage to

keep a closer eye on management. They are willing to look beyond short-term jumps in stock price or profits to ask where things are headed in the future. Are we seeing all the financials? Could trouble be hidden away somewhere? Does the CEO's strategy make sense in the long term? Are we ready for the next downturn?

Yes, the next downturn. At this writing, a few indicators have taken a chill, though there are always a few signs of slowdown somewhere to keep the bears happy. The next recession is certain to come sooner or later—economics assures us of that. This cloudy horizon should give any CEO who has not yet learned the fear of God (or any director who thinks he or she might finally be able to grab 40 winks) pause. The pressure on boards to truly hold management accountable, to exercise strong oversight, and to increase shareholder value has been quietly building during a time of economic growth. Gee, what will it be like when the next recession actually hits?

The final clues that boards have irrevocably changed as we start a new century are to be found *on the board itself.* Changes in board membership, structure, and pay have not slackened since the revolts of 1992–93. Indeed, they have accelerated. Some aspects of governance that were not even considered five years ago, such as paying directors at least partly in stock, have rushed from oddball experiments to becoming the paradigm. Shareholder resolutions are moving beyond director pay and benefit issues to mandate the basics of good governance, like canning directors who miss too many meetings or limiting the number of board seats directors can hold.

Yet such investor pressures, unrelenting as they are, remain externals. *Professionalism* has become the buzzword for board structure and oversight. Shareholder value, good supervision, and active involvement with management to gain results have grafted themselves onto the genetic code of corporate America. We can judge their results by what we see within U.S. corporate boards, by the new people, new practices, and new purpose of the twenty-first-century board.

26

The New Directors:
"Who Are Those Guys?"

- Corporate boards in the United States consist of talented, tough-minded individuals who combine corporate status with shrewd business insight.
- Corporate boards in the United States are filled with homogenous, unchallenging mediocrities selected because they are unlikely to disagree with the CEO.

These two statements express today's breadth of common wisdom regarding who is named to corporate boards and what they do once they get there. The reason we have such trouble dealing with current board issues is that both statements, as contradictory as they seem, both accurately describe U.S. boards of directors. Indeed, in some cases, the ultimate paradox occurs—the same board is both tough and passive, sometimes at the same meeting.

There are several reasons for this. The first, and most obvious, is that in a culture with rapidly converging management techniques, the board of directors remains amazingly idiosyncratic. Every board of directors is different from all others, a unique corporate fingerprint reflecting the business's hierarchy, its markets, its history, its strategy, its management, and, of course, its board membership. As noted earlier, the scholarship and study of corporate boards is still a largely ignored field. Corporate management techniques have benefited (however questionably) from several generations of business school research and training. Millions of MBAs can be depended on to make management a discipline, if nothing else. Armies of consultants are eager to offer companies an ever-changing lineup of management models and buzzwords.

In the boardroom, however, there remains little more than shared wisdom and rules of thumb for decisions as central as precisely what the Audit Committee is supposed to audit. State charter requirements, SEC and exchange standards, and accepted fiduciary norms form a defensive perimeter of legal minimums the board must respect. Legal precedent and corporate counsel impose checklists on a few crucial matters. Beyond this, though, the board is largely on its own. This ad hoc nature should allow innovation to flourish, but instead it often forces boards to continually reinvent the wheel. And too often, they invent square wheels at that.

A more subtle quandary is that corporate board members are at once very unique, yet very alike. I have always found it odd when media coverage of a corporate board imbroglio uses phrases like "The board was concerned" or "The board expressed its doubts." The image is presented of a seamless Greek chorus, commenting on the action with one voice. Yet the board of directors of a major company is made up of individuals, and often very *individualistic* individuals at that. Despite media images to the contrary, these are not people who tend to follow like sheep. Particularly at the Fortune 500 level, modern outside corporate directors are people who have already made a major mark in life. Chief executive officers, former presidential cabinet officials, retired legislators, top academic administrators, senior law firm partners, entrepreneurs—such people are comfortable with wielding power. Indeed, they have often reached a point in their professional lives where they can make a decision and expect it to be enacted. Yet the board, to be effective both in a legal and a practical sense, must be collegial. There must be give and take, and at least a semblance of equality.

Despite these battling egos and creeping diversity, corporate boards remain a very homogenous group. According to the 1995 Korn/Ferry survey of the directors of major corporations, only 7% of corporate directors are women, and 2% of the director population is black.[1] Given the popular profile of an outside corporate director as either a current or recently retired CEO, age also becomes a unifying factor, typically extending from the late-40s to the mid-60s. However, the homogeneity of most boards goes beyond these

---

1. *Korn/Ferry International Board of Directors Survey,* 1993, 1995.

external factors and extends into the members' vitae. Particularly in midwestern, midcap companies, directors tend to be hometown guys with similar backgrounds, education, and career paths. Aside from wanting somebody with finance background to chair the Audit Committee, the concept of strategic board recruitment is still fairly new. Thus, it remains permissible to present a roster of outside directors who, though seasoned and proven executives, pretty well know the same things and view matters from about the same perspective.

The board then acts like our solar system, with a balance of forces that keep the group together, while others drive it apart. The result is a body that tends toward stasis. One's attention can only be divided so many ways, and the position of director on a particular company's board is usually only one of the many hats this individual wears. The traditional emphasis on naming CEOs to the board in itself assures that a director will have most of his or her energies diverted elsewhere. If the director also sits on other boards—well, you cannot be everywhere at once. The fact that our corporate board structure has proven itself in dealing with crises suggests that it is still too distracted to *prevent* crises.

Inside directors, the company employees representing management (aside from the CEO/chair), would seem to be at a disadvantage in this very fast company. Their status and power derive solely from their position with the corporation, and besides, they are shrinking in numbers. Yet inside directors consistently have the odds in their favor. First, they no doubt owe their seat on the board to the chair/CEO and are the last directors to pipe up with anything the CEO prefers left unsaid. This makes their continued presence and influence a CEO priority. In making the strategic ententes and alliances needed for boardroom success, the CEO can be quite sure that inside directors represent votes in his or her pocket. I should note that this is not always the case. At Dow Chemical, noted for its insider-dominated board, employee directors were willing to rise up against CEO Zoltan Merszei in 1978, replacing him with Paul Oreffice. However, Dow at the time also had a separate chairman, former CEO Ben Branch. It is likely this Dow coup would have been impossible without such division at the top.

Inside directors have another advantage in the boardroom rough-and-tumble. These directors are tapped into the corporate pipeline far more than even the most attentive outside director can hope to be. If the CFO, for example, sits on the board, it is unlikely that any inside financials reaching the other directors will be numbers that the CFO has not signed off on. Should the CEO then make it clear to the CFO that he or she need not bother the board with certain unpleasant numbers, the outside directors will start out with two strikes against them in gaining good intelligence.

This matter of loyalty makes inside directors inherently suspect. The board of directors serves as the corporation's superego, watching and judging the actions of management. When three or four or half of the board represent that very management, such independent judgment goes out the window. Managers are asked to supervise themselves and, not surprisingly, are unlikely to give themselves a good talking to. The rise of the professional manager brought heavy concentrations of inside directors into the boardroom, and as late as 1973 insiders held 38% of the seats on the average large company board. By 1993, however, that ratio had fallen to 25% although it has been stuck at this figure for several years. The 1995 Korn/Ferry Board of Directors survey found that most directors felt the most effective board has 12 members, nine from outside and three insiders, including the chair.[2]

What is the attraction of this one-quarter inside/three-quarters outside formula? Despite the objections noted above (there is no urgent need for any employee other than the CEO to hold a board seat), there is value in having insiders on the board. The insider's information pipeline, though it may seem compromised, gives the board an informed source on what the company is doing and needs to do. Board status makes this employee that much more accessible, plus gives him or her a measure of added clout to strengthen this input. The growing "committee-ization" (to coin an ugly term) of the board helps segregate insiders from areas where they should not tread, such as setting their own pay or auditing their own results. Finally, if push comes to shove and the board must get tough with the CEO, it will need to build links with crucial executive offices, such as the corporate counsel and finance. An inside board member could see which way the tide is turning and might prove valuable.

The decline in inside board membership has stalled and will probably not fall much further in the foreseeable future. The in-

2. Ibid.

sider/outsider mix has, according to Korn/Ferry, been stuck at three-to-one since 1990, as has the average board size of 12. When boards were declining in size, it was easiest to shed employee directors. But board size seems to have reached a plateau. The increased duties of directors, plus the needs of committees, make it difficult for most boards to fall below 10 to 12 members without overstressing everyone. A few recent shareholder resolutions have been advanced to cut all insiders from some boards, with the exception of the CEO, but it is uncertain whether this is another of the "procedural frills" that distracts from real issues. Short of any new exchange or SEC rules, look for boardrooms to stay at 12 apostles, with a quarter of them insiders.

27

New Board Needs, New Board Talents

Numbers in the boardroom may be static, but who goes into those numbers, and how and why they are recruited, continues to change. Traditionally, people were nominated to the board through the suggestion and support of the CEO. This was the beginning and end of the matter, with endorsement by the nominating committee (if one existed) and approval by shareholders serving only as legal punctuation for the process. As long as directors were selected on the strength of their connections and malleability by the CEO, this was an adequate process. But as board work grew more demanding over the past two decades, the country club approach became less and less practical. Board work required more time and effort of candidates and added to their legal liabilities. Prize CEOs became more and more difficult to recruit to boards (which may have been a factor driving director compensation: Business 101 told us that as supply falls, prices increase). Boards and CEOs began asking the executive recruiters they had already worked with for years if they could help find someone to take Old Joe's place on the board when he retired. And while you're at it, could you make sure that he or she has serious credentials in international consumer products marketing? With greater use being made of the board's skills, what a director knows has become vital. Expertise is being sought in the following areas:

Telecommunications and technology. Research and development, capital needs, market shifts, competitive intelligence, and personnel all have unique aspects in a technology company, and boards need a director who understands these demands. For a long time this has been of obvious value to high-technology companies, but today *all* companies are becoming high-tech, so board savvy in the field is a real asset.

Marketing.   And more specifically, a board candidate with marketing smarts where the company wants to go. New acquisitions or diversifications can take the corporation out of its comfortable core of expertise. Without some knowledgeable, board-based marketing talent for these ventures, disaster could be waiting. At Morrison-Knudsen, William Agee led the construction company into the wholly new field (at least for MK) of building and remanufacturing railcars. If someone on the board had had any experience in this market, perhaps they could have warned of a yawning money pit ahead.

International markets.   Yes, the world is going global, whether we want it to or not, and even firms that never looked beyond the central time zone in the past are now assessing how to market their goods in the European Union. A director with strong experience at a foreign company, background in a target region or nation, or seasoning with an overseas subsidiary could help your board avoid cultural or political gaffes. The global corporations of the next century will go beyond the "multinational" model, with U.S. headquarters and foreign outposts. Rather, they will become firms with virtual headquarters as much in New York as in Singapore or Zurich. Boards will need to be likewise borderless. The ideal candidate for the board would be a foreign national with transnational experience. (I will discuss these international directors later.)

Top-level finance.   At the beginning of 1994, financial derivatives were a spooky, esoteric subject limited to currency traders, a subject of which corporate boards knew little and cared less. By the spring of 1994, though, firms such as Gibson Greetings, Procter & Gamble, and Metallgesellschaft AG reported derivatives trading losses in the hundreds of millions of dollars, and so to speak, the fertilizer hit the ventilator. As consultant Charles M. Seeger wrote, the Procter & Gamble board "learned a quick lesson on the topic" when it was forced to write off $157 million on soured deals and had a heck of a time explaining where the money went.[1] Boards across the world suddenly were expected to tell investors how exposed the company was to derivatives deals and how carefully the board was monitoring this exposure. Boards that included experienced financial executives were at least able to learn that the sky was not falling and would know precisely to whom in the company they should be directing tough questions. Corporate finances will grow even more complex in the future, and financial markets and instruments more sophisticated and fast moving. Boards will want to assure that the next derivatives panic does not catch them napping.

Restructuring. The last decade has seen a tidal wave of restructuring in corporate America, yet "corporate restructuring has cured nothing for most companies," wrote John Parkington of the Wyatt Company in 1994. His research on major restructuring initiatives found that only 46% met their profitability improvement goals, only a third increased productivity, and barely 60% even reduced expenses.[2] Parkington found that restructuring was most successful with close attention to strategic oversight, long-term goals, and a "nothing is sacred" mind-set imposed from the very top. Who can provide such omnipotent control of the restructuring process, with the power to tell even the CEO what ballast to drop? Guess who. If the board is to oversee a continuous process of restructuring, which seems to be the pattern of the future, it needs a director with experience at doing a restructuring right.

Entrepreneurial skills. Goal: Corporations wish to be more nimble, creative, and fast thinking. Problem: The Fortune 500 corporation has traditionally been as fleet-footed as a water buffalo. Solution: Add proven entrepreneurial talent at strategic points. Perhaps the best spot to add such thinking is the corporate board. When a successful start-up company is acquired, the entrepreneurs who launched the venture are often the most valuable part of the acquisition. Corporations should consider adding some of this drive to their boards as well. Entrepreneurs have the ability to see oppor-

---

1. "Derivatives: A Board Briefing," Charles M. Seeger, *Corporate Board,* July/ August 1994, p. 11.
2. "The Board's Role in Restructuring," John J. Parkington, *Corporate Board,* January/February 1994, p. 12.

tunities a mile off, and almost define the term "problem solvers." Particularly in acquisitions, board membership will help bring the entrepreneur into the action and help avoid the frustration that can stifle the contributions of founders after they sell. If nothing else, they can liven up the boardroom procedures.

Service industries.   The U.S. economy's shift from traditional manufacturing fields to the service sector is well known. However, the talent for managing many service industries productively and with strategic vision is less common. Finance, health care, entertainment, communications, and consulting have grown spectacularly in recent years and will grow even faster in the years ahead. Business leaders who have shown brilliance in such fields are valued by boards as they expand into the service sector.

28

Board Diversity—Expect the Unexpected

Perhaps the most powerful trend in board makeup is increased diversity. Despite 20 years of effort to add women and minorities to corporate boards, most still look like the cynical tag applied to Richard Nixon's first cabinet—"twelve gray-haired white guys named George." The concept of affirmative action has faced some strong criticism of late, and there is debate on whether the widely discussed shrinkage of white males in the twenty-first-century workforce will really be as sharp as predicted. Nonetheless, the current gender and ethnic makeup of the boardroom has grown ever harder to defend.

In 1995, a Catalyst survey found that 81% of Fortune 500 companies had a woman serving on their corporate boards. This sounds pretty diverse and was, indeed, a 7% jump over the previous year. But 59% of the companies had only a lone female on their boards, and of all board seats on the Fortune 500, only 9.5% were held by women.[1] Further, in a world of multiple, interlocking board seats, women are even busier than men. Certain "estimable women" (I can think of no better term for them) take up an unusually high number of the seats held by females. Lilyan Affinito, Carla Hills, Juanita Kreps, Ann McLaughlin, Wendy Gramm, Marina Whitman, and Barbara Hackman Franklin are leading members of this elite. I know several of these women and have found them savvy, strong, and an asset to any board. But there must be more women out there who can meet these qualifications. Indeed, Affinito was one of the directors mentioned in a 1995 *Business Week*

---

1. *1995 Catalyst Census of Female Board Directors of the Fortune 500*, pp. 3–7.

article asking, "Are These 10 [Directors] Stretched Too Thin?" The article tasked these directors (including Affinito, former Defense Secretary Frank Carlucci, and Goldman Sachs Chairman John L. Weinberg) with not only sitting on too many boards, but also serving on the boards of companies with performance problems. A relationship between the overstretch and poor results was hinted.[2]

But, very recently, the glacial progress of women into the boardroom has rumbled forward a few more inches. Catalyst found that one-third of Fortune 500 companies had at least two women on their boards in 1995 and that the number with three women shot up 40% in the same year. The Korn/Ferry survey asked women directors about their influence in the boardroom and found them largely optimistic about the future. Women directors rated themselves on par with male directors for their influence on such company policies as finance, strategy, succession, and executive pay. Women directors also see themselves as mentors and enablers for women in the company's executive ranks. Thirty-four percent say they use their board role to encourage greater hiring of female executives.

However, even after they make it into the boardroom, women directors face barriers to their effectiveness. A recent study by Diana Bilimoria from Case Western University found that women on boards tend to be shuffled off to certain committees, usually those with the least clout. Male directors were most likely to staff the executive, compensation, and finance committees. Women directors had the strongest presence only on public affairs committees, which are largely responsible for making the corporation *look* responsible. "Their gender often keeps [women] off the boards' most powerful committees and propels them toward less central ones."[3] Bilimoria faults the board nomination process for the slow pace of adding women to boards. Even in cases where the CEO/chair makes good use of a nominating committee, this committee, usually made up of senior directors, tends to look quite a bit like most CEOs—older, white, and male. The trait that Rosabeth Moss Kanter calls "homosocial reproduction" causes directors to replenish the board with people who pretty much look like themselves.

---

2. "Are These 10 Stretched Too Thin?" *Business Week*, November 13, 1995, p. 78.
3. "Women Directors: The Quiet Discrimination," Diana Bilimoria, *Corporate Board*, July/August 1995, p. 11.

This looks a bit bleak, but suggests that women's boardroom inroads should accelerate as we enter the next century. As the current cadre of women directors grows and gains seniority, their influence on board thinking will increase. A board candidate that "looks like us" will lose the Waspy male absolutes, tremendously broadening the pool of director prospects.

At Avon Corporation, CEO James Preston has committed his company to push the concept of women in the boardroom even further. In late 1995, he announced that he would work toward full "gender equity" in the Avon boardroom—a board that is half male and half female. The current 12-member Avon board has four female directors, with a targeted 50-50 split to be achieved through attrition among current members and an active effort to recruit women. According to Preston, the idea of board gender equity is not a universal need. "On other boards, this would be imprudent. But 99 percent of our customer sales reps are women, and Avon is essentially a women's company. Our company should represent the markets we serve." For Avon, tapping the expertise of female directors has already shown dividends. A few years back, the company mulled a move into apparel, but the volatility and dangers of the rag trade generated great uncertainty within the firm. The idea was nonetheless presented to the Avon board, where the women directors were enthusiastic about Avon apparel. "They said women don't like to buy at department stores, where selections are picked over, and that they thought the idea would be successful," recalls Preston. Fashions were added to the Avon line, where they proved "a runaway success."[4]

The expanding minority presence in the boardroom has followed a similar upward track, though less resoundingly. Korn/Ferry found that in 1995, 44% of studied corporate boards had a person of color as a member. Thirty-one percent of boards had a black member, representing the greatest single group of minorities. However, only 2% of the total board population was black, and these directors are if anything even busier than the women.[5] Names such as Vernon Jordan, William Gray, John Brooks Slaughter, Clifton Wharton, and Claudine Malone lead the list of noted black directors —and pretty well complete the list as well. Despite the presence of

---

4. Author interview, January 1996.
5. *Korn/Ferry International Board of Directors Survey,* 1995.

hundreds of black directors on U.S. boards, blacks remain both overused and underrepresented. In 1994, *Ebony* magazine found that only 146 board seats at the Fortune 500 were held by blacks, and many of these were multiple directorships. Vernon Jordan held seats with 10 companies, Andrew Brimmer with eight, Sybil Mobley six. Almost one-third of the black directors (32.9%) were academics.[6] Vernon Jordan notes that, when it comes to expanding the black directors club, "Companies haven't looked hard enough, and they always look in the same place."[7] Although other ethnic groups, particularly Latinos and Asians, have an even smaller board presence, the rate of growth for these groups is actually somewhat larger.

The relatively small pool of current black board candidates has made their recruitment a boom industry. *Forbes* magazine quotes a Paul Ray Berndtson recruiter as saying that diversity searches now make up about half of his firm's board business, and SpencerStuart's board practice was seeking minority prospects for 30 board seats.[8] In 1993, Los Angeles business celebrity Peter Ueberroth joined with a west coast recruiting firm to develop a Corporate Board Candidate Portfolio of black board prospects. This profile of 73 black business, civic, and education leaders is intended to add new faces to the board search shortlist.

These varying rates of progress suggest that the token group of "women, minorities, etc." to be represented in the boardroom is breaking down. This change is to the advantage of women, but is leaving other groups behind.

---

6. "America's Top Black Directors," *Ebony,* October 1994, pp. 36–43.
7. "Pool of Qualified Blacks Expands, but Very Few Sit on Corporate Boards," *Wall Street Journal,* June 28, 1994, p. B1.
8. "Diversity Hucksters," *Forbes,* May 22, 1995, p. 176.

29

Replacing Old Joe

Despite these "help wanted" changes, some of the traditional rules of director recruiting remain. Both CEOs and the board still prefer to add a director who is already a CEO. CEOs remain the gold standard for board candidates for reasons other than status. The CEO/chair wants to deal with a director who has walked in the CEO's shoes, with whom he or she can share peer-to-peer respect. Another CEO or retired CEO brings a special perspective to the board on the isolating, pressured task the CEO faces. The corporate CEO also has a more flexible schedule that can be of great value in board work. It can be difficult for an executive vice president to sneak away from a day job to serve on the board. The CEO, however, pretty well plays by his or her own rules on scheduling.

Often, the preference for CEOs has been taken to odd extremes. In *Directors: Myth and Reality*, Myles Mace gives anecdotes on some of the mating rituals of corporate boards and director prospects. He notes how the president/CEO title seemed valued above ability and experience. The president of a small midwestern firm was offered numerous board invitations, until he left to take the vice presidency of a much larger company. Abruptly, board offers ceased. "Now that I am only an executive vice president, there is no more attraction. Yet I am the same person, with more experience." A corporate president was even more emphatic: "You can't downgrade the prestige of our board membership by inviting, say, a promising vice president to serve as a board member."[1]

---

1. *Directors: Myth and Reality*, Myles Mace, Harvard Business School, 1971, pp. 86–88.

This preference has grown too cumbersome for several reasons. The time demands of board service (not to mention the demands of being a CEO) have grown so burdensome that the great name Fortune 500 bosses are simply "boarded up." The grand days when Goldman, Sachs's Sidney Weinberg could serve on 35 boards, Ralph Lowell of Boston Safe Deposit Trust on 42, and Hulett Clinton Merritt a truly heroic 138 are long passed. CEOs, particularly name CEOs, are sharply limiting their board commitments. If they do not, as noted earlier in the *Business Week* article on directors who are stretched too thin, their effectiveness and contribution might face close questioning.[2] Spencer Stuart search firm honcho Dennis Carey sees the outside board commitments of director candidates becoming a real factor in nominations. "If someone is already on three or four other boards, the CEOs throw their hands up and say 'they clearly won't have enough time for us.' " Carey also sees some breaking down of the resistance to considering talent from below the CEO's office, due to necessity. "Companies are assuming more risk—they have to due to the [board] time demands. They have to rely on more emerging talents, people who are not yet serving on boards."[3]

I see several trends coming together here, to everyone's benefit, under the umbrella of strategic board recruitment. Boards need, and increasingly want, directors who can bring strong talents in specific areas. The beauty of such a meritocracy is that it is so democratic. Remember that board search candidate I mentioned earlier, the replacement for Old Joe? The board sought someone with excellent, current background in international consumer products marketing. While those parameters tell us some valuable clues about Old Joe's replacement, they also suggest several attributes that the target prospect need *not* have. He does not need to have attended the CEO's alma mater. He does not have to be white and past 50. He does not have to be a CEO. And he does not even have to be a "he." Strategic board recruitment places more emphasis on what the board candidate knows, and what he or she can do, and less on titles.

This not only levels the playing field for women and minorities, it can actually give them a leg up on the Good Old Boys. Some of

2. "Are These 10 Stretched Too Thin?" *Business Week,* November 13, 1995, p. 78.
3. Author interview, January 1996.

the more sought-after board skills, such as technology, international markets, entrepreneurialism, and diversity background, are nontraditional fields that attract nontraditional talent. Says National Women's Economic Alliance President Patricia Harrison, "The search is on for truly qualified people to serve as outside directors, and increasingly those qualified people are women."[4] Women have driven the boom in the service sector, and high technology and communications have become another U.S. immigrant success story.

---

4. *A Seat at the Table*, Patricia Harrison, Mastermedia Limited, 1994, p. 114.

30

The Global Director

Immigration—and emigration—are important to another board recruitment trend, the international director. This term encompasses many different life experiences among directors and may in fact be overly broad. It includes directors who are foreign nationals who have immigrated to the United States. It includes those who have been based in a number of different countries or perhaps in one target country of interest to the recruiting firm. It can even be a top executive of a foreign company who may have limited experience in the United States. However he or she is defined, the international director is eagerly sought by many U.S. boards for several valuable characteristics.

The ideal international director is, like most other board ideals, a CEO, in this case the leader of a major multinational corporation. However, the commitments and the logistics involved in adding the chair of a Nestle, Hanson PLC, or Shell make it even less likely that a U.S. board will be electing one of them anytime soon. But the broad definition of an international director allows companies to custom-tune a candidate for their governance needs. Expertise in particular markets, in multinational trade and regulation, in national development trends, and in identifying overseas power centers can be blended to give the board a cosmopolitan flair. In fact, this broadened viewpoint within the board can be the greatest asset of adding international talent. Heidrick & Struggles partner Ted Jadick notes that the diplomatic skills of these global directors can loosen up board members "accustomed to imposing dictates based on their parochial cultural experience."[1]

---

1. "Recruiting Global Directors," Theodore Jadick, *Corporate Board*, January/February 1996, p. 12.

Global directors are paying off for a number of forward-looking companies. Campbell Soup in 1995 elected David K. P. Li, deputy chairman and CEO of the Bank of East Asia in Hong Kong. Both Campbell and Li carefully negotiated in advance to assure that Li could meet the needs of a working board while based on the other side of the globe. "Neither we nor he wanted him to just come on as some kind of a figurehead," says a Campbell spokesman.[2] The board of Amoco, meanwhile, has added directors from Holland and Canada, and Sara Lee's board gains insights from a former European Community commissioner and an Australian.

A few cautions are advised for recruiting an international board member. Prepare for a lengthier, more frustrating search. This will not be one of the guys from the country club, and tracking down the talent you seek will take effort. Also, as Campbell's negotiations with David Li show, adding a director from the antipodes can be a logistical nightmare. Prepare for a few culture clashes as well. Jadick writes about a multinational corporation that was pleased to have recruited a talented Japanese CEO to its board—until he sat through the first two meetings silent as a stone. Some one-on-one discussion revealed that the new member was dutifully acting the way a director should behave—in Japan. There, matters are discussed between directors before the board actually meets, and the directors convene largely to ratify what has already been agreed to. Once clued in to the more freewheeling style of U.S. boards, the Japanese director became a valuable player.

Many of the board membership changes discussed above will require a shift in how board recruitment is handled. By seeking tactical board members rather than just folks we are familiar with, a new problem arises—how do you recruit someone when you do not know them, or how to find them?

Nominating committees of the board are taking their jobs more seriously today. They now serve as the nexus for bringing together the qualifications for a strategic recruitment. Nominating committees have grown in popularity over the past decade, and today they are the third most common board committee, found at 71% of major corporations. I will consider their changing roles in more detail later, but for now note that the act of adding a committee to do *anything* in corporate America tends to give the function a life of its own. With the nominating committee, however, this

---

2. "Welcome!" *Industry Week,* February 19, 1996, p. 33.

effect has been for the good, adding a measure of planning and objectivity to the traditional recruitment routine—the CEO saying, "Well, there's a fellow I know . . ." Even if, as Jonathan Charkham estimates, 90% of board recruits are still known by the CEO in advance,[3] board nominees will be vetted by a body that might have a few better ideas on meeting a need for expertise.

Still, including members of the nominating committee will not widen the horizons enough for a fully talent-based board search. More professional search savvy is needed. Corporations have rarely suffered a need that consultants have not rushed to fill, and director recruitment has turned into a definite need. According to Roger Kenny, president of search firm Kenny, Kindler Hunt, & Howe, at the end of the 1980s, perhaps 12% of Fortune 500 board searches made use of a search firm. "Today, it's probably close to 50 percent. And there is no such thing as a generic board search assignment today. . . . We don't see any without specific skill and experience levels."[4] Search firms are able to bring their extensive contacts and background checking abilities to the board search process. They can expand the board's circle of acquaintance to an almost limitless horizon, adding geographic breadth and variety in expertise. While I do not want to give board recruiting firms a plug (or at least not for free), their use fits in with the general pattern of growing boardroom professionalism.

---

3. *Keeping Good Company,* Jonathan Charkham, Clarendon, 1994, p. 190.
4. Author interview, November 1995.

31

The "Professional" Director

And what about the future of board "professionalism?" The above trends pretty well limit themselves to tinkering with the present paradigm—directors who are amateurs. Not amateurish (or at least not necessarily), but *amateur*—interested hobbyists, people who act as directors in a part-time, dabblers' way. Their interests and attention are devoted to the board only occasionally, barring a major crisis. One estimate finds that the average outside director spends only 163 hours annually on board business, including preparation and travel. That is a little over 20 working days yearly and includes an average of eight board meetings.[1] While these numbers have increased in recent years and are higher for the largest industrials, it remains easy to see how the CEO of a major company could handle a few board seats on the side without any serious time squeeze.

The current board structure is built upon the outline of the old-style board in much the way a 1996 auto still has the basic elements of a carriage from 100 years ago. Greater demands are being made of a governance model ill-suited for heavy service. The board has long been ideally designed for the dilettante and was both shaped to and by their needs. Seventy-five years ago, when Daddy Warbucks put his representatives on the boards of the companies he held, they were no doubt there to protect his interests, but these were among many other interests. If the large investor felt a necessity for day-to-day monitoring and oversight of his company, he would as likely just fire the president and do it himself.

---

1. *Korn/Ferry International Board of Directors Survey,* 1995.

With the coming-of-age of managers, directorship became even more of a loafer's delight. Those $20 gold pieces outside directors received seemed a reasonable tip for busy men who had to be getting back to the office. As pay and perks increased, the desirability of serving on a board rose, although the time and effort involved did not. The busy directors mentioned earlier, with their double-digit board seats, were likely providing all the effort and oversight demanded of them. When Penn Central director Howard Butcher III faced charges for unloading his company stock shortly before the rail line declared bankruptcy, he responded by resigning from the 70 other outside directorships he held. Did he feel contrite, overstretched, blindsided? Naaah. "The potential liability of being a director has become too great for the active, experienced businessman to suffer," he observed. It was also Butcher who, when asked why he had not seen financials showing that the railroad faced disastrous losses, replied, "Because they didn't show them to me— that's why."[2]

Although the numbers of board seats have declined, the workload has risen, and the liabilities actually have caught up with Butcher's complaint, the board structure remains the amateur's playground. If a director is also a major company CEO and happens to be an avid art collector, he likely spends more time on his hobby than on his board service. It is interesting to note that both corporate boards and our judicial jury system face current, harsh criticism for their efficacy and relevance. Both consist of a panel of 12 people who would rather be someplace else, instead of having to judge the arguments of people who know far more about the matter at hand than they do, receiving no thanks if their decision is a good one, and catching hell if it is not. And, in both cases, those impaneled are essentially amateurs dealing with professionals.

Well, in that case, why not *professional* directors in the formal sense of the word? There have been a number of proposals for such arrangements over the years. Most would call for skilled people to serve exclusively as directors of a limited number of corporations or even a single company. In 1940, William O. Douglas, then serving a tumultuous term as chairman of the SEC, suggested a new class of "salaried, professional experts [who] would bring a new responsibility and authority to directorates."[3]

---

2. *Corporate Leadership,* Stanley C. Vance, McGraw-Hill, 1983, p. 166.
3. Quoted in *Taming the Giant Corporation,* Ralph Nader, W. W. Norton, 1976, p. 121.

In his 1976 manifesto for federal corporate chartering, *Taming the Giant Corporation,* the ever-creative Ralph Nader proposed total shareholder nomination and election of directors, all of whom could serve on only one board. These "public" directors would each be assigned a distinct interest to represent, with a director for such concerns as "Employee welfare . . . consumer protection . . . environmental protection . . . shareholder rights."[4] Nader offered no information on how these directors would be found, qualified, or paid.

Recent years have brought some better researched and more viable proposals for professional directors. Academics Ronald Gilson and Reinier Kraakman in 1991 suggested "a novel position, that of the professional outside director, that would exist prior to, and apart from, the election of other directors."[5] This pro director would be elected by institutional shareholders (or more likely, a coalition of institutions) to serve the boards of up to six of their portfolio companies. The director would not be a full-time director for a single company, which as the authors note, would make this person "no longer an *outside* director at all." Rather, he or she would be full-time in commitment to board service for a portfolio of companies— and full-time in commitment to their institutional investor sponsor.

In an intriguing *Stanford Law Review* article (with footnotes that include economist jokes and Dr. Seuss poetry), Gilson and Kraakman sketch out how such a full-time director would be able to devote far more time to individual companies, even while holding six board seats. If paid in accordance with usual director compensation norms, such a role would add up to an attractive income, able to draw talented people, but divided so as to avoid co-option by a single board seat or management. This director could become more deeply involved in committee work and monitoring and, by holding his or her board seat solely through the sponsorship of an institution, would have the ultimate incentive to work for investor interests.

The idea of such a professional director would shake up the board/management/investor paradigm more than most of the other board reforms discussed. As far back as the writings of Adam Smith, business thinkers have mulled how to make managers act

---

4. Ibid., p.126.
5. "Reinventing the Outside Director," Ronald J. Gilson and Reinier Kraakman, *Stanford Law Review,* April 1991, p. 884.

more like owners. As we have seen, the board of directors has proven an imperfect tool for enforcing such a balance, usually because the board joins management on its end of the teeter-totter. The professional director could finally fulfill the faith in governance, it is said, by offering a core of board members (Gilson and Kraakman suggest a quarter to a third of the board) who are not nominated or endorsed by, or beholden to, management in any way. Such an overhaul, while a radical change, would be fully practical within current securities law. Indeed, the idea was proposed before passage of the 1992 SEC shareholder communications rule changes, which would make the concept even more practical. The professional directors, as a minority on the board, could not impose the will of the institutions on the company but would have to make their effect felt through compromise and coalitions. As "delegates," wholly dependent on the shareholder groups for their mandate, these directors would, it is claimed, be the ultimate pipeline between those who own and those who manage.

The Gilson and Kraakman concept has had a busy life in the footnotes of other governance writers (including this one) but, in the five years since its presentation, has resulted in no action. Part of the problem may be that all professional director proposals have an underlying goal of "opening up" the boardroom beyond those who currently form our director corps. Gilson and Kraakman's writings on the subject of where to find their new all-pro directors hint at this hidden agenda. They suggest a "professor of finance at a graduate school of business" as their first hypothetical candidate,[6] which if nothing else would do wonders for keeping college faculty members off the dole. Top accounting or consulting firm partners are also offered as good boardroom monitors. The authors suggest that the institutional investors form a clearinghouse to vet candidates.

How these candidates would work in the boardroom is also a concern. Even the authors suggest that factions could develop, with a three-way split between current inside board members, current outsiders, and the institutional pros. CEOs and chairs might object that this would harm board collegiality, but the authors write that "they see no reason to lament the possible loss of collegiality."[7]

---

6. Ibid., p. 885.
7. Ibid., p. 889.

Given the dubious effectiveness of U.S. corporate governance, what is there to lose? As to the objection that academics and consultants are not the sort we have come to accept as ideal directors, the authors might respond that that is the whole point.

As a final note on the professional director concept, such directors in a sense already exist. If we define "professional director" as somebody who serves on corporate boards as a more or less exclusive trade, there are many examples. Each election cycle loosens a torrent of former politicos into the corporate world, and some find boardrooms the ideal roost. Upon leaving office in 1977, President Gerald R. Ford constructed a bustling portfolio of directorships, including Amax, Santa Fe International, and Twentieth Century-Fox, while offering advisory services to such corporations as American Express. Former U.S. defense secretaries, such as Harold Brown, Robert McNamara, and Frank Carlucci (one of *Business Week*'s "overstretched" directors) have proven especially desirable to defense-related corporations and have made careers from board service.

There are some current professionals who do without this government service seasoning altogether. Awhile back, I interviewed director Raymond Troubh for the *Corporate Board*. I titled the interview "America's Busiest Director," which Troubh may just be. He serves on 16 corporate boards, including Time-Warner, Manville Corporation, Petrie Stores, Triarc, and American Maize Products, and board service is his only job. "I'm a full time, professional director," he observes, spending from 30 to 50 hours weekly on his "job." "I'm constantly on call, like a doctor. It's absolutely full time." Troubh, who is an attorney by training, finds that his specialization has made him an expert on corporate governance and allows him to share the best ideas between boards. "I can serve as a bridge from one company to another."[8] His status as a completely independent director with so many seats means he can offer his expertise to all but is dependent on none. In speaking with him, I was impressed with his savvy on the mechanics of board service, though he likewise did not impress me as someone who would be leading any boardroom revolutions. *Forbes* magazine estimated his 1995 annual board pay at more than $650,000.[9]

8. Troubh interview, *Corporate Board*, July/August 1995, p. 32.
9. "The Cosseted Director," *Forbes*, May 22, 1995, p. 172.

Are the ex-politicos and Raymond Troubh a harbinger of the future or a sign of what is wrong with governance today? Despite their specialty in board work, many governance observers object to someone holding such a large number of board seats. Stetson University Professor of Law Charles Elson observes that "if you sit on many boards, it's probably a sign that you're not a very good director."[10] Heavy board commitments have been a long-time complaint of governance observers and have drawn criticism from critics as different as Nell Minow and William Allen of the Delaware Chancery Court. It is interesting that some of the very people who would most strongly endorse the idea of dedicated, professional directors would likely find a board portfolio such as Raymond Troubh's to be part of the problem. They do not see someone as a professional because they serve on a lot of boards. Instead, they view exclusive service on boards as the end result of a professionalizing process. That leads us to how we decide who gets to *be* a professional.

---

10. "Are These 10 Stretched Too Thin?" *Business Week*, November 13, 1995, p. 78.

32

Flash Forward: Director Certification

You look in the mirror and decide that you are due for a haircut, especially with that big conference coming up next week. You set an appointment with Tina, or Antoine, or whomever, the person you really trust with your tresses. When you arrive for your appointment, you find to your chagrin that your favorite cutter has had to leave town suddenly, a sick relative or personality crisis or some such situation. Would you care to go ahead with Tina or Antoine's backup? Probably it is no serious matter to you, and you go under the scissors with little concern. Why? Well, if nothing else, the sub must know *something* about the business of hair. After all, he or she must have completed a certified course of training from a state-approved school of barbering or cosmetology. Further, this person must then have been tested by the state authority who handles such weighty matters and was then duly licensed to perform the haircutting trade. Finally, Mr. or Ms. Snips must renew that license on a regular basis. Possibly he or she will not know how to deal with that little flip you have in back, but at least you can be confident of getting a serviceable cut. After all, the cutter is *licensed*, right?

Yet if that same cutter were to be nominated to the board of a multibillion dollar Fortune 500 corporation, there could very well be no other reason than that the CEO likes the way he or she swings those scissors. That, in analogy form, is the argument for one of the hotter upcoming debates on corporate governance—director certification. Before proceeding, let me define the terms of qualifying directors as they have evolved in recent years. Qualification could take two basic forms—certification or licensing.

Certification would vouch for the director having completed a corporate governance training program. It could also verify (though this is less likely) that he or she has accumulated a certain level of breadth and experience in business, finance, actual board service, or other relevant trade. Certification would likely be awarded by an educational, professional, or investor group and in most proposals would be voluntary. However, with time, certification could assume a de facto compulsion if it became so widespread and universally recognized that no one could gain a board seat without it. For the time being, certification would likely work in the same way the Wizard of Oz was able to give the Scarecrow wisdom, the Tin Woodsman a heart, and the Lion courage—by providing them with impressive pieces of paper.

Licensing is the next stage in qualifying directors, and at present has few adherents. To be effective, it would need to be mandatory. Without a license one could not legally serve as the director of a corporation, a requirement probably subject to a number of loopholes regarding company size, ownership structure, and so forth. One reason that most board observers have shied away from licensing is that it would require us to pin down hard, fast rules on director skills and abilities, and then separate the sheep from the goats. Every interest group with two cents to contribute on the subject of business management would likely chip in on these parameters, bringing a hellish political debate. No doubt some excellent directors would be unable or unwilling to meet some aspect of the licensing requirements. Who would decide exactly what makes a good director? Who would do the licensing—the SEC, the stock exchanges, or a new independent body? Would director performance be regularly rated and considered in renewing the license?

Despite such uncertainties, discussion on the need for better boards, a better nominating process, and less director dependence on management all point to some form of qualifying directors as the next bright idea in governance. Why should the people we elect to govern our corporations not have to be trained, certified, and perhaps even rated for their effectiveness? The idea of director certification has fermented for some time in those usual yeast pots of business thinking—academia, consultancies, and government. In 1978, Stanley Sporkin, then head of the SEC's Enforcement Division, endorsed the idea of certification. Sporkin envisioned it as the end product of a formal education program for corporate directors, possibly as an outgrowth of university graduate business programs.

"There is a foreign service school that produces an elite corps for the State Department, so there could also be a school that would produce qualified directors."[1]

In 1980, the National Association of Corporate Directors launched a major effort to certify directors through NACD's Director's Institute program. The goal was to offer a professional title of competence, similar to those conferred as a Certified Public Accountant or as a member of the Society of American Engineers. The initials CPA or SAE after someone's name tells us a great deal about their field of specialty and qualifications, not to mention giving them an impressive business card. Why not provide directors with their own badge of initials? The NACD proposed the title "certified corporate director" (CCD) for their graduates and awarded this certification to graduates of the group's first session held in October 1980 at Saint Simons Island, Georgia. These weeklong programs combined many elements of current NACD programs, including the history of boards, committee organization, liabilities, and the design of board information systems. Although such a seminar no doubt resulted in better-educated directors, the brief training sessions, as well as the lack of certification on the directors' previous experience, limited their effectiveness. The NACD still offers a number of valuable training seminars, but the Director's Institute today serves more as a basic tutorial for freshman directors, and we do not see CCD emblazoned on anyone's business card.

Nonetheless, the NACD has continued to keep the idea of director certification alive. The group convened a roundtable on future trends in corporate governance in 1994 and found wide diversity of views on the subject of certifying directors. Philip R. Lochner Jr., a vice president at Time Warner and former SEC commissioner, was unimpressed with the concept. He was concerned that certification could lead us toward a generation of directors who are "expert at taking courses" rather than in the actual chemistry of the boardroom.[2] He supported continuing education rather than licensing. Ralph Whitworth, former president of the United Shareholders Association and a longtime advocate of board reform, is also unconvinced on the topic of certifying directors, either on a man-

---

1. Quoted in *Corporate Leadership,* Stanley C. Vance, McGraw-Hill, 1983, p. 260.
2. Corporate Governance Roundtable, NACD and Deloitte & Touche LLP, 1994.

datory or voluntary basis. He argues that director education cannot substitute for motivation.

Ira Millstein, also a panel member, was more optimistic on the matter of accrediting directors. "I wouldn't write off the certification notion," he told the NACD conferees. "Next year, no. Five years, no. Maybe ten years, yes . . ."[3] However, even Millstein saw board certification as less important than board professionalism. Millstein, by the way, was much less sanguine on the topic when I spoke with him in 1995. Asked whether director certification would come to pass, he responded, "I hope we don't. Other than from academia, I haven't seen many proposals for it here, and I would not endorse the concept."[4] Corporate governance scholar Jay Lorsch questioned whether director certification would be practical in the United States, with its large, dispersed population, diverse industries, and tradition of state law in governance matters.

If not the United States, how about elsewhere? One of the NACD roundtable participants had firsthand experience with a national director certification system and found it successful—in Australia. E. Graham Stubington is CEO of the Australian Institute of Company Directors (AICD), a director education and professional group. As summarized by the NACD, AICD offers a director accreditation course covering the legal and financial aspects of serving as a corporate director in Australia. Directors who complete the course receive a certificate, but those who are also willing to take an exam on governance receive a diploma. Directors who achieve this sheepskin level and serve as a director for five years reach the highest level, status as an AICD Fellow.

According to Stubington, director certification has proven more popular in Australia than in the United States because of Australia's unique business and legal environment. Although Australia has a state-based corporate tradition like the United States, changes during the 1990s have given the federal government a stronger role in corporation oversight. The result has been more uniformity in national governance requirements and procedures, increased federal willingness to intervene, and greater value in a uniform certification process. Also, the role of major institutional investors is even more powerful in Australia than in the United States. With a few big

---

3. Ibid.
4. Millstein interview, *Corporate Board*, November/December 1995, p. 32.

institutions owning large chunks (up to 10%) of relatively fewer corporations, investor/board relations tend to be cozier. But this puts more clout in the hands of institutions, who are usually more impressed with the idea of certifying directors. This link between Australian institutional investors and certification offers a lesson for the United States and hints that any accreditation process here will proceed just as far as the institutions back it.

Other players have an interest in certifying or licensing directors. Some directors' and officers' insurance companies have expressed support for certification as a risk management tool. Consulting firms and business school academics occasionally weigh in with support—especially if the training and certification is to be handled by consultants and business schools. Leslie Levy, president of the Institute for Research on Boards of Directors, observes that "the only 'certified' directors to date are those who have been recognized for completing training of some sort, without anyone's knowing if the training actually changed them or if any new 'qualifications' they developed through training were likely to affect subsequent performance."[5]

Today, NACD President John Nash is less convinced of the value of certification. "Broad director certification would be hard to accomplish. You'd have to go state to state for approval. What we're seeing in the future looks more like accreditation, deciding what education directors need to keep abreast of trends."[6] The NACD convened a new Blue Ribbon panel in 1996 to study director evaluation and is making the certification issue part of its mandate.

Ultimately, director certification is an idea with few real enemies, but as yet even fewer real supporters. It is a concept that smolders, waiting to catch flame, with a number of compelling arguments on its side and a larger number of practical stumbling blocks opposing it. The negatives come to the surface when we ask a simple, yet subtle, question: *What makes a good corporate director?*

Over the years, I have encountered, edited, and (I confess) written a few lists of what makes a good corporate board member. All have many common characteristics. A typical director checklist was prepared a couple of years ago by the NACD Blue Ribbon Commission on Performance Evaluation of Chief Executive Offi-

---

5. Author interview, January, 1996.
6. Author interview, February, 1996.

cers, Boards, and Directors. The following are among the qualities in its ideal director profile:

- Integrity. A director should display the highest ethical standards, maturity, and responsibility. Objectivity, fairness, and forthrightness are required.
- Experience. A director should have a background that offers useful skills to the board and the corporation and bring these talents to bear on board duties.
- Judgment and knowledge. A director should have the intelligence to knowledgeably assess company strategy, business plans, and the abilities of management. He or she must be aware of changes in business and market conditions.
- Time and commitment. A director should have the time available to fulfill his or her duties, to learn about the company, to prepare for meetings, and to review company information.
- Teamwork abilities. A director needs the ability to work with other members of the board in a collegial manner.
- Absence of conflicts. A director should have no conflicts of interest that could interfere with board service or that could cause others to question his or her duty of loyalty.[7]

What could possibly be wrong with such a list of qualifiers for board service? Certainly we should want such people serving on our corporate boards. Yet the very broadness and generality of these inventories suggests their weakness. I call them "Boy Scout lists." To commitment, teamwork, and integrity, we need add only cleanliness, thrift, and reverence to gain our merit badges. Such lists do little for narrowing down who really qualifies to represent shareholders at major corporations by vetting potential candidates. Indeed, to publicly accuse a person of *lacking* some of these attributes would probably be libelous.

In reviewing directorship over the years with some people far more experienced than myself, I have found that no matter their

7. *Report of the Blue Ribbon Commission on Performance Evaluation of Chief Executive Officers, Boards and Directors*, National Association of Corporate Directors, 1994, pp. 8–9.

technical qualifications, authority, or board experience, they likewise opt for generalities when defining the good director. Robert Charpie, former chairman of the Cabot Corporation and a member of numerous major boards, recently offered a list of factors that make a good director including experience, judgment, teamwork, communication . . . Well, you get the idea.[8] Thomas Neff, president and CEO of director search firm SpencerStuart, writes of director candidates requiring "interest and enthusiasm . . . sound business judgment . . . dedication to the highest ethical standards."[9]

Now both of these men are respected business leaders with proven talents for knowing who makes a good director. Yet they are recommending board qualifications that seem both broad and obvious. While it could mean that such luminaries are snowing the world, I do not think so. Likewise, I do not believe that such all-inclusive talents qualify anyone with a higher than two-digit IQ and a modicum of conscience to serve as a corporate director. Possibly it is the trait we see among artists and other highly talented creative professionals of possessing genius themselves but being wholly unable to teach or even express it to another. As J. D. Salinger wrote about a sublime artist (but middling art teacher) in *De Daumier-Smith's Blue Period*, "It was not . . . that he was consciously or unconsciously being frugal of his talent, or deliberately unprodigal of it, but that it simply wasn't his to give away."[10]

Perhaps our problem is to view the Boy Scout lists of director attributes as job descriptions. More likely they are only the first stage, a *basic floor* for board membership. Of course we seek these qualities in a director . . . but then we move on to the specific talents we actually need. This could be the ultimate argument against trying to license corporate directors. The process of seeking agreement on certification terms would bring an endless debate over expressing the inexpressible. The most likely result: "least common denominator" qualifications. We would then give the above Boy Scout oath the force of law. The vagueness of these attributes would not only give director licenses to lots of people no board would ever touch,

---

8. *Directorship Magazine Special Report, 1996,* Robert A. Charpie (contrib.), pp. 5-1-2.

9. "What Boards Are Asking Before They Look for a New Director," monograph, Thomas Neff, SpencerStuart & Associates.

10. *Nine Stories,* J. D. Salinger, Little, Brown 1953, p. 143–144.

but could exclude enough worthies to nurture a thriving new branch for tort law.

After we began licensing directors as to their moral and intellectual fiber, individual companies would then move on to the real point of vetting them for their specific skills and attributes. A licensed corporate director who would be ideal for a fast-growing west coast software firm might be useless on the board of a century-old midwest regional metal bender. On the other hand, he or she might just have the unique blend of talents needed. If so, the director's permit would still serve as no more than a sort of union card.

This is not to wholly discourage the idea of certifying board members. In a world where boards are going far afield to find specific talents, dealing more often through intermediaries and with unknown candidates, there could be some value in basic certification, particularly on an international basis. An unknown board prospect from the other side of the world might look good, but wouldn't you like to know if he or she had done time for tax fraud? Beyond this, director certification would seem to be a new layer of bureaucracy for the already overloaded board.

33

Q: Why Is Board Education like Sex Education?

Certifying U.S. directors is a topic for the future, with few current adherents and dim prospects. Training, educating, and raising the standard for directors, however, is an idea of the here and now, with strong boosters, a flowering infrastructure, and ambitious goals.

The subject of director education covers several elements. First is an *orientation* process for the new outside director joining a board. It is likely this novice knows no more about the corporation than would any other experienced layperson from the outside. As companies search further afield for directors with strategic skills, they may end up talking with someone who literally never heard of the company before, so orientation becomes even more important. A second aspect of director education is *ongoing learning* about the corporation and its industry. The speed of business change and the generation of new data means that directors have an obligation to know what is happening in the firm, what *will be* happening in the firm, and where trends in the industry and economy at large are headed. Finally, there are the *governance basics*, the Directorship 101 aspects of board service. This includes the function and organization of committees, board responsibilities, legal liabilities, compensation design, investor relations, financial and operating review, and boardroom rules and procedures.

Two comments on these three main colleges within the boardroom university: First, I have listed them in their traditional (if cockeyed) order of priority at most companies. We start out by adding good prospects to the board, teach them about the company, make sure they stay up-to-date, and then educate them about governance procedures as the need arises. This turns the goals of most board accreditation advocates upside down. The idea that anyone should have training on the basics of governance before they set foot in the boardroom is simply not the way things are currently done. Governance activists and "great thinkers" might add a final "Yeah, we can tell by the results" to that thought.

The second comment is that these elements of education, notwithstanding their order, are applied very haphazardly, when they are applied at all. Indeed, I have found that there are probably more good how-to books available on *nonprofit* board training than for the boards of commercial corporations. Too often new directors join the board of a corporation, even very large ones, with little more background than the info package a new office employee might receive from personnel. Updates on the company, its people, and the industry may be limited to the board meeting envelope the director usually has too little time to review anyway. As to training on governance procedures and issues, this often consists of putting out fires. When companies reported big losses on financial derivatives transactions a couple of years ago, many boards suddenly demanded information on how derivatives work and where their companies stood. Had director education been a priority at these companies, the board would already have known.

Smart novice directors, especially since the liability scare of the 1980s, do some serious background checking before joining a company's board. If you sleep with a dog, you will get fleas. I know of one case where a nominee was elected to a board without anyone bothering to tell him that he was walking into a pending lawsuit against the directors.

The board, as well as management, should make a structured, comprehensive *orientation* program available to all fledgling directors. A Heidrick Partners survey of Fortune 1000 companies found that as of 1995, half offered structured orientations for new directors, up from 36% in 1989. Orientation was most common at larger industrial firms, 60% of those with sales exceeding $4 billion, as well as "progressive" corporations, those with more women and minorities on the board. Directors in companies with orientation programs rated a statement of corporate strategy, info on senior management, and the balance sheet as the information they most needed to see. Heidrick CEO Robert Heidrick observes that "companies with structured orientation programs overwhelmingly report that these programs contribute to better informed, more knowledgeable boards."[1]

Illinova corporation, an Illinois power producer, has been one of the more progressive corporations in board policy and designed a solid orientation program for its new directors. A package is prepared for board novices that includes the basics (the latest annual report, 10-Ks, and the articles of incorporation), but Illinova adds much more in a complete director's handbook. This includes a company history, bylaws, meeting schedules, a statement of director duties and responsibilities, full particulars on director pay and benefits, plant locations, stock information, insider trading laws, and data on outside counsel and major Illinova investors. As a utility, Illinova bears a heavier regulatory burden than most other corporations, so material on relevant utility laws, rules, and governing bodies is part of the handbook.

But if a corporation is still sluggish about orientating new directors, why not do it yourself? A woman named Jamie Baxter wrote for us a few years back on how she developed her own self-guided orientation program over the course of joining several boards, including Banta Corporation, a Chicago-area savings and loan, and a major mutual fund. The description of her wise, step-by-step process formed one of our most useful articles.

Baxter joined her boards from a background in nonprofits and privately held companies, so she set herself ambitious goals for coming up to speed on governance in general and her companies in particular. She started out by securing all the written information on her companies. A great deal of this is available, just waiting to be requested by the new director. "Getting to know the company is the easiest starting point, and probably the most effective. . . . Volumes of written material are readily available."[2] She suggests the basics, of course, such as recent annual reports and other SEC filings. But she also examines company bylaws, sales and marketing plans, the strategic plan, and laws and regulations relating to the

---

1. "Board Orientation Programs," Robert L. Heidrick, *Corporate Board*, March/April 1995, p. 18.
2. "The Freshman Director," Jameson Baxter, *Corporate Board*, November/December 1992, pp. 10–14.

specific industry. I would also add any board or committee charters, recent board and committee minutes, and the various stock analysts' reports on the company. The latter offer valuable insights on how the company looks from the outside.

Baxter made a special point of touring company facilities. "The company's pulse and personality came through on these visits in ways not possible in a board report. A true understanding of some functions or equipment is only possible by being on-site."[3] Such visits help directors visualize their responsibilities, to see the people and communities that depend on their judgment. They also give a human face and understanding to how the processes and chemistry of the company really work. At the pricing room of her mutual fund, for example, Baxter discovered that the flow of work is fairly smooth during the day but turns into a short-lived frenzy right after the markets close as all the fund's securities are updated and information on the new prices are dispatched. By including the shop floor, the back offices, the field sites, the warehouses, the labs, and the production line in your orientation, you learn what the company's work looks like and smells like and how it feels to be on the spot with the employees.

Those employees are another benefit of adding field trips to orientation. Workers discover that someone on the board of directors is interested in them, in what they do, and in what they have to say. Plant managers, marketing directors, and production people can take you closer to the front lines of what customers are really seeking. Gaining a strategic view of the company from the top down will be one of the goals of your orientation, but also make it a point to build tactical knowledge of the company from the bottom up.

One-on-one communication is valuable for the new director, and Baxter made it a point to gain face time with the CEO and top managers for personal views on the company's position, goals, and future. Ask the CEO what he or she really wants from a board member, and make it clear that you are there to be of service to the company. Does the CEO want a working board, with strong operational input from directors, regular assignments, and solid committee work? Does the CEO want a hands-off director who nods when told (in which case, ask, "Then why the hell am I here?") Time spent with the CFO, the corporate secretary, the company

---

3. Ibid.

counsel, and the audit staff will round out your personal feel for operations and build relationships that could be of value in the future.

Also, put in some quality time with other directors, who will likely be more than willing to show you the ropes. Although the idea of naming a lead director for the board is fairly new, informal lead directors have long been common. They are usually the most experienced, senior directors and come to the board with the most impressive outside credentials. (And, as I discussed earlier, they are usually the linchpin of efforts to oust underperforming CEOs). Spend some time with the director who serves this role on your new board. As the board's "rabbi," his or her insights are priceless. The lead director "can speak with authority, backed by a record of consistently sound judgment and thorough knowledge," according to Baxter.[4] The lead director's judgment is valued by other board members, even the CEO/chair, and his or her discussion points always receive a hearing.

The lead director is also a good source for deep background (or gossip, if you will) on the board's working relationships and pecking order. Someone may be touchy, someone else brash, another hesitant to challenge. These two may get along like fire and gasoline; Director X can always be depended on to support Director Y. Factor this intelligence into your own estimate of the board. New directors will find a few hours spent with the lead director to be one of the most valuable aspects of their board education.

Board orientation also includes specific orientation for committees as well. The new director who joins your audit committee, for instance, should receive a copy of that committee's charter (and it *does* have one, right?), information on accounting policies, the company's audit plan, background on the internal and outside audit staff, and any relevant financial filings not already received. A schedule of audit activities that go with the plan and opinions on unusual audit issues facing the company or any pending litigation or tax issues could round out this committee package.

The next element of the board curriculum is *ongoing education.* The pace of restructuring alone dictates that directors need strong, continuous information flow from the company. Changes in competition, regulations, financial markets, strategy, and tech-

---

4. Ibid.

nology have a strong impact on the company's prospects and demands. Insist that presentations to the board by staff not be happy-
face dog and pony shows, but instead, forward looking, carefully
examining risk factors or any wild cards that may lie ahead. Management may be carefully watching for the next blindside hit—or
it may not. Assuring long-term value is a board job, and part of it
is to make sure that *management* is watching out for long-term
value. The board can use its lessons to assure that the CEO has a
lesson plan.

Finally, directors need to know more about the *rules and duties*
of corporate governance. Much of the written knowledge on how
to be a director is little better than the director job descriptions I
mentioned earlier. However, there are a few specific areas of board
practice where most directors need some training.

Directorship 101.   What is the legal status of the board? What are
the functions of the committees, their mandates, their resources,
their legal authority? What parliamentary procedures does this
board use? Is there an executive committee, and if so, what are its
powers? Are there evaluation procedures for the board? For the
CEO? How is the agenda assembled and the minutes compiled and
approved? How are board, committee, and special meetings scheduled? Such basics are valuable as part of your original board orientation, but they can also be of use to current directors, who may
not know as much about the essentials as they should.

Time management.   With growing demands on directors, the raw
time demanded for responsibly serving on a board has grown tremendously. If the director is already CEO of another corporation,
not to mention sitting on the boards of companies X, Y, and Z, the
load can grow overwhelming. Directors who face such a schedule
unprepared will give poorer value to their boards. Teaching directors tips and techniques to schedule the unique demands of board
service is cheap insurance of good governance.

Compensation.   Few areas of board service have grown more complex than setting, monitoring, and accounting for executive and
board pay. If annual pay for the CEO or top executives exceeds $1
million, IRS rules now require the board to set a compensation plan

with performance targets and verification measures to keep the pay deductible. Boards have dealt with these rules in various ways, from assembling plans that meet the rules to exploring and using a variety of loopholes (more on this later).

However boards cope with the new headaches of executive pay, they have had to devote more time and *much* more expertise to the matter. The technical requirements just in understanding how to value stock options, what peer companies are paying, or the mystical aspects of pay deferral are enough to dumbfound most of us. Although there are plenty of internal tax staffers and outside consultants to design such masterpieces (the CEO will make sure of that), the board must have a working knowledge of these intricacies, be able to justify the plan, and be able to attest to its value as a motivator. The compensation committee will have the greatest need for this intelligence, but the board as a whole benefits from training on new pay rules.

Liabilities. Stephanie Joseph is founder of the Director's Network, a New York firm that specializes in board training. I asked her in which area the directors of major corporations feel the most ill at ease, and she immediately answered, "Liability. They're *all* nervous about liability."[5] It is hard to blame them. Since the big director liability scare of a decade ago, the battle between corporations seeking new liability defenses and clever plaintiffs' attorneys finding ways around them has taken on an almost biological air, antibiotic-resistant germs and such. Liability for directors (and, indeed, for the company as a whole) takes many forms, a constantly shifting field of threats and cautioners. Insider trading, the environment, currency transfers, equal opportunity, sexual harassment, and securities laws are a few.

Education is a particularly effective vaccine against some of these liabilities. For example the insider trading violations that make headlines involve tipping and trading venality. But the majority of insider trading violations by directors are minor technical goof-ups. Someone forgot to file an SEC form on time for an otherwise legal transaction. A director slips up and converts some options a few days too soon. These missteps are minor, but they still bring fines

---

5. Author interview, November, 1995.

and unwanted attention. A bit more internal info on dos and don'ts can usually prevent them.

In December 1995 the United States Congress overrode President Clinton's veto of a major liability reform bill. How will this new federal law affect the liability of directors and corporations? In many companies, the board might never find out. In a few more, the corporate counsel's staff might give a presentation on the law's basics. A few enlightened companies, though, will arrange a solid board training program as part of a liability risk management program. Which directors do you think will sleep better at night?

Outside relationships.   The growing public role of outside directors can lead to gaffes, misstatements, and contradictions unless boards are kept up-to-date on who says what. In 1995, after the Archer-Daniels-Midland Company was charged with price fixing and bribery, it was vital for everyone to keep quiet and say nothing that was not reviewed by counsel. But in October, an ADM director, the irrepressible F. Ross Johnson, gave comments to a college audience slamming the FBI's handling of the case and the main witness against ADM, former executive Mark Whitacre. While many might quietly agree with some of Johnson's views, the media jumped upon his remarks as a sign that ADM directors were whitewashing the case. Good board training and briefings from company legal and media staff might have prevented such an imbroglio.

Directors usually bring a businessperson's good sense about holding their cards close to their chests. However, someone who comes from his or her own business as an owner or CEO is used to setting the communications agenda and may slip up when the subject concerns someone else's company. Directors know that what goes on in the boardroom stays in the boardroom, but as the Ross Johnson case shows, a director's comments need not be ex cathedra to catch fire.

Offhand remarks about the corporation's prospects can also come back to haunt both directors and the company, especially when a rosy forecast is followed by a dip in results. Although the new securities lawsuit reforms of December 1995 widen the safe harbors for forecasts, they do little good if a director pops off with something out of line at an analyst's meeting. The windows of liability from projections remain large and uncertain. The director's offhand comment to a business reporter, a remark on the accuracy of an analyst's projections, a prediction that varies from the official company projections—all can cause the stock price to flutter, and all can start a stampede to the courthouse. Training sessions with the corporation's investor relations staff, media relations, and corporate counsel should be requirements in the board curriculum. While the message of training should not be (and likely could not be) that directors keep their yaps shut, procedures should be laid out on common messages, who the "point man" should be on communications, and how to handle major events. It is vital that everyone be singing from the same hymnal.

Crisis management. Training for crises has connections to the above, especially since someone from CNN might be sticking a microphone in a director's face and asking how he or she could have let such a disaster happen. But crises come in many shapes and urgencies: environmental disasters, such as the Exxon Valdez or Union Carbide's Bhopal, India, plant; legal debacles, such as ADM's; public image fiascoes, such as the messy, public leadership battle at W. R. Grace; or safety emergencies, such as poisoned Tylenol or pop cans with syringes inside being discovered on store shelves. Some will pop up instantly, when some technician at a plant in the middle of nowhere turns the wrong valve. Others will build over time, such as black eyes on plant closings or legal investigations.

Most major companies have crisis plans, teams, and procedures in place, but has the board been brought into the process? What is its role? A few years ago, the board's involvement in crisis planning was to make sure that someone had put a plan together and then to stay out of the way if it was ever needed. But directors are on the front lines today and must know how to handle themselves. Educate them by assigning crisis responsibilities (including specific roles for directors), making them a part of practice sessions, and routing them critiques on how these "fire drill" sessions came off, as well as reviews of how other companies handled a crisis.

Through most of corporate history, the training of directors has been handled with the same shoulder-shrugging awkwardness our society has shown sex education. With novice directors, as with adolescents, we hope for the best and let them pick it up as they go along. That is not enough for companies today and will be even worse down the road. Boards have powers and responsibilities unimagined a generation ago and must know how to use them. Management, in particular, should encourage improved training and education for directors. The age of the imperial CEO is winding down, and boards will hold far more power over management, whether the CEO wants them to or not. If you are a CEO, you want your board to be smart enough to use that power responsibly.

34

Making the Modern Board Work

So far we have discussed how a future of smarter, more independent, more strategic corporate directors is coming together for the twenty-first-century boardroom. But what will they do once they convene there? How will they manage their new duties, exert their powers, and structure themselves? Board makeup is only part of the story. New board processes and organization are also reshaping governance.

In the literature and thinking on modern corporate governance, much of this change remains uncharted territory. The scholarship of boards concentrates on the great themes of independence, oversight, shareholder value, motivation, and fiduciary duty. Once we've chewed on these for awhile, we can move on to the big issues, like paying in stock, splitting the CEO/chair roles, or the power of institutional shareholders. However, when I talk with directors about the real information they need to be more effective, I find them far more interested in essential housekeeping matters. Exactly what should (and shouldn't) the audit committee be examining? How do we set up an evaluation program? How do we gently prod the CEO on succession planning? What is the best way to ease non-contributing members off the board?

While these may not qualify as the subjects that get academics and consultants published, they are the real-world minutiae that make corporate governance work. Most great concerns in our society, from government, to education, to health care, to law, to corporate governance, have a similar split. There are people on the outside who discuss the weighty issues and revolutionary changes. And then there are the people on the inside, thinking, doing, wrestling with life in the day-to-day and more concerned with fixing the plumbing and paying the bills. In corporate governance as in the other arenas, those on either side of this divide may sniff at the other as pointy-headed busybodies or as pedestrian dullards.

There is no doubt that the thinkers provide long-term goals for the doers. However, there is also no doubt that the doers, in our case those who serve on the corporate boards of the United States, need better tools and procedures to do their jobs. Only by overhauling these board procedures can we build a practical foundation for permanent board change. The changes in what boards do are dictating much of this overhaul. When the board's oversight power became divorced from ownership earlier in the present century, the board lost its indirect vigor, and its legal and administrative functions declined into formalities.

Looking back over board history, by the post–World War II era the board had evolved into an almost ceremonial body. When an institution that once held real power is outstripped by events, yet survives, it tends to grow decadent, placing importance on form over substance. Corporate boards, up until fairly recent times, were a disquieting example: the classic, walnut-paneled boardroom, the strict rules on what was and was not to be said, the legalistic, ornate terminology, even the occasional member nodding off. Board meetings came to resemble one of those baroque rituals of British royalty that has long lost its original purpose. All we need are formal Beefeaters with pikestaffs outside the boardroom door being photographed by tourists.

Building a twenty-first-century board marked by utility, power, and speed upon such a historic framework is proving a real challenge. Think of upgrading a one-horse shay to compete at Indy. Even assuming that the original model and legal functions of the board had purpose and value, that blueprint will not do us much good in the future. Those squires sitting about their corporate plank may have been damned good, attentive trustees in Adam Smith's day, but new archetypes are required for the next century. We are demanding something very new from the idea of the corporate board—strong, involved governance oversight from people who are not major owners of the company. I will discuss the matter of director stockholdings later, but even firm advocates of the idea would not envision turning anyone on the board into a major investor in the corporation. Directors who accumulated a nice piece of equity over years of service would still own but a drop in the bucket of all company shares. However this turns out, we are left with a problem, the need to create a governance function that has never truly existed before. *How do we give directors the strength, motivation, and tools to govern corporations they do not own?*

We are making a start on this voyage of discovery by reshaping the board structure, a process that has gone on for at least a couple of decades. Shifts in who is named to the board based on race, sex, and insider/outsider status have been under way for some time now. These trends show signs of accelerating and will likely expand as a by-product of adding new talents to the board.

Lesser noted, but ultimately more helpful, has been the growing professionalism and infrastructure of *how* the board does its work. Use of committees, willingness to tap outside talent, and moves toward the true *working* board show how a number of small changes can add up to major results.

35

Staffing the Board

Much of this change is shaped by a simple equation: greater demands *of* boards = greater time demands *on* boards. The time, work, commitment, and brainpower required of an outside director today is far greater than it was even a decade ago. In 1995, the average corporate director dedicated 163 hours yearly to service on a single board. This equals about 20 days a year. As recently as 1988, the average director spent only about 14 days a year on board service. Further, at the largest industrial corporations ($5 billion and over), the director time commitment climbs to as much as 187 hours yearly.

The Conference Board found that in 1995, most corporate boards met around five to six times per year, although this climbs to eight per year at the largest manufacturing corporations, and monthly board meetings are not rare.[1] On top of this, the average company has three or four committees (five at the largest corporations), the most common being audit, compensation, executive, and nominating. Each of these committees typically holds three to four meetings yearly. Committee work alone keeps some directors hopping. In 1991, a writer in the *Corporate Board* estimated that yearly committee assignments for directors came to 46 at ITT and 33 at General Motors. At GM, this was the year *before* the board was tied up in sacking the CEO. According to Korn/Ferry, directors received for their services in 1995 an average of $31,415 in annual retainer and meeting fees, plus another $8,000 or so for committee fees and meetings, for an average total pay of $39,707.

---

1. *Corporate Directors' Compensation,* 1996 ed., Conference Board, 1996.

This may sound like good money for about four weeks' work every year, but directors earn their keep. The modern working board essentially gives the CEO (and the shareholders) talents from many fields. The board serves a bit as an auditor, legal department, top-level consultant, strategic advisor, long-term planner, investor relations, and pay consultant, all at a bargain price. Rather than finding fault with how and how much we pay directors for their yearly workload, we should marvel at how they manage to cram so many full-time roles into so little time.

One reason for this greatly increased workload is management acceptance of the new board role. CEOs (not all, of course, but some; the more progressive trendsetters) have come to realize that a more active, involved board is a reality of the coming business age. So if you must live with a busy board, why not put them to work? As Hicks Waldron notes, "CEOs began to look at their boards more for help rather than as a pain."[2] Directors are handling assignments for the CEO, for the board as a whole, and for the company on a scale unknown a decade ago. The payment of consulting fees to directors for their services has grown controversial but obscures the fact that directors are doing far more consulting work that goes unpaid as part of their normal duties.

To support the growth of the working board, corporations are increasing the amount of staff time dedicated to their efforts. This is a fairly new idea. Most of the board's support needs have traditionally been handled as side activities by various top management offices. Foremost of these is the corporate secretary's office, but the CEO's office, corporate counsel, and the CFO's staff also pitch in. This has worked reasonably well over the years but obviously tends to make the board more dependent on management, as well as keeping board support services diffused and erratic.

In 1972, Arthur Goldberg, a retired justice of the U.S. Supreme Court, made corporate waves when he resigned after less than two years on the board of TWA. What stirred the waters was his announced reason for leaving the board. For several months Goldberg had lobbied TWA management and his fellow directors to create a committee of outside directors to oversee the effectiveness of both the board and of management (this was an early version of the board Corporate Governance committee). He further pro-

---

2. Author interview, November 1995.

posed to fund a modest support and technical staff answerable solely to the TWA board. Aside from administrative functions, this staff was to include talent in science, economics, and finance. The board staff would have stood outside the influence of management and would have aided the board in reviewing and judging management reports and policies. Goldberg was concerned that all results, projections, and appraisals *of* management were first filtered *through* management and that directors were, with the current system, unable to gain any independent view of results. He proposed a truly autonomous back channel for the board to circumvent this bias of the system. Such an unthinkable act left management aghast, and the other directors sided with the CEO in rejecting any such idea. Goldberg, stating that he "did not find it possible to fulfill my legal and public obligation as a member of the Board," in October 1972 resigned as a TWA director.[3]

As with other aspects of corporate governance, a trend once battled as a reform proposal is now creeping in the back door as a housekeeping aid. The information and oversight we demand of boards today, as well as that demanded by boards themselves, are forcing corporations to reconsider how they staff and support their directors. Harvard Professor John Pound commented on this in his proposal of a "political" model for the board of directors. According to Pound, calls for stronger accountability, stakeholder consideration, and public oversight, plus the rise of constituency directors, are making corporate governance look less like a market function and more like a political, public sector affair.[4] Taking the analogy a bit further, why not give these semipublic boards their own staff, like the "hill rats" buzzing about the offices of Congress?

The idea of using government bureaucracy as a model for staffing the boardroom does not stir many hearts. But some see glimmers of a boardroom staff model in other areas of government. Attorney John Gardner writes that a good starting point for a board staff could be found elsewhere in Washington, at the White House. The White House chief of staff, or the staff secretary's office, could well serve as a model for a board "secretariat." This secretariat, according to Gardner, would answer directly to the board, and be

---

3. *Managing the Managers,* Edward McSweeney, Harper & Row, 1978, p. 110.
4. "The Rise of the Political Model of Corporate Governance and Corporate Control," John Pound, *New York University Law Review,* 1993.

responsible for improving information flow to directors. It would serve a less radical purpose than Goldberg's idea, being more a simple conduit and liaison for information, both through management and through back channel sources. The board secretariat would be staffed with no more than half a dozen people, would be inexpensive, and would lift the burden on boards to dig out information by creating an in-house process.

The board secretariat would not require any of the more contentious board proposals, such as corporate governance committees or splitting the CEO and chair roles, to be effective. However, it could dovetail neatly with either idea if they should be put in place. Further, the secretariat would be accountable to the *board*, not to shareholders. While this would help strengthen the board's hand in working with management, it would also help keep governance power in the boardroom, avoiding the concerns that arise from proposals for outside shareholder committees.

Gardner's government/governance comparison may turn off some strong free-marketeers, but the small size of such a secretariat avoids the concern over a new layer of bureaucracy. Further, some of the government models he mentions, such as the National Security Council and the Joint Chiefs of Staff, have proven quite effective at compiling, sifting, and processing information. *Some* aspects of government decision making are pretty good, the IRS and EPA notwithstanding. As a clincher, Gardner points out that William Agee was long able to pursue his failed strategies at Morrison-Knudsen without board challenge—until he made the mistake of adding two former National Security Advisors to the board, William Clark and Zbigniew Brzezinski. "Their careers were built on receiving and evaluating information . . . and they are accustomed to moving quickly."[5] Within a year, Agee was out.

---

5. "Independent Staffs for Boards of Directors," John S. Gardner, Harvard Business School paper, 1995, p. 72.

36

Hey, Committees Aren't All Bad

Although boards are putting in more time and effort today, that does not necessarily mean they spend more time locked in the boardroom. Perhaps the most underreported change in how boards function is the increased use of board committees as working bodies. The greater specialization and intricacy of modern board work is one reason for this. Boards that once nodded their heads and approved what was placed before them could afford interchangeable directors. With more diverse, specialized membership, more technical demands, and limited time, it makes more sense to break tasks down to their components at the committee level. Further, legal, regulatory, and accounting mandates over the years have set high independence standards for board committees. When we add growing concerns over board interlocks, it's wisest to have people with "Caesar's wife" unimpeachability on most committees.

No longer legal niceties, board committees are becoming power centers in their own right. And as the board faces new demands, the committee system is proving versatile. Although some new committees are showing up with such concerns as governance, compliance, and corporate responsibility, many new board tasks are being taken on by the current committee structure, particularly the audit, nominating, and compensation committees. Why?

Most of the newer demands on boards are outgrowths of their traditional responsibilities. The job of setting, structuring, reviewing, and verifying executive pay has become much more complex, but it is still essentially a comp committee job. As for the audit committee, it has a tightly written mandate to monitor and certify financial statements, and this oversight function can be applied to many other areas, such as regulatory compliance.

Although board work is more specialized today, it is also more inter-related. In years past, two of the more common board committees were a salary and bonus committee and a committee for executive stock options. Indeed, writing in 1966, Juran and Louden found these committees more common than the audit committee at man-ufacturers.[1] But as executive pay became an octopus of stock, op-tions, long- and short-term incentives, base pay, deferred compen-sation, benefits, and perks (all with complex tax and accounting concerns), it made more sense to consolidate the whole jumble into one committee.

The present committee structure has certain norms that give their work legal cover. The membership and independence of the audit com-mittee, for example, is shaped by the rules and standards of the SEC, the stock exchanges, and accounting bodies. This structure of man-dates gives the committee a "Good Housekeeping seal" of inde-pendence and helps validate its decisions when the committee looks into other areas.

Time demands on the board are growing. Adding new committee burdens to this would only complicate already tricky scheduling. Even if new committees for corporate responsibility or environment only meet a couple of times a year, they drain time, effort, and resources away from the board's other duties. It is more efficient to broaden the mandate of the current committees to include these matters.

The committees focus accountability in known groups. While the board as a legal unit always retains responsibility for the work of its committees, committees make it more likely that a particular job will be done right. A duty that remains diffused throughout the board as a whole too often becomes lost in the shuffle. By empow-ering a committee, the board can prevent a governance task from becoming "everyone's responsibility, but no one's job."

---

1. *The Corporate Director,* J. M. Juran and J. Keith Louden, American Manage-ment Association, 1966, p. 246.

Another committee of the board, common, powerful, but rarely examined, is the executive committee. The executive committee has varying functions but is best viewed as a management-based condensed version of the board empowered to act in its stead between full board meetings. It usually includes the CEO/chair, but he or she need not chair it.

The changing powers of the major board committees offer fascinating clues as to where boards are heading, and each deserves its own consideration.

37

Audit Committees: The Busy Watchdog

Audit is the most structured committee of the modern board. Indeed, there might be more regulation of who serves on audit and how the committee discharges its role than there is for the board as a whole. Yet the rapid growth in its importance and its wide usefulness as a watchdog has caused much uncertainty as to its role. Even the SEC rules pertaining to the audit committee, while stressing its importance, remain vague on exactly what it is supposed to do. No group of directors, despite their skills or scope, will be able to spot all errors, misapplications, or chicanery that might crop up when they only meet about four times yearly. But that is not the audit committee's job. Rather, the committee exists to audit the *company's* internal and external mechanisms for catching problems. The audit committee is the group that watches the watchers.

The idea of a discrete board audit committee was first kicked around in the 1930s, but audit committees remained quite rare for years. As late as 1967, only about 19% of major corporations had one, and membership was an undemanding sinecure, a holding tank for novice directors and the less brilliant board luminaries.[1] Audit committees received their big boost in 1978, when they were required for all New York Stock Exchange companies. However, audit committees lacked a clear portfolio until 1987, when the Treadway Commission report on fraudulent financial reporting was released. This commission, named for its chair, former SEC commissioner James Treadway, was sponsored by the American Institute of CPAs,

---

1. *Corporate Leadership*, Stanley C. Vance, McGraw-Hill, 1983, p. 66.

the American Accounting Association, and the Financial Executives Institute, among others.

The Treadway report found the key to cutting audit mischief was to set the proper tone from the top and that one of the most powerful tools for this ethical leadership was the board audit committee. The commission urged the SEC to require all public companies to form audit committees (this has not happened, by the way, but since the percentage of corporations with an audit committee is in the high 90s, a mandate now seems unnecessary). Audit committees should have a written charter, should be strong and independent, should review the reports and oversight of both inside and outside auditors and management, and should oversee all company financial filings, including interim reports. Although the Treadway Commission report did not carry the weight of law, its recommendations have since become standards for judging the work of all audit committees.

The wide view of company financials that goes with audit committee service makes it a popular spot to break in new directors. While this has value, it is important for the audit committee to retain a core of sharp, experienced members. Continuity is vital for maintaining purpose and consistency in oversight, as well as the ability to ask why an item is being treated differently today than it was two or three years ago. Staggered terms for the board as a whole may be controversial, but for the audit committee they make good sense.

Deciding who goes on the audit committee has usually been handled by the CEO/chair, with board approval, but more collaboration between the CEO, the board, and the current committee chair is becoming the rule. Committee members should have broad, solid knowledge of business and ideally should have a bit more time available than other directors. At least one or two audit members need a background in corporate finance, and one of these finance members will make the best chair. It would seem a foregone conclusion that anyone named to the audit committee be an independent director, but the definition of "independent" has grown tighter recently and deserves consideration. Audit committee members obviously should not be employees of the company, but this extends to parent companies, subsidiaries, and divisions. Directors affiliated with major customers or suppliers should likewise be excused, as should former employees, at least for a period of several years after leaving the firm. Employees of joint ventures or firms in which the company has a significant ownership interest may be acceptable, but the relationship deserves a second look. Close family or personal relationships with management may likewise present a problem of appearance.

Orientation for service on the audit committee requires a few added subjects. Are there any unusual transactions, financial instruments, or accounting treatments that apply to the company? Does the company and its industry face specific regulatory or reporting requirements? Are there disagreements between internal and outside auditors on how a rule is applied? Audit committee functions and norms are unique to each company. Bringing new members up to speed on these quirks not only makes these directors more effective faster but prompts fresh thinking on just why the committee handles items the way it does.

As boards are breaking themselves down into committees to better specialize their tasks, the audit committee itself is taking a team approach. A committee member with strong background in finance, for instance, can specialize in different areas from a committee member with legal qualifications. The audit committee chair should assign the members each to their own skill while directing the overall effort.

The broad oversight potential of this committee makes it easy for audit to overextend itself. By looking into too many areas, audit can diffuse its talents on jobs best left to others. This need for focus, plus the value of giving audit a strong mandate, make it important to have a solid, up-to-date audit committee charter.

- The charter should specify the experience and skill requirements for its members. At least one member should have a strong financial background. Also, the charter should attend to basic housekeeping matters, such as maximum and minimum size of the committee (four is the average), member rotation and term limits, and the required degree of independence from the company and from management.
- The charter should lay out the essential areas and levels for the committee's oversight. These would include financial controls, company financial reporting, the work of internal and outside auditors, and company compliance with financial laws and regulations. These are the oversight basics, but

audit committees are extending their talents to such new fields as regulatory compliance, assessment of potential environmental liabilities, and review of corporate ethics codes.

- The charter serves as the board's warrant to the committee, giving it the power and discretion to look where it feels it must. A charter should specify areas of oversight with enough precision to make the committee's authority clear but not enough to hobble it from looking into related spheres. If there is any one unit of the corporate board that should be fearless at poking its nose into matters, it is the audit committee.

- The charter provides a master schedule and playbook for the audit process. It sets guidelines for meetings and reporting relationships with both the internal and outside audit staff, as well as the frequency of these meetings and their basic itinerary. It also specifies the committee's role in selecting and retaining the external auditor.

The audit committee might seem like the area of the board with the least human contact, concentrating itself on dry financial figures. Yet the modern audit committee finds itself most effective when it builds strong personal relationships with auditors and management. Warning flags that might get lost among spreadsheets and reports can come to the surface one-on-one. Barbara Hackman Franklin has an impressive résumé of service on the audit committees of such companies as Dow Chemical and Aetna. She recently told me that she sees "directors paying more attention to their private sessions with the internal and outside auditors, and with management. . . . They're not always coming from the same place, so I can do a nonconfrontational check-and-balance."[2] Hackman Franklin also sets time aside for frequent personal meetings with company internal audit staff, as well as the other members of her committee. This helps keep surprises from being so surprising.

The essentials of financial reporting review keep the audit committee busy, but audit is being put to work in many new, innovative areas.

---

2. Hackman Franklin interview, *Corporate Board*, November/December 1994, p. 32.

- Reviewing corporate compliance programs and codes of conduct for their value, reach, and effectiveness. Are internal controls really effective? Will regulatory or reporting changes require a compliance overhaul? What changes in law or regulation are on the horizon, and how will they affect company programs?

- Overseeing financial derivatives risk management. Do the people in the company who manage derivatives know what they are doing? Has the company enacted a code for uses, acceptable risks, reporting, and oversight of derivatives? Is it effective? Are company incentives for employees who manage derivatives in line with the code (do they discourage risky speculation on paper but reward it in practice?) How effective are the company's risk assessment and monitoring tools?

- Tax and accounting impact of executive and board compensation. Although this borders on the work of the compensation committee, there are many areas that require audit committee thought. How is the company managing tax aspects of the $1 million pay cap for top executives? At this writing, a bill has been introduced in Congress to extend this tax treatment to other highly paid managers. How would this affect pay deductibility throughout the company? Is the corporation keeping up with the debate on the accounting treatment for stock-based pay?

- Committee oversight (if any) of nontraditional items. How involved is audit with quarterly financial reporting, financial press releases, or the Management Discussion and Analysis section in the annual report? Should the audit committee chair also prepare a letter for the annual report?

- How does the company account for potential environmental liabilities? What contingencies have been made? Are management's assumptions on environmental liability potential realistic? This could fit in well with board crisis planning.

- Investigatory functions. Although the board unusually forms a special committee to look into unusual matters, the audit committee's independence and financial base often makes it the ideal candidate. Audit should be considered for poking into conflicts of interest, the propriety of director consulting fees, and the suitability of sensitive or questionable company payments.

The audit committee will need plenty of "maintenance" in the future to keep up with the new demands being placed on it. Continuing education is probably more important here than in any other committee. Presentations on current issues by management and finance staff or inside/outside auditors would be a valuable part of every meeting. Although audit meeting time is precious, consider devoting a session every year or two to in-service training and updates. These can be conducted by the audit staff, either internal or external, but can also call on legal counsel, environmental consultants, tax counselors, or technical experts.

The training would offer an in-depth look at major issues affecting audit: pending changes in FASB, SEC, AICPA, IRS, or stock exchange rules; the effects of operational changes; new technology and its audit impact (especially electronic data processing); or organizational or policy changes at the external auditor. But they should not have to come to you. Visit company sites for fact-finding tours or even committee meetings, especially sites that have been audit trouble spots. Outside seminars and workshops should also be part of the committee member's schedule. Indeed, the board may consider setting up a continuing education requirement for audit committee members.

The modern audit committee can hardly pass judgment on the results of others unless it is willing to regularly pass judgment on itself. The committee should implement a periodic self-assessment/ evaluation program. Shaun O'Malley, former chairman of Price Waterhouse, suggested a committee evaluation every three years in a 1994 article in the *Corporate Board*.[3] A 1995 Arthur Andersen report ups this to every two years, suggesting how rapidly the audit committee has gained importance. The committee evaluation should examine its charter, the contribution of its members, its independence, its access, its information flow, its relationships (inside

---

3. "Improving Audit Committee Performance," Shaun F. O'Malley, *Corporate Board*, May/June 1994, p. 11.

and outside auditors, management), and the scope of its oversight. The audit committee should also take comments from the rest of the board, the inside and outside auditors, and the CEO on how well it does its job. The single most important task for any audit committee is to audit itself.

38

Compensation Committees: The Struggle for Respect

Serious money draws serious attention, and pressures on the comp committee have shot up at the same speed as executive pay. Certainly when the CEO's pay package was simple and modest, the efforts (and brainpower) of the board devoted to voting "aye" were likewise undemanding. But stronger efforts to make executives accountable for their pay—combined with much closer attention to their pay levels—have made the comp committee's work a more serious job.

As noted, CEO and top executive pay is gaining more attention today, which puts the comp committee in an unusual (and no doubt awkward) position. Audit committees, despite the weight of their work, the growth in their mandate, and their increased professionalism, labor in relative obscurity. Oh, they may uncover a fraud, with lawsuits and people being led away in handcuffs. But the vast majority of audit committee work is no more pulse pounding than any other area of accountancy. Members can rest assured that they will not make splashy business headlines with their decisions on the accounting treatment of long-lived assets.

But this is *precisely* the risk that the compensation committee of a major corporate board faces. What they decide about paying the CEO can land their company on the cover of *Fortune* or *Business Week*, and maybe even the business items in *Newsweek* or *CNN*. In the worst case, the CEO pay package the comp committee worked so hard to shape with reasonable rewards and wise incentives will end up being noted by a national news columnist or wire service info-bit, in these cases no doubt in close proximity to the words "obscene" and "greed."

The saddest aspect of this is that the compensation committee usually tries very hard to be good. It takes surveys, compiles good information, and works with well-informed outside consultants to design a package that both retains management and motivates it to do its best. Unfortunately, the comp committee has for too long faced a system designed to increase executive pay despite results and has had to swim upstream to overcome this bias. Real change came to the system only a few years ago with regulatory mandates to clean up the house of executive pay setting. In 1992 the SEC issued rules regarding the disclosure and reporting of executive pay, including a careful statement of the company's pay policy (causing quite a flurry in itself because few companies *had* executive pay policies). In 1994, the IRS followed up with its own strictures, including the infamous "$1 million pay deductibility cap" that required much tighter board oversight. Yet despite these mandates, comp committees are only now gaining the strength and motivation to shape pay that works. The root of this dysfunction is found in the history of the compensation committee itself.

The comp committee goes back even further in corporate history than the audit committee, although it has more complex genesis. As noted earlier, most boards of 30 to 40 years ago handled executive stock compensation, salary, and benefits as separate functions, sometimes with specific committees for each. This loose, ill-coordinated process was too often dominated by the very insiders whose pay was being decided, drawing early shareholder and regulatory criticism.

The compensation committee collected these scattered functions together under the purview of a specialized group of outside directors and helped CEOs maintain that the board was indeed in charge of pay setting. The committee proved quite popular and caught on rapidly. Indeed, a 1973 Korn/Ferry survey found comp committees were more common than audit committees at big companies.[1] The comp committee pay-setting process developed a number of tools over the years to shape pay that would be competitive and reasonable. Surveys were usually made of other companies to

---

1. "Board Composition and Governance: 1973–82," Lester B. Korn, *Corporate Board*, March/April 1983, p. 20.

develop pay norms based on company size, industry, profitability, and location. A large network of sophisticated compensation consultants developed to offer in-depth research on pay practices and trends. The tax and accounting treatment of pay elements could be precisely calculated. The executive pay levels that resulted seemed both reasonable and defensible, though often hard to decipher.

The flaws of this pay regimen became apparent in the 1980s, when executive pay began to soar upward with little apparent relationship to performance. In earlier years, the average CEO's pay was typically about 80% base salary and 20% in the form of bonuses. As the pay-setting infrastructure became more sophisticated, however, "at-risk" compensation in the form of incentives, bonuses, and stock options grew much more popular. Today, base salary is usually only a third to a quarter of the CEO's yearly take.

If we accept the idea that CEOs are economic animals as much as the rest of humanity (although with far more tools to do things about it), the reason for this shift is obvious. While it may have been impolitic for the management team to seek hefty increases in base pay, there was an unending stream of new ideas for supercharging the compensation mix with incentives. These could be quite obscure compared to the black-and-white simplicity of base pay and could soar to enormous amounts, at least on paper. Incentives could also overlap, allowing double, triple, or even quadruple dipping. Best of all, they could be so crafted that the performance needed to trigger them was negligible, a brief jump in the stock price, a no-brainer financial goal, or just not dropping dead before the end of the year. As Robert Monks observed, "The most disturbing trend in compensation is its ability to change with the times, always appearing to be designed to reward management for performance, but rarely actually doing so."[2]

The board compensation committee has traditionally been a partner in this dubious process, usually convincing itself that its actions were for the good of the company. Graef Crystal's 1991 *In Search of Excess* describes the comp committee as near the bottom of the heap in committee prestige, and Crystal himself has little use for either the committee's talent or toughness. "Compensation committees never spend enough time studying complex compen-

---

2. *Power and Accountability,* Robert A. G. Monks and Nell Minow, Harper Business, 1991, p. 171.

sation schemes."[3] Indeed, under "Compensation Committees," the index of Crystal's book lists such heartwarming topics as "bias of," "as culprits," and "problems with." Crystal is not alone in viewing the compensation committee as part of an executive pay problem. Even as sympathetic a commentator as the Conference Board in 1987 admitted that "it is not difficult for a chief executive to have an influence . . . on the committee's thinking as far as his own pay is concerned."[4] Rather than serving as a pay watchdog, the comp committee was assailed as (and, too often, was) a pay lapdog.

Thus, the comp committee, like the consultants, the surveys, the incentives, the stock options, and all the other safeguards that were developed to keep management pay in line, has become a tool that in fact helped management pay to soar far beyond any link to performance. However, signs of hope are showing in this process. While the mechanism of executive pay setting has been corrupted in the past, it is also apparent that a strong infrastructure has been built that *can* be used to make CEO pay effective. Consider an analogy from General Motors. GM has long been bashed as poorly managed, spending too much to build out-of-touch cars that are ineptly marketed. Yet GM is also the largest corporation in the world, with enormous reserves of engineering, sales, finance, and marketing talent. It has world-class technical and manufacturing facilities. If it is able to rouse itself (though this would be no small feat), it could use the same people, resources, and structure that currently seem hapless to build the best, most popular cars in the world. All it needs is resolve and wisdom. Likewise, the board compensation committee already has the tools and assets needed to create pay that truly motivates and rewards. It just needs to find itself. The process starts with good membership and a good committee charter.

Although it would seem obvious that insiders do not belong on the committee that decides their own pay, employee directors were a common feature of comp committees until quite recently. However, the IRS pay deductibility changes affecting pay over $1 million mandated that all committee members be independent, squeezing out the last of the employees. Nomination to the comp

---

3. *In Search of Excess*, Graef S. Crystal, W. W. Norton, 1991, p. 226.
4. *Corporate Directorship Practices: The Compensation Committee*, Conference Board, 1987, p. 12.

committee has also changed, with CEO selection of members, and especially CEO naming of the committee chair, on their way out.

The board should select comp members based on their general business acumen and ability to deal with complex pay issues. Stock options, restricted stock, pay deferral, bonuses, contract negotiation, golden parachutes, retirement benefits, and perquisites all feature very intricate valuation, timing, and deductibility considerations. When these and other components are mixed together, the decision making transcends arithmetic and turns into algebra. This complexity is one of the reasons executive pay packages have turned into runaways.

Members should have a knowledge of these components, but they no more need to be experts than audit committee members need be accountants. Pay consultants have developed excellent training materials on the value and impact of pay elements and are available to answer questions. Knowledge of the company's strategic plan and performance goals are also important. Unless you have a working knowledge of where the corporation needs to go, how can you judge whether the CEO is properly leading it there?

Compensation committee members must also bring a tough, iconoclastic viewpoint to their work. Too often in the past they have been willing to accept the utility of pay packages on face value. While they need not be cynical toward the proposals of the CEO and pay consultants, they have every right to study recommendations with a jaundiced eye. How much of management pay is really at risk here? Are rewards simply being shuffled from an old heading to a new one? Will the CEO get seriously rich if results are spectacular? Good! Will he or she also get seriously rich if the company merely stagnates? Not so good.

I noted earlier that the IRS now sets tough independence rules for members of the compensation committee. In fact, these rules were at first so tough as to stir some controversy in themselves. As proposed, the rules would have banned current employees, former employees who received any recent payments from the company, corporate officers, or anyone whose employer received any fees from the corporation. The last stricture was so broadly drawn that, as an author wrote in the *Corporate Board*, directors could be banned from the comp committee "if they were an employee of an entity, such as a local telephone company or electric utility, from which the corporation purchases more than $60,000."[5] Particularly in smaller, midcap corporations with boards of eminent locals, this could have left few directors with clean hands. Fortunately, the IRS watered down the rules a bit in the comment phase, but it is still wise to seek advice from counsel or the tax staff before adding a new member to the comp committee.

A final concern on the independence of comp committee members is to avoid board interlocks. If two CEOs serve on the compensation committees of each other's board, the temptation is to subtly help "one hand wash the other." Cases of one director/CEO blatantly conspiring with another to prod the pay process upward are uncommon but would rarely need to be so overt. Even in cases where the directors made an effort to be religious, there would be a problem of appearance. And besides, both the SEC and IRS frown on such pay interlocks.

After restocking with skeptical, smart, clean membership (if not before), directors should prepare a solid charter for the compensation committee. This charter may need even more defining than that of the audit committee. While audit has a known central purpose (to assure that mechanisms are in place to monitor and certify financial reporting), comp is trickier. We can say that its purpose is to set top management pay (or, in years past, to rationalize it), but that tells us little. Using what bases? What business results and executive action does the company seek to reward? How will the results be monitored and enforced? Will pay recommendations start with management and be vetted by the committee, or will they be comp committee productions all the way through? Which of its decisions must be ratified by the full board? Without a tightly written committee charter, the comp committee could be subject to end runs by the CEO, or aspects of the comp process could be fumbled between the committee and the full board.

The comp committee charter details the pay-setting philosophy and policy of the company. It also defines the committee's (and by implication, the board's) role in fulfilling that policy. The following are among the items the charter should address:

- State the company's compensation philosophy and goals (try to make this substantive).

5. "The New Era of Executive Pay," Clint Stretch and Bill Wilson, *Corporate Board*, May/June 1994, p. 17.

- Discuss the committee's role in reviewing and setting pay, and for whom (just the CEO? Top managers? The other directors?)
- State whether the committee will generate these recommendations itself or whether it will instead review recommendations from management.
- Discuss the compensation elements to be used by the company in shaping executive pay (base salary, incentives, stock option plans, deferred compensation, etc.). Full definitions of how each of these elements will be interpreted within the company should be included as subheadings or as a separate appendix.
- Provide formulas for summing up these elements into a total executive pay plan (X% of this, Y% of that, etc.). This may be too specific for the charter but can be addressed as part of a yearly compensation committee report. Also, this recipe can be revised by updating the charter on a regular basis.
- Define committee authority to assess the performance of managers under performance-based elements of the pay package. These standards must be spelled out, the tools for their assessment defined, and the result of the achievement/nonachievement detailed.
- Assert the committee's authority to set and review executive benefit and pension plans, and spell out elements that will be used in shaping these plans.
- Assert the board's authority to work with resources and authorities both within and outside of the company (consultants, tax counselors, investor relations) as the committee sees fit.
- Lay out boundary lines between the compensation committee and other committees with which there might be overlap, for example a pensions or stock option committee, if one exists, or the nominating committee for human resource matters.

This may sound like quite a full plate for committee members, yet it is only the basic outline to be filled in. Compliance with the new SEC and IRS guidelines is forcing the comp committee to develop very complex plans, including graphs, that show how the company pays its executives and how this pay is justified by results. The SEC rules require issuance of a yearly "Board Compensation Committee Report on Executive Disclosure" (the committee even has to put its *name* on it). The report must detail company compensation policies, including how executive pay is related to performance. Specific indicators are sought, and the SEC frowns on boilerplate language.

The committee must show company performance with a line graph that charts total shareholder return over the past five years compared to a broad market index or a peer group of companies in the same industry. If a shareholder invested $1,000 in your company five years ago, how would the results compare to those of your competitors? One of the specific concerns that prompted the SEC rules was executive pay disclosure that was so obscure and buried throughout the annual report as to be indecipherable. The comp committee must now do better, with standard tables detailing the following: a summary table of all compensation from all sources for the CEO and four other top executives during the past three years; option/stock appreciation rights grants (including potential gain or value); option/stock appreciation right exercises; and long-term incentives.

These SEC rules do not have a *direct* effect on how companies pay the CEO and other top executives. Nonetheless, they impose a discipline on the compensation committee. They force it to publicly detail both how and how much it pays company executives and whether there is any relationship between this pay and company performance. If the comp committee fails to do its job, there is now no place to hide.

If the SEC rules have affected appearances, 1993 IRS deductibility rules can bring a direct hit on the bottom line by cutting the deductibility of pay beyond a set level. As enacted in 1993, the deductibility rules—Internal Revenue Code Section 162(m) among friends—were a populist plank in the Clinton deficit-cutting plan. Yearly pay beyond $1 million would be nondeductible for the CEO and four other top-paid executives. Pay beyond the ceiling could be deducted only if it was performance based as determined by the board of directors—a role thanklessly delegated to the compensation committee (which faced further independence guidelines similar to those above). The comp committee is required to base the outlier pay on objective corporate performance criteria, although there is a wide variety of criteria available. Terms of the performance agreement must be disclosed to shareholders and approved by a shareholder vote. The committee then must certify that the performance goal has been achieved before payouts are made. Stock option plans that are based on a preset increase in stock price are exempt from the ceiling if the committee sets a maximum number of options to be granted and general option terms, such as the price.

The IRS rules sound pretty comprehensive, but results since they took effect in 1994 have been mixed. First, companies that paid their CEO less than $1 million rapidly inflated pay up to just under the magic number. For those who did come under the rule, within months it became apparent that comp committees, consultants, and executives were devoting serious attention to the search for loopholes. They were successful. During the first full year of compliance, the average CEO pay increased by more than 10%. While a few affected companies simply ignored the rules (and only about a third of U.S. corporations pay at a level to be affected), it is hard to defend simply giving away a large chunk of wage deductibility. Therefore, coping strategies are at a premium.

Most corporations were swiftly able to comply with the rules, but in ways that make us question whether the rules really did any good. Compensation deferred until after retirement is exempt, so CEOs and other top execs near retirement are now pushing a lot of their gains forward a few years. Comp committees let younger execs defer outlier compensation forward to years when their pay may fall beneath the cap amount. Committees are also using "negative discretion" allowed under approved pay plans in a very unusual way. Negative discretion lets them cut rewards if performance is not up to standards outlined in the plan. The committee can thus seek approval of a plan with reasonable performance goals but huge potential rewards. When the executives deliver only modest results, the board then cuts pay back to a smaller figure that was the actual goal in the first place.

Certainly many corporations have altered their pay plans to honestly reward executive performance. But the effort and ingenuity some have devoted to turning IRS Section 162(m) on its head does not build confidence that compensation committees have seen the light yet. The pay cap coping strategies cited above may help shelter executive pay, but what effect do they have on the company? In the deferral cases, the firm must carry a growing amount of pay liability on its books. And how much incentive does an executive gain from an assured nest egg down the road? As to setting high rewards and then backing off, aren't you really telling the CEO it's OK to dog it next year? Only by crafting plans that truly reward for success and punish for failure can the comp committee live up to its promise.

There are other areas where the compensation committee is valuable, sometimes more so than in dealing with CEO pay. As I mentioned above, the comp committee is proving a natural home for the management of director pay and benefits. How we pay the board has become one of the hottest topics in corporate governance lately, one that I will examine in more detail later. But a first matter in any discussion of director pay is who should set that pay. Boards of directors are one of the few bodies that get to decide how much to pay themselves, and this obvious conflict has always generated unease and opportunism. As I mentioned earlier, certain CEOs have worked to convince the board to up its own pay as a tool to make them more generous in viewing CEO pay.

The board has generally handled its compensation in an uncertain manner, with little in the way of goals, motivation, or strategy. In the 1995 National Association of Corporate Directors Blue Ribbon Commission report on director compensation, the group named good process as a priority in board pay setting. The board as a whole should assign pay setting to a committee. Given the contacts and structure it already possesses, the compensation committee is cited by the report as a natural home. In essence, if the board must handle a job with inherent conflicts of interest, it is best to do it with a well-established, strong line of accountability.[6]

A number of other concerns increasingly come within the comp committee's ambit. The status and health of company profit sharing and pension programs have become part of the board's fiduciary responsibility. Lacking a pensions committee, the comp committee offers a good fit for keeping an eye on these liabilities. One factor in General Motors's cash flow disasters of the early 1990s was Roger Smith's decision to impose unduly rosy assumptions on

---

6. "Director Compensation: From Philosophy to Practice," *Director's Monthly*, August 1995, p. 3.

GM's pension fund liability. The decisions caught up with the company after Robert Stempel took over, when low funding and low interest rates brought a staggering $24 billion unfunded pension debt for 1992. The GM board's audit committee had not commented on this black hole in the making. Perhaps if the compensation committee had also been watching over pensions, the result would have been different.

Although its pay-setting mandate usually extends no further than the top executive team, the comp committee should periodically examine compensation levels and design further down in the company. This could be in the form of a report from the CEO (who bears the line responsibility here). Do company pay levels, pay mix, benefits, incentives, and pay schedules motivate, attract, and retain the talent needed? How does the company's compensation mix compare with peer companies? Is there enough flexibility (or is there *too* much, allowing abuse)? Many pay critics like to bash corporations with dark comparisons of how the CEO makes 100 or 150 times the company's lowest-paid workers. The comp committee can choose to play such games or not, but it should at least know what such multipliers look like for the firm.

If the comp committee expects the CEO to evaluate the corporation's pay setup, it is only fair that the committee evaluate *itself* every year or two. Is it living up to the various components of its charter? Are there elements that have proven unnecessary, too limited, too broad, or better handled by another committee? Are all committee members pulling their weight? Are new talents needed on the committee? Have any changes developed among members that could raise doubts of their independence? Could relationships with outside consultants and inside resources be more effective? Is the committee receiving all the information it needs? Are compensation disclosures being made according to all the rules?

The comp committee should also evaluate the results of its pay-setting work at least as often as it evaluates the CEO. Are pay incentives bringing the results desired? Can each element be justified as results receiving their due rewards (as opposed to rewards in search of a rationalization)? Are shareholders satisfied with the executive pay program, or is there a large element of opposition? Does the executive pay plan make the best use of tax and accounting rules?

The compensation committee still lags after the audit committee in the quest for legitimacy and conviction. Where dereliction by audit can leave the company open to criminal charges and potential ruin, laxity on the comp committee has, up to the present, been winked at as a venial sin. The CEO lines his pockets, the board justifies it and takes its own cut, and no one is really hurt. But new demands by regulators and shareholders have made this boardroom baksheesh too expensive to accept in the future. Only by approaching compensation as a reward to be earned, rather than rationalized, will the board compensation committee meet its duties.

39

Nominating Committees:
Talent Scouts, etc.

O f the major committees, nominating is one of the newest and least defined. The goals of audit committees are apparent to all. Compensation committees, despite their shortcomings, have a solid (and expanding) mandate. The nominating committee is ... Well, what is it? The simplest definition is that it is a committee to fill vacancies on the board. Yet even with increased director turnover in recent years, such a stripped-down job description would scarcely fill one meeting a year. However, nominating committees are gaining rapidly in corporate popularity. The 1995 Korn/Ferry survey found 71% of major companies have one (though the prevalence declines among smaller corporations). In 1973 the same survey found them at a negligible 2.4% of corporations.[1] In 1994, Ted Jadick of Heidrick & Struggles called nominating committees "the most striking example of a board committee coming of age."[2]

What brought about this sudden boom? As I noted earlier, one of the first major beefs about boards of directors was their inbred sameness. Directors were wealthy, middle-aged white guys who too often both looked and thought alike. Such concerns fit in well with the spirit of the '60s and '70s. Indeed, the 1972 *Fortune* magazine article I mentioned awhile back, "Change Invades the Boardroom," had little to do with liability, institutional shareholders, or the SEC, but was much concerned with the addition of minorities and women

---

1. *Korn/Ferry International Board of Directors Survey,* 1995.
2. "Board Committee Trends," Theodore Jadick, *Corporate Board,* July/August 1994, p. 9.

to boards.[3] In an era when the board was a quiet sinecure, it seemed a harmless public relations boon to add women, minorities, and consumer interests as directors. But finding this fresh blood was a problem. One criticism of the insular board was that it was self-generating. The CEO/chairman would suggest another CEO of his acquaintance as an impressive addition to the board, and the CEOs and inside directors who already constituted the board would duly agree. The perspective was limited to the proverbial small circle of friends. Also, by the late 1970s the SEC governance reforms and proposed federal chartering legislation were bringing pressure for more independent outsiders on boards and encouraging a formal board nomination procedure. The nominating committee sprung up almost overnight to meet these needs.

The nominating committee added a patina of professionalism and objectivity to the process of deciding board membership needs. Although right up to the present day, suggestions for new directors still typically come from the CEO, the nominating committee has both supported and compelled better strategic consideration of the board's roster. Committees being committees, the nominating committee tended to create a function for itself.

Nominating committees rapidly took on the basic form that they have today. They average four or five members, dominated by outside directors. The trend today is for the nominating committee to be made up exclusively of outsiders, although the CEO still sits on many of these committees or is a nonvoting member. Independence is considered so important that a number of companies have faced recent proxy proposals requiring an independent nominating committee, though the proposals gain few votes.[4] In the past the committees met on average twice yearly, but today the Korn/Ferry survey finds this has increased to an average of three times a year, possibly reflecting the committee's growing utility.[5]

Beyond these basics, membership of the nominating committee should meet many of the standards of the audit and compensation committee, though the independence level demanded is not

---

3. "Change Invades the Boardroom," Peter Vanderwicken, *Fortune*, May 1972, p. 156.
4. *Getting Listed on Wall Street,* Carolyn Kay Brancato, Irwin Professional Publishing, 1996, p. 179.
5. *Korn/Ferry,* 1995.

as rigorous. Board diversity concerns make the nominating committee a natural perch for women and minority board members. This has the advantage of bringing fresh thinking on who would make a good director to the place where it will do the most good. Be careful, though, that nominating is not turned into a boardroom dead-end street, where the company displays its social conscience but provides low status and too little real influence.

Committee members will also benefit by past or current exposure to human resource matters. This could include working with executive search firms, background on other board nominating committees, contracting with consultants, and dealing with major trends, like reengineering, reorganizations, or diversity. It helps if someone on the committee has contact with a key shareholder or stakeholder influence, such as institutional investors, unions, regulators, or community groups. This will add outside intelligence to the recipe when the time comes to cook up a new board member. Unlike the other major committees, which are concerned with internal corporate matters, the nominating committee demands an outward-looking aspect. If the board lacks a public affairs committee, nominating can serve as its eyes to the world, keeping the board up-to-date on stakeholder concerns, pay issues, governance trends, and sources of outside expertise.

As with the other committees, it is important for the nominating committee to have a charter, especially given the vagueness of its function. The NACD's 1994 Blue Ribbon commission on CEO and board evaluation suggested that at a minimum the committee should consider the following:

- board philosophy
- current situation of the company
- size and composition of the board
- specific board needs, including diversity of age, experience, gender, race, geography, and business background.[6]

Every year or two, the committee should review the board for the above factors, decide where membership weaknesses lie, and

---

6. *Report of the Blue Ribbon Commission on Performance Evaluation of Chief Executive Officers, Boards and Directors,* National Association of Corporate Directors, 1994, p. 9.

discuss options for solving them. The nominating committee charter is also valuable for demarcating turf between itself and other committees. Such an overlap is most likely with compensation. Not only should their charters be written to assure that committees do not have the same duties, they should be negotiated between committees to make sure that a task does not fall between two stools. Better still, charter negotiation can help on matters that require interaction between committee functions. Nominating and compensation can hardly function properly without sharing notes.

The nominating committee seeks board candidates from many sources. The traditional route, with the CEO suggesting a splendid fellow he knows, is still quite common, but it will become less defensible as we move into the next century. If the only function of the nominating committee is to validate the CEO's candidates, who needs it? Better to use the outward focus of the committee to broaden a pool of nominees that can meet the board's needs. By naming people to the nominating committee who have wide experience, diversity, and contacts, you can put these good mixers to work, tapping their contacts in the wide world.

An effective nominating committee will use many other resources for finding strategic board candidates. Contacts at other firms, databases of business leaders, major business and governance organizations, and major shareholder groups are examples. A word about the latter: In cases where a big investor is campaigning to add representatives to the board, the nominating committee can serve as a valuable gatekeeper. With a strong, independent committee and a charter that spells out objective procedures and priorities for adding new membership, it becomes harder to claim that the company is merely stonewalling.

Nominating also gives a good arm's-length approach to working with search consultants. As I mentioned earlier, the use of search firms to find qualified directors has increased sharply of late, especially among the larger corporations. The search will be more effective if the firm has a central contact within the company that can offer agreed-upon, objective criteria for candidates. Also, by adding another layer in removing the search process from the hands of management, director nomination gains a greater air of independence.

When filling a specific vacancy on the board, the nominating committee should develop a list of several candidates for consideration by the full board. This again helps avoid the appearance of the management tail wagging the board dog in naming directors, although one of the candidates may still be a clear favorite. However, there should be no attempt to merely pad out the field for a sure winner. All director candidates the nominating committee suggests should be quality contenders.

One way to improve everyone's chances is to present candidates with a variety of skills and credentials. Since any board will always need more talent from more areas than it can ever hope to accommodate, select a slate of finalists that juggles abilities from different target areas. The board as a whole is then the best judge of who meets corporate needs most precisely. This stage of weighing the contenders may be the best time to bring the CEO into the selection process. Although management may have suggested one or more of the nominees, it is best to bring the CEO's views in later rather than earlier to keep the process independent. However, the CEO/chair needs a say in who will finally be added to the board slate. Good chemistry and a constructive relationship are important for the board and CEO to work together well. If the CEO has any strong objections to Candidate X, let him or her detail them to the whole board. Although most CEOs can find more subtle ways to sidetrack a candidate, a solid nomination process from beginning to end at least adds a layer of protection.

One final comment about the typical board search: Handle the candidate review phase diplomatically and swiftly. Most boards like to have the nominating committee, various board members, and the CEO meet with the candidates to measure the cut of their jib, but too often the company will drag its feet in the process. While carefully judging the fit of a finalist is important, a leisurely "Don't call us, we'll call you" muddle-through will turn off the best candidates. The CEO of a major corporation is not interested in pitching him or herself repeatedly in a prolonged job interview and will politely (or impolitely) decline. It is more effective to do the maximum amount of homework on finalists before the formal interview stage and limit the actual interviewing to a final candidate or two.

The value of the nominating committee to the board has grown as directors realize that it is a handy "Swiss army knife," versatile far beyond its basic functions of figuring out who the board needs and tracking them down. The board profiling and appraisal that are part of the committee's duties lead naturally into another hot topic—board and CEO evaluation. Evaluating the board for its effectiveness, membership, and oversight is becoming one of the most popular, practical tools for improving corporate governance. A Russell Reynolds survey of U.S. fund managers and institutional investors found 78% view regular, formal evaluation of the board as a high priority.[7]

Meanwhile, board evaluation of the CEO has become a shareholder must. At the *Corporate Board*, we produced a special report on evaluation in 1995, and the NACD also considered the subject in a Blue Ribbon Commission report. Structured evaluation of both the board and of the CEO is one of those topics that fits in so smoothly with current business concerns that it seems a natural. Productivity, pay for performance, shareholder accountability— evaluation touches on all of these and may even be a mandatory prerequisite. Which committee of the board would be the most likely to take on such a personnel-related job as evaluation? Who else?

While the entire board shares responsibility for its evaluation process, the nominating committee is an excellent organizer and go-between. It can handle scheduling, subassignments, compilation of results, and writing up the final conclusions. The committee also makes a good recruiter and liaison if an outside consultant is sought to assist with the evaluation (an outsider is valuable for bringing third-party objectivity to the process). Board evaluation examines such topics as the chair's influence and effectiveness; the board's input, structure, and contribution; and the value of the present meeting, committee, and communications systems.

Evaluation of the CEO follows a similar track. The process is usually simpler and less bureaucratic but has a more immediate impact on setting rewards. The committee could be assigned to develop an evaluation form using the CEO's current job description as a blueprint (how well has the CEO lived up to this outline?) It can then grade the CEO's performance against this standard. More likely, though, the committee will facilitate a review by all the outside directors of the board. Individual directors can provide their appraisals, which would then be compiled into a total report card by the committee. Such a shared administrative effort would com-

---

7. "U.S. Boardrooms," *Governance*, January 1996, p. 1.

bine the independence and expertise of nominating with validation by the board as a whole.

The nominating committee's human resources edge also proves handy for assessing the company's total employment strategy. The management team of a corporation ultimately takes on a look and structure that meets the CEO's needs. But is this management structure the one that best meets the *company's* needs? Are rising stars being identified and tapped for an effective grooming program? And whose standards are being used to identify these talents, anyway? Do executive headhunters have a suspiciously easy time luring away your top talent? Such a long-term, strategic take on the corporation's leadership is an ideal role for the board, and the nominating committee is the ideal body to make sure it happens.

If the nominating committee looks at the evolving management structure, should it not keep an eye on CEO succession planning too? In talking with board members, I hear many concerns and beefs about the CEO, ranging from the crisis grade to the trivial. But one chronic problem pops up consistently—CEOs who drag their feet on succession planning. I will not belabor you with all the psychological theory of why a CEO procrastinates on, fudges, and at times even sabotages succession planning. Perhaps the board should not try to play the psychoanalyst either. Still, the board has an obligation to assure that various plans are in place. These range from having known, proven talent in the bull pen, to laying out an emergency plan if the current CEO gets hit by a falling satellite (or whatever).

While modern nominating committees are taking on this responsibility, they are also doing their own looking around at potential leadership talent outside the company. With boards more willing to sack lagging CEOs, this reserve is important. If the CEO must go, the board may view his or her planned inside successor as part of the problem. Also, willingness to go outside the company can break loose a succession deadlock that may have developed on the inside. One reason the Chrysler board looked outside the company to lure Robert Eaton as CEO was Lee Iacocca's unwillingness to step down if President Bob Lutz were to take over. Nurturing such an effective dark horse requires both the overview talents of a corporate board and the specific skills of the nominating committee.

Though the nominating committee remains more of a supporting player for the board, its role is rapidly growing and evolving. With new, radical demands on the human capital of a corporation, demands that reach from the boardroom all the way to the shop floor, the nominating committee will become even more vital in the years to come.

40

New Committees for a New Century

Although the committees above are finding many new roles for themselves, the number of committees on a corporate board is also increasing. Some of these are hatched to meet company-specific needs, but others may point the way for new board roles in the next century.

Corporate Governance Committees. Corporations may find that the increasingly strict demands of governance reform are too serious to be imposed on the traditional committee structure. Such tasks as shareholder liaison, succession planning, and board and CEO evaluation are delicate, prone to management influence, and have serious long-term consequences for the company. Adding them to the roles of the audit, nominating, or compensation committees may be more efficient, but will the ultimate results be as good? Also, dividing governance matters among several committees, even with a tight chartering process, will increase overlaps and turf disputes. More companies are discovering the value of a distinct corporate governance committee.

This committee goes by various names at different companies, making it very hard to get a precise handle on either its popularity or duties. The Conference Board found corporate governance committees at only 7% of its 1995 survey companies.[1] However, the 1995 Korn/Ferry board survey found committees on "board organization" at 28% of its firms. Such committees are made up ex-

---

1. *Corporate Directors' Compensation*, Conference Board, 1996.

clusively of outside directors, and in the Korn/Ferry sample, had an average of five members and three meetings yearly.[2] Tom Neff of search consultant SpencerStuart in 1992 proposed a "committee on directors" as an outgrowth of the nominating committee, although it would also have handled some director appraisal matters (including the ouster of underperforming directors). IBM formed a corporate governance committee in 1993, with its key function to improve shareholder relations. At General Motors, a committee on director affairs handles most review and evaluation procedures (and is mandated in the 1994 GM Board Guidelines).

Campbell Soup's governance committee "will annually assess Board and Committee effectiveness," according to Campbell's 1995 proxy report. To fulfill this duty, the Campbell governance committee has three main functions, according to CEO David Johnson:

- The organization and structure of the board.
- Setting qualifications for director candidates.
- Judging the role and effectiveness of the board and its committees as part of the Campbell corporate governance process.[3]

These three functions sum up the role of most such committees, no matter what they are called. However, they cover a lot of turf and, with the booming interest in improved governance, are wide open for definition. For example, should a governance committee also be evaluating the CEO? The NACD considers this an option. Also, should it serve as the board contact with major investors? How does it coordinate its evaluation function with the pay-setting duties of the compensation committee? The blurring of roles is such that the corporate governance committee is sometimes only a new name given to an older committee to reflect added duties. Most commonly this morphing occurs with the nominating committee.

Forming a separate committee to monitor the quality of gov-

---

2. *Korn/Ferry International Board of Directors Survey,* 1995.
3. "Walking in the Shoes of the Shareowners," interview with David W. Johnson, *Director's Monthly,* December 1995, p. 3.

ernance can send a strong signal to shareholders that good governance is important to the board and management. The active institutional shareholders have yet to make governance committees a specific plank in their platforms. But with investors such as CalPERS pushing toward more independent, empowered outside directors and increased board self-evaluation, the means and the end will likely align. I suspect that the use of governance committees (and their powers) will continue to expand, and we will see more standardization of their duties and mandate.

Compliance Committees. Regulatory burdens have become massive in many industries, and the punishments for noncompliance frightening. In a 1994 article in the *Corporate Board,* former U.S. Assistant Attorney General Stephen Markman estimated that there were approximately 10,000 federal regulatory requirements with potential criminal sanctions.[4] Environmental laws impose harsh measures for infractions and factor the scope and efficacy of company compliance systems into decisions to prosecute and sentencing. Insider trading, exports, currency and banking, occupational hazards, employment law and defense contracting are a few of the other areas where companies face draconian penalties that include fines and damages in the tens of millions of dollars and personal criminal liability for violations.

These infractions may often be technical, questionable, unknown (and unknowable), and related more to process than results. However, violations can wreck lives and ruin companies. In a case cited by Stephen Markman, Louisiana Pacific, found in violation of the Clean Air Act, was compelled to impose new management procedures, purchase new equipment, name new supervising managers, and fund extensive training programs. Another company, for an environmental violation that occurred without willful intent, was hit with an $11 million fine and ordered to purchase $70 million in new equipment. And in California, corporate officers can face three-year prison terms for failure to notify the state of "concealed dangers" in the workplace—which prompts the question; If the dan-

---

4. "Criminalizing Business Law," Stephen J. Markman, *Corporate Board,* September/October 1994, p. 7.

gers are concealed, how are corporate officers supposed to know about them?[5]

Government sentencing guidelines have an answer for such treacherous questions. They offer points off in sentencing if companies have effective compliance programs built into their corporate procedures. These procedures are meant to extend throughout the company and must show due diligence in preventing, discovering, containing, and reporting violations. They can include all manner of tools, from audit procedures, to paperwork, to monitoring, to personnel. Such programs require disclosure of violations and even up-front admissions of responsibility to be effective. In some cases, they are not even all that effective in easing liability, compelling corporations to spill everything to the government and hope for mercy. However, when they are accepted by prosecutors and courts, an effective corporate compliance program can cut the level of fines under the federal sentencing guidelines as much as 90%.

So how are such compliance programs made and kept effective? First, by being thorough, sincere, and consistent. If the company's compliance efforts are weak, sporadic, or consist largely of legal-sounding paperwork, courts will consider them useless when making their calls. The courts might even find such lax compliance efforts worse than no efforts at all. Done right, though, sentencing guidelines will give the company credit. An inside trade, a chemical spill, or a kickback will then be viewed as an aberration by an isolated bad egg in the company—but only if the corporation has a top-down system for discouraging such behavior.

This "top-down" element is where the board comes in. If the company's board makes compliance procedures and mechanisms a part of its agenda, that should not only help set a tone of compliance from the top, it should help *prove* that compliance is taken seriously. The logical next step for some corporations: Why not a *committee* dedicated to auditing company compliance programs? This compliance committee would hold a regular review of the corporation's compliance liabilities and structures. What are the major legal and regulatory exposures of the company based on its industry, operations, and facilities? What changes and new interpretations are pending under these laws? What compliance structures does the company

---

5. Ibid.

have to meet these mandates? Have they been independently reviewed for their value? Have there been any violations, errors, or inadequacies uncovered since the last review? Who are the people in the company's compliance chain of command? Are any revisions needed? Will changes in company operations require updates in compliance procedures? Unlike some of the other committees discussed, compliance will benefit from having at least one inside director to act as liaison with staff on the technical and legal matters. In fact, this manager could be in charge of developing the periodic reports on compliance measures needed by the committee.

The most common compliance dangers seem to be environmental, so many compliance committees are outgrowths of board environmental committees. In these cases the committee will also tie in broader green concerns, such as liaison with major environmental groups and monitoring of environment-related issues and how they will affect business (such as the use of dangerous chemicals or product recycling). Environmental compliance committees thus have a public relations as well as legal mandate.

The work of the compliance committee would be largely a matter of reviewing the staff's compliance work, and there are probably a limited number of companies for which such a committee will be worthwhile. Compliance committees at present seem confined to high-risk industries, such as chemicals, petroleum, and waste management. Indeed, in some cases when these companies are found guilty of a regulatory violation, a board compliance committee was mandated as part of the settlement. Although compliance committees will remain valuable, expect their use to be limited. It is likely the rest of the board committees will gain increased respect for compliance concerns and build them into their own portfolios.

Special Committees. There are some board issues of such pitch and moment that the best response is to form a special-purpose, short-lived committee to cope with them. There are several advantages to this technique. Membership can be crafted to deal with particular concerns of independence, background, or skill. Certain board members may need to stay as far away from this committee as possible for legal or appearance reasons. Also, standing committees have their own agendas, workloads, and schedules. A special-purpose committee lets the board clear the deck to meet an emergency.

However, special-purpose committee members face perhaps the greatest pressure of any job on the board. They must make short-notice, closely watched decisions that are fraught with legal second-guessing. Most special committees are like a SWAT team—they are not needed until matters have already gotten very, very serious.

Special committees are by definition unique for each purpose, but there are some common uses. Major structural changes, such as large acquisitions, mergers, or buyouts, benefit from a searching overview by a committee of tough-minded outsiders. Perhaps the most famous of these was the special committee of RJR Nabisco directors appointed to oversee the auction of the company in late 1988. Despite the public outcry over "greed" on the battle over who would win the company, the RJR Nabisco committee worked hard to increase shareholder value. Its efforts turned what could have been a lowball walkover for the F. Ross Johnson team into a real bidding war. A transaction committee works closely with sources inside the company, such as corporate counsel, but should also be free to secure outside advisory services on such matters as legal opinions, valuations, and financing.

Investigative or demand committees are sort of the negative twin of a transaction committee. If the transaction committee convenes to assure that no monkey business occurs, the investigative committee is named because someone thinks monkey business *has* occurred. An investigation committee is convened to study internal or external allegations that the company is somehow involved in wrongdoing. An employee is accused in a kickback scheme, someone in management is committing fraud, a member of the board is accused of suspicious transactions—there are as many charges for an investigative committee as there are varieties of human venality. A "litigation demand committee" is similar, though externally based. A shareholder may deliver a "demand" to the board alleging that management, employees, or the board has committed a tort against the corporation that caused shareholdings to lose value. The shareholder demands that the board investigate the matter, seek damages, fire whoever is alleged to be at fault, or take some other action.

It is obvious that service on such special committees involves stressful matters (or, as a writer on boards in 1947 sweetly termed them, "unpleasant tasks").[6] These special committees will often wrestle with matters that have an inherent conflict of interest—approving a management buyout, a decision to take the company private, criminal charges against a personal friend, reviewing a merger agreement that would leave the directors out of a job. Therefore, the most stringent standards of objectivity must be observed. Documentation and supporting valuations must be scrupulously maintained. In such treacherous activity, fraught with conflicts, the board should go in *assuming* that someone will sue, and document their decision as if they were preparing a defense brief. The usual board standard of reticence outside of meetings should be upped a few notches. Not only should members avoid discussing their deliberations with members of management, they should even keep other members of the board in the dark until a final report is ready.

Directors selected for the special committee should be able to devote a solid block of time to their work, at least for a brief period. Likewise, it is helpful if they are centered around a convenient geographic area to allow for practical short-notice meetings. These special committees are usually formed to put out fires, and long hours and emergency huddles for the duration are the rule.

The corporate board committee structure will only grow in importance during the years ahead. The time demands, special skills, and practicality of specializing board work will drive a greater reliance on committees and more attention to their needs. As it becomes more difficult to assemble the full board for regular meetings, look for the formal boardroom sessions to become less common but quick committee confabs to grow. Technology is starting to support this, with greater use of telephone and video conferencing. I'll look into high-tech board meetings in more detail later, but they are proving more practical for committee work than meetings of the full board. They can be quickly arranged and transcend the restraints of geography. Also, high-tech conferences are most practical for groups of three to five people discussing a

---

6. *The Board of Directors and Business Management,* Melvin T. Copeland and Andrew R. Towl, Greenwood, New York, 1947, 1968, p. 115.

limited range of topics for a brief period—which neatly describes most committee meetings. In the future, expect corporate boards to look less like a circle of dour faces collected occasionally around a large mahogany table and more like a busy confederation of ever-shifting committees.

41

The Chair/CEO:
How We Achieved Oneness

Boards may have grown busier and more byzantine, but who is the boss? The distinct roles of chief executive officer and board chair are less than distinct in most U.S. boardrooms. Unlike many other Western nations, most companies in the United States combine the role of CEO and chair in a single person. A 1996 Conference Board survey found that 68% of companies combine the two roles, although this was down from 72% the previous year.[1] Other studies of the topic place the percentage at anywhere from 65% to 75% depending on the companies examined. It is safe to say that any corporate form that includes two-thirds to three-quarters of companies is our national model. Determining *why* it became the model is a more complex subject.

The evolution of top corporate roles is a murky area, partly because definitions keep changing. Indeed, the term "chief executive officer" is a fairly new one—through most of corporate history the manager in charge of running things was the company president. The board chairman was sometimes a major investor or a former president of the company who had been bumped up to emeritus status. He might also be an investor representative who took over during a corporate crisis to sort things out. As governance consultant Leslie Levy observes, "The chairman's title was awarded in an almost unlimited range of situations, and to all manner of people."[2]

1. *Corporate Directors' Compensation,* 1996 ed., Conference Board, 1996, p. 7.
2. "Separate Chairmen of the Board," Leslie Levy, *Corporate Board Special Report,* 1993, p. 7.

Although the position of board chairman held impressive symbolic status, chairmen rarely exerted any serious power in running the corporation or governance of its affairs.

Consolidation of the chair and CEO positions began on a large scale after World War II. Alfred Chandler credits General Motors's Bunkie Knudsen with starting the trend during the 1940s, although Alfred Sloan long after retained at least the title of GM chairman. During an era when the board consisted primarily of insiders, there was a certain logic for the chair to be likewise a company employee. And if the board chair is an employee, it would hardly do for him or her to be anyone except the top employee of the company.

It is notable that the slow rise in board powers up to the 1980s and the solidification of the combined CEO/chair office seem related. It is possible that as CEOs sensed the rising responsibilities of the board, they thought it prudent to establish themselves in the chair's seat. Vice versa is also possible—by staking their claim on the chair, CEOs were empowering the board with their leadership. Also, the rising percentage of outsiders on boards presented the CEO with a growing power center outside his or her immediate control. Note that the CEO/president slowly took over the position of chair, rather than the other way around. This suggests that the chair's role was seen by the person who already had power (the CEO) as a way to add to that power.

Whatever the genesis, by the current business era, it had long been business as usual for major U.S. corporations to combine the roles of chair and CEO. Yet the U.S. pattern remains uncommon in most of the world. In the United Kingdom, the proportions are a mirror image of the United States, with two-thirds to three-quarters of chairs being separate nonexecutives. Britain's Cadbury Commission, which several years ago developed a set of "best practices" rules and recommendations for U.K. boards, recommended the split role almost as a matter of course. Germany, with its bi-level supervisory and management boards, has two "chairmen" for each company. In Japan, the pattern is similar to that of the United States 50 years ago. Corporate boards are large and made up chiefly of inside directors. A chair is elected but is traditionally a retired senior officer of the company with largely ceremonial duties, and the company's president holds the actual reins of power.

The U.S. model, then, is an outlier in much of the developed world. As a result, the CEO/chair combination has come in for much questioning and criticism both in the United States and overseas. Foreign business observers consider the joint CEO/chair model to be one of our distinctly oddball U.S. corporate traits, right up there with massive liability suits and equally massive executive pay. A 1995 worldwide governance study by the International Capital Markets Group noted a trend in the United States toward separating the roles but offered little evidence to back its assertion.[3] Authors Ada Demb and Friedrich Neubauer surveyed European executives in 1992 and found that 56% preferred to see the jobs split. Only 26% endorsed the combined role, and most of these supporters qualified their answers, saying that the combination depended on a number of background and industry factors to be successful.[4]

If overseas business observers are puzzled on why U.S. companies should want to put all of their governance eggs in one basket, U.S. critics are often downright contemptuous. In 1978, SEC Chairman Harold Williams proposed that CEOs should not be chairs of the board (and also proposed that all inside directors, save the CEO, be banned). Jay Lorsch of Harvard called for separation of the roles in his famous 1989 book *Pawns or Potentates* and has been an articulate supporter of "bifurcation" since.[5] Shareholder activism on the separation issue peaked in the aftermath of the boardroom revolts of 1992 and 1993. During the 1992–93 proxy season, shareholder proposals to rend asunder the jobs of CEO and chair were submitted at such companies as IBM, Polaroid, Sears, and Westinghouse. In a 1992 report, the NACD's John Nash predicted that half of all Fortune 500 companies would split the two jobs within five years.[6] Judith Dobryzynski in late 1992 enthused that splitting the roles of chair and CEO was "the way to go,"[7] and in 1993 CalPERS General Counsel Dick Koppes complained that "when you combine the two positions, you end up with the same person grading his own papers."[8] But the most compelling argu-

3. *Who Holds the Reins?* International Capital Markets Group, 1995, p. 58.
4. *The Corporate Board,* Ada Demb and Friedrich Neubauer, Oxford University Press, 1992, p. 138.
5. *Pawns or Potentates,* Jay Lorsch, Harvard Business School Press, 1989.
6. *Investor Responsibility Research Center Corporate Governance Bulletin,* November/December 1992, p. 8.
7. "A GM Postmortem," Judith H. Dobrzynski, *Business Week,* November 9, 1992, p. 87.
8. "How CalPERS Can Ruin a CEO's Day," *Global Finance,* February 1993, p. 37.

ment for divided governance came with the GM coup in 1992. John Smale assumed the chairmanship, while Jack Smith led the charge as CEO. If the biggest corporation in the world is willing to do it, why not everyone?

There are many compelling arguments for splitting the positions of chair and CEO. Shareholder groups hold religiously to a separation between the board of directors and management. The board represents the shareholders and is there to monitor the works of management. If the same person is top dog both on the management side and on the governance side, how can there be any pretense of accountability? The triangle of management-board-shareholders becomes badly tilted as the two inside entities are joined under one leader. The rhetorical question of "Who watches the watchers?" takes on an introverted twist. Indeed, if the CEO slowly took over the position of chair to cope with increasing board power, why not then use the position to limit that power? Countertrends such as having independent directors evaluate the CEO or ensuring more independent committees can tip the scales back toward the board. But, as we've seen, such moves remain nascent and limited while the CEO serving as board chair is the well-established standard.

Critics point to too many examples of companies going astray without any system of boardroom checks and balances. General Motors, IBM, Sears, K-Mart, Archer-Daniels-Midland . . . companies with the same person in charge of both managing the company and supervising the managers, allowing problems to grow into disasters unchecked.

All of the arguments against combining the position of chair and CEO in one person seem irresistible. So why does it continue unabated? First, the concept has fewer real enemies than it seems. The closer we get to the front lines of running a corporation, the less concern is expressed over having the same person hold the roles of chair and CEO. Investor Robert Monks, usually on the cutting edge of shareholder activist issues, quotes without comment a 1992 Korn/Ferry survey that found 60% of corporate directors are neutral on the idea of splitting the two jobs.[9] It would be hard to lead

---

9. *Corporate Governance,* Robert A. G. Monks and Nell Minow, Blackwell, 1995, p. 190.

any boardroom revolution on the issue with that many conscientious objectors.

If anything, the past few years have seen this disinterest stiffen into active support for a combined role. A Korn/Ferry director survey from 1995 finds that while 23% of the directors' boards have separate CEOs and chairs, 67% are not considering the idea at all, and only 10% are looking into the idea. At the largest industrials, those with over $5 billion in sales, the share of boards flirting with the idea of a split-up is even smaller, only 6%.[10] This is a telling difference. Most big governance reform ideas, such as adding outsiders to the board, independent committees, and CEO evaluation, first took root in the largest companies and worked their way down the food chain. If the big corporations remain unimpressed with the idea of split roles, don't expect to see the notion spreading very quickly.

We should expect current CEO/chairs to view the combined role as a splendid idea. But solid defense for the joint position also comes from others in the corporate world, even some of those we would expect to support shareholder empowerment. Robert Pozen, general counsel and a managing director with Fidelity Investments, sees the matter of whether or not the CEO also sits in the chair's seat as a "procedural frill." He is unimpressed with "the push for a chairman separate from the CEO: although this separation may be fruitful for a particular company, there is no evidence that as a general rule it benefits public companies."[11]

This criticism goes to the heart of the debate. Most research on the matter of splitting the CEO and chair roles is contradictory and limited, and arguments are more often than not based on anecdotes. A 1995 study by a group that included professors James Brickley and Gregg Jarrell of the Simon School of Business suggests that a split CEO/chair arrangement is associated with lower cash flows and value.[12] But Compaq Computer put the role of separate chair to good use in 1991 when Chairman Ben Rosen was able to fire CEO Rod Canion and then spearhead a splendid turnaround.

---

10. *Korn/Ferry International Board of Directors Survey*, 1995.

11. "Institutional Investors: The Reluctant Activists," Robert C. Pozen, *Harvard Business Review*, January/February 1994, p. 146.

12. *Corporate Leadership Structure*, James A. Brickley and Gregg Jarrell, William E. Simon Graduate School of Business at the University of Rochester, 1995.

At Apple, however, major investor Mike Markkula took the position of chairman after firing John Sculley in 1993, installing Michael Spindler as CEO, and pitching in to help with a company turnaround. To no avail. By 1996 Apple had fired Spindler and was foundering.

And what about the most famous instance of splitting the roles of CEO and chair, General Motors? The tag team of Jack Smith and John Smale was seized upon by activists and investors as showing the potential of a split role. In a famous 1995 *New York Times* piece, Judith Dobrzynski wrote glowingly of the success of "Jack and John" in turning the automaker around. She quoted Smale's enthusiasm on the CEO/chair split: it was "very difficult to defend any other format."[13]

But in late 1995, the GM board announced that Smale was passing the mantle of chairmanship to Jack Smith as of January 1, 1996. "It's clear that GM's management team under Jack Smith has turned GM around," said John Smale in a board statement, his only comment on the change.[14] The GM reunion luffed much of the wind from the sails of the job-split supporters, but there had long been hints that Smale and GM management did not intend to keep the split permanent. The 1994 release of GM's 28-point Corporate Governance Guidelines was widely applauded as a sign that GM had seen the light. CalPERS even used the statement as a launchpad for one of its corporate campaigns, sending a copy of the GM Magna Carta to its owned companies and asking them to discuss how their governance principles compared.

A closer reading of the GM governance guidelines, however, shows that despite some solid reforms, many of the governance tools to be used were carefully left blank. In 1994 I wrote that there was "too much lawyerly evasion" in the guidelines, with items such as the committee structure, board size, mix of inside and outside directors, and former CEO board membership waffled with "as the board may consider appropriate" qualifiers.[15] The most notable dodge was the very first heading, "Selection of Chairman and CEO." Indeed, at the same time GM was receiving business press

---

13. "Jack and John: Two for the Road at GM," Judith Dobrzynski, *New York Times,* July 9, 1995, p. F11.
14. General Motors press release, December 1995.
15. Unpublished letter to the *Wall Street Journal,* 1994.

praise for the perestroika of its guidelines and for its success in splitting the CEO and chair jobs, the automaker was saying in black and white that it would "make this choice any way that seems best for the company at a given point in time."[16] The guideline on chair and CEO structure reads almost like a legal waiver, going to great pains to forswear any preference on the matter one way or the other.

That GM would eventually let Jack Smith wear both hats was no surprise because such a move fits in with the history of CEO and chair splits. A review of the recent past shows that most cases of U.S. companies using a separate chair and CEO are transitional. Companies rarely deign to keep a permanent wall between the two jobs, but rather split them up as a temporary expedient and reunite them at the first opportunity. A common example is the crisis situation as was seen at GM, but also at Salomon and K-Mart. The company is in trouble. The board rouses itself, fires the chair/CEO, names a new CEO, but keeps one of its own on watch as separate chair. This was the pattern of the glitzy boardroom coups of 1992 and 1993, but less noticed was the trend of the separate chair to pass the reins back to the CEO after the crisis passed.

The people who have risen to take over the chair in these emergencies, such as John Smale at GM or Donald Perkins at K-Mart, tend to be very estimable businesspeople, experienced, proven, respected, and likely recognized as the dean of their boardroom. They know how to run a large enterprise and are used to doing so. They are not shrinking violets and likely have quite healthy egos. Yet, though they managed to seize the reins of a massive enterprise, they make no apparent effort to stay in power. After a brief period, they hand those reins back to the new CEO. Why not stay in charge? The taboo against maintaining a separate chair is so great that these people make no effort to linger in power and would no doubt face censure for opportunism if they tried. Also, they may find that holding power as the separate chair of a corporation is not as powerful as it seems. Remember, the CEO/president took over the role of chair rather than vice versa. This suggests that, legal definitions aside, the chair of a corporate board derives muscle from also being the CEO, rather than the other way around. Hanging on as separate

---

16. *General Motors' Board Guidelines on Significant Corporate Governance Issues,* 1994.

chair once the new management team is humming along might make you less a power behind the throne than a fifth wheel.

But such crises, though they grab the headlines, have been the exceptions for separate chairs. As Leslie Levy noted in her 1993 special report on separate chairs for the *Corporate Board,* "At least 90 percent of all separate chairmen appear in connection with orderly transition from a retiring chairman/CEO to his successor."[17] Such instances are so common and unremarkable that it is almost difficult to name examples, although FMC, Citicorp, and Transamerica have used this technique. A similar arrangement is the formation of an "office of the chief executive," which combines two or more people in a shifting group marriage of chair, president, and CEO. These likewise tend to be transitional structures.

Most commonly, the former CEO/chair is on his or her way up and out and retains the chair on a temporary basis for various personal or political reasons. Possibly the new CEO is considered to be on probation, and the old CEO wants to keep an eye on him or her. The company may also be restructuring from a merger, with one too many top dogs. In this case, the leader of the acquired company may assume the chair role as an honorific to keep his or her hand in until retirement, at which point the acquiring company honcho takes up the chair's title. In cases where there is an "office of" multiperson hodgepodge, roles tend to be even less defined. But in a typical scenario, the former CEO might be elevated to the chair to allow two or more potential successors to prove their mettle. After one candidate emerges as the leader, all the vague-sounding reasons for constructing an "office of" are swept aside and a single person is named CEO/chair. Such extended offices were a trend in the 1970s but still pop up to the current day.

In all of these "on the way out" cases, the separate chair is assumed to be at most a background presence, keeping a weather eye on the grooming process but doing very little. Indeed, the only problems that usually arise come when the emeritus chair *does* try to exert control. After Harold Geneen retired as CEO of ITT in the 1970s, he remained as a separate chairman of the board while Lyman Hamilton took the reins as CEO. But Geneen disliked the way Hamilton was handling those reins, and in less than two years, Hamilton was out. Successor Rand Aroskog proved much more adept at

---

17. "Separate Chairmen," Levy, p. 18.

dealing with his separate chairman and had an unthreatened term as CEO—after securing the job of chairman for himself.

None of these models are quite what the academic supporters of separate chairs had in mind. Rather than a relief pitcher or bench warmer, they seek a chair who comes from outside the company and is able to serve as a helpful, yet effective counterweight and superego to the CEO. Independent, yet engaged; loyal to the owners, not the managers; comfortable with the company, but able to make hard calls, this outside chair would act as the true boardroom leader.

Yet corporate reality seems to have eroded the bright promise of the separate chair, turning the idea within less than half a decade from coming trend to great disappointment. As noted, supporters among those who naturally run corporations are few, even those who tend to be iconoclasts on how to run a company. Al Dunlap, the stormy former CEO and chairman of Scott Paper, has been a loud proponent of boardroom change and made headlines with his 1994 plan to pay the Scott board wholly in stock. But on the matter of splitting the chair and CEO jobs, Dunlap is a staunch conservative. "Separate chairmanship might pay well and look good, but it's not right. If the chief executive isn't good enough to be the chairman, fire him." (Dunlap also claims to have seen the payoff of splitting the positions up close in two countries where it is popular, Australia and Great Britain. "The chairmen there who are not the chief executive don't have a clue as to what's going on.")[18]

Most of the arguments against the separate chair have a similar wake-up-and-smell-the-coffee toughness. One person is needed to captain the ship. The CEO/chair split can only work if you have an ideal personal chemistry between the two—and how often do we encounter the ideal in corporate America? How exactly would you split the many overlapping duties of a CEO and chair? What about divided loyalties among subordinates (who is really in charge?) Would the outside chair's special status subject him or her to greater liability dangers? And how exactly do you pay a separate chair?

While these practical objections have merit, I think they obscure a deeper, unspoken problem with the separate chair idea. The independent outside board chair, who has no other connection to the company, simply would not have enough muscle yet to make a difference. Despite the new powers and self-confidence the boards

---

18. Albert J. Dunlap, speech, Stetson University, 1995.

of major corporations have gained, they still lack the day-to-day strength to counterweigh management. As Jay Lorsch wrote, "In most instances, directors understand the company through the CEO's eyes."[19] The CEO is a daily presence in the corporation and controls the conduits of information, and every employee works for him or her. The chair, on the other hand, has the board's legal authority and the occasional support of shareholders. Which army would you rather lead? The effectiveness of the chair as a distinct office cannot be separated from the effectiveness of the board. Too often today, the board still lacks this muscle.

This does not mean that we should give up on the idea of a separate chair, but rather that supporters may have been too early with the idea for it yet to be effective. The logistical concerns of "Who's the boss around here?" or the chemistry between the CEO and chair are ones that would work themselves out if real separate chairs came to power. If boards had the strength to field an effective separate chair, then they would have the strength to make it work. But, as of yet, few corporate boards do. Boards are rapidly increasing their power and legitimacy through internal changes and shareholder empowerment. However, only the future will tell if they gain the capacity to create a true separate chair.

---

19. *Pawns or Potentates,* Lorsch, p. 171.

42

Take Me to Your Lead Director

So if the board cannot yet field an effective separate chair, who should represent its interests to management? Governance thinkers have developed a fallback position called the "lead director." The lead director would be an outside director of the board who served in various representative roles. He or she would be the board's agent, its dean, its negotiator, its ombudsman, its spokesperson. The lead director would be designated by the board on the strength of his or her experience, status, professional achievement, and leadership abilities. The lead director is "not a position, it's a role," according to Jay Lorsch, a strong advocate.[1] In most proposals, the lead director would also have distinct administrative duties, such as chairing meetings of the outside directors, conducting the CEO's evaluation, and consulting with the CEO/chair on such tasks as shaping board agendas and making committee assignments.

The lead director has some big advantages over the separate chair. First, someone with this role is already found on most boards. This is the outside director recognized by others as a sort of guru, the fixer, the one who is not easily overawed, the organizer. Those who led the 1990s boardroom coups were their boards' ad hoc lead directors—Smale at GM, James Burke at IBM, Rawleigh Warner at American Express, and Don Perkins at K-Mart. If such talent and leadership is already on the board, goes the thinking, shouldn't we use it? Would it not be better to formally elect this lead director so he or she can prevent crises rather than try to build consensus after disaster has struck?

---

1. *Pawns or Potentates,* Jay Lorsch, Harvard Business School Press, 1989.

The lead director could also prove valuable in serving as "wrangler" for the growing structure of board committees and committee chairs. The audit, compensation, nominating, and other functional and monitoring committees are gaining more independence and duties. With more of the board's work being handled at the committee level, it becomes handy to have someone greasing the wheels and coordinating the work of the committees. It seems odd that while more committee work and functions like evaluation are handled by outsiders, the board's overseer who synchronizes it all remains the ultimate insider. Yet membership is increasingly made up of outside directors. Some of the new board charters, such as those at GM and Campbell Soup, mandate meetings of the outside directors, as well as independent board review of the CEO's performance. These tasks obviously must be supervised by an independent, outside director, and a lead director is the natural candidate.

A final plus of the lead director role lies in its very limitedness and informality. As noted, the lead director job would be largely administrative and limited to the board itself. Chemistry between the lead director and the chair/CEO, as well as between this director and the rest of the board, should be no problem because the lead director has the trust of both. The CEO would have less reason for turf disputes with a lead director than a separate chair because of the lead director's limited role. The question of who is the boss would not come up because outside the board setting there would be only one boss. Within the board, the lead director would hold his or her status through consensus of the other directors, and much of his or her power would be informal. In the hands of a true leader such vagueness would be an asset rather than a handicap. The CEO would feel less threatened, and the other directors could have faith that the lead director was their agent rather than a power seeker. More than one lead director could even be recognized, representing various areas of expertise, although how many board leaders would prove practical is a difficult question to answer.

But the lead director concept grows unwieldy when we talk about making it a formal office, as do such supporters as Martin Lipton and Jay Lorsch. If the lead director should be voted into the office, run board meetings, and automatically take over if the board fired the CEO, how would he or she differ from a separate chair? Korn/Ferry finds that even fewer boards are considering the lead director idea than that of a separate chair, with 78% saying "no."[2] In his 1989 book *Pawns or Potentates,* Lorsch proposes an early draft of the lead director idea, a presiding director who, though elected as the board's representative, would function only in emergencies, such as CEO incapacitation or when a majority of the board votes to empower the presiding director as a step toward replacing the CEO. This director would then function like the federal vice president as part of an emergency succession plan. Likely the presiding director would be a formal, contingent recognition of the person who was already serving as the informal lead director.

The naming of formal lead directors also runs into many of the same stumbling blocks as the separate chairs. How do you pay them? Do they bear more liability? Do they require their own staff? How exactly would their boardroom role differ from that of the chair? When John Smale resigned as chairman of GM at the beginning of 1996, he was named chairman of the GM board's executive committee. This might be a way of formalizing the lead director's role without trying to invent a new position. Someone obviously has to chair the executive committee, and this role has a more powerful day-to-day presence than chairs of other board committees or likely even more than a separate chair trying to invent a new role.

The separate chair and the lead director, both formal and informal, show that the board of directors is shaping itself into a true power center and is searching for its own leadership. The board coups of recent years implied a sort of spontaneous generation for this leadership in response to emergencies, but they also suggest how waiting for lightning to strike when a leader is needed can bring change that is too little and too late. Ralph Whitworth, former president of the United Shareholders Association, notes that "you have to invest these roles with some real stature and some real authority so that along the way they can pull a trigger or raise a flag, or blow a whistle."[3] As boards become more powerful, it is inevitable that they will develop their own leadership. Most attempts thus far have been abortive, but that is because most boards, even in 1996, are not yet strong enough to make their leader effective. For the boards of 2001, however, it might be another story.

---

2. *Korn/Ferry International Board of Directors Survey,* 1995.
3. Corporate Governance Roundtable, NACD and Deloitte & Touche LLP, 1994.

43

Boards without Borders

As I mentioned earlier, the separate board chair has proven quite workable in the context of Great Britain, or Germany, or Japan. As business and governance become more international, we should ask what other boardroom ideas we may be importing in the twenty-first century. These make up two main areas, narrowly defined governance and boardroom techniques, such as the separate chair, and larger affairs, such as issues that U.S. boards will have to face in the next century that are already making waves overseas.

Each of the major nations has a distinct corporate form that has evolved from unique national roots. In some cases, different countries use the same terms to describe quite different functions. The typical chair of a U.S. corporation, for example, fills a role quite different from the nonexecutive chair of a British firm. However, overseas corporations tend to have a few shared corporate characteristics that distinguish them from companies in the United States.

Labor representation. Germany, by law and tradition, has a two-level board. The *Aufsichsrat* (supervisory board) represents shareholders and employees. It in turn names a *Vorstand* (management board) made up of the company's top managers. Both elect chairs, and by law, there is no overlapping of membership. The closest U.S. analogy might be if the CEO chaired a board of inside directors, and an outside chair headed a separate board of outsiders. Although most members of the supervisory board are elected by shareholders, a percentage of seats have been required for the corporation's labor representatives since the 1970s. This gives German corporations a mandated labor presence on the board, and the power of company unions and workers' councils gives this presence substantial clout.

Employees also have a boardroom presence in France, although not as voting members. By law, employee representatives are allowed to attend all meetings of the *conseil d'administration* (board of directors). While this does not directly affect deliberations, it obviously crimps the board's style. The Dutch do not require a board labor presence, but give company "works councils" mandated input on certain corporate decisions.

If the definition of boardroom "employee involvement" is expanded beyond lunch-bucket workers to management, we find that there is strong employee board involvement in other countries as well. In the United Kingdom, the typical board mix of inside/outside directors is roughly three-to-one, the reverse of the United States with its majority outside boards. Japan's large corporate boards (30 to 40 members) are made up almost exclusively of employee directors who have worked their way up in the company.

In the United States, labor representation on boards has progressed over the years from nonexistent to minuscule. When Chrysler added UAW President Douglas Fraser to its board in 1979, it was seen as a milestone, but after Fraser retired, there was corporate resistance to retaining his replacement, Owen Bieber, on the board. According to Lee Iacocca, the addition of Fraser to Chrysler's board was based as much on Fraser's personal abilities as on his union affiliation, so the board seat was never intended as a union set-aside. "I thought someone was going to put up a monument to me in some park for bringing a good union guy onto the board, but after Fraser left, it just didn't work," Iacocca recalls.[1]

Employee-owned companies have seen more boardroom progress in the United States. As of the mid-1980s, 4% of Employee Stock Ownership Program (ESOP) companies included nonmanagement employee representatives on their boards, and in companies with majority employee ownership, this increases to 15%.[2] However, this has been the limit of direct employee presence on corporate boards in the United States. If anyone seems to be changing, it might be the foreign corporations. British companies are edging away from their dependence on employee directors, and in Ger-

---

1. Iacocca interview, *Corporate Board*, September/October 1993, p. 2.
2. *Employee Ownership*, Joseph R. Blasi, Harper Business, 1988, p. 202.

many there is discussion of limiting the size and power of supervisory boards.

Environmental issues. While U.S. boards have plenty of experience in dealing with legal and public concerns on the environment, other countries, especially those in Europe, have developed unique aspects that are finding their way here. Environmental concerns are far more politicized in Europe, with Green Parties a strong political force in Germany, France, and Scandinavian countries. Although the United States has the lead in certain pollution-control policies (such as auto air emissions), some green ideas that are brewing in Europe will find their way into U.S. boardrooms.

"Recoverability" statutes require that certain products and packaging be designed for ease in disassembly and recycling—and often compel manufacturers to take the products back for disposal. Pending German legislation on electronic equipment recycling, for example, has prompted Siemens Nixdorf AG to redesign its personal computers for ease of disposal (plastic PC housings are no longer painted to assure recyclability, for instance). The firm has also built a major disassembly facility in Paderborn. The recycling plan was initiated at the Siemens Nixdorf board level, and the recycling program manager is only one reporting stage away from the board itself.[3] As the European Union becomes more involved in environmental rule making, look for such considerations to spread across the continent. These new green laws will be of concern to any U.S. board doing business in Europe. Beyond that, expect them to pop up on the U.S. agenda sooner rather than later.

Executive and board pay. A few aspects of U.S. society have become staples of foreign news, the quickie info-bit items that help convince them of how crazy the Yankees are. Among these are U.S. firearm deaths, huge liability judgments, U.S. commuting distances—and, last but not least, outrageous CEO pay.

Graef Crystal has made a career of documenting the latter. In his 1991 book *In Search of Excess,* Crystal fired off statistics that would be footnoted around the world: the average U.S. CEO is paid 160 times that of a typical worker, while in the United Kingdom CEOs earn only 35 times more, and in Japan the differential

3. "Disassembly by Design," *Business and the Environment,* December 1995, p. 5.

is less than 20 times.[4] Even in cases where foreign CEOs do bring home handsome rewards, pay disclosure in most countries, particularly Britain and France, is weak, so shareholders rarely get angry about what they do not know. Director pay in the United States is likewise considered excessive compared to that of other countries, in most of which board compensation is rarely an issue. However, the fact that directors in Europe and Japan are more likely to also be company employees muddies the waters a bit. This means that it is hard to tell if, compared to their U.S. counterparts, foreign directors are underpaid a bit as directors or underpaid *a lot* as employees. Although France and the United Kingdom have some stock option payment benefits for directors, most foreign director pay is in flat fees and retainers.

However, the rate of executive and director pay has begun to climb in some countries, particularly Britain, and various governance observers, such as the Cadbury Commission in the United Kingdom, have grown concerned. Here is another case where the international flow of corporate governance influence is spreading from the United States to other nations. In 1994, British Gas CEO Cedric Brown was awarded a 76% pay increase at the same time the utility was laying off 25,000 employees. The company's 1995 annual meeting brought outraged shareholder protests over corporate greed, including a 350-pound pig named for the chairman. Swedish industrialist Peter Wallenberg received a $1 million consulting fee from a company on whose board he served, a fee carefully hidden in an annual report footnote. A newspaper dubbed him "The Greediest Man in Sweden." In France, a 1995 government report on executive stock option payments called for much stricter reporting requirements, concluding that the current slippery accounting standards encourage "fraudulent behavior."[5]

Increased attention by foreign investors is causing part of the flap. Foreign investors now hold more than 20% of French shareholdings and 16.3% in the United Kingdom.[6] As the nosy Yanks and other foreigners demand more disclosure on the companies in which

---

4. *In Search of Excess,* Graef S. Crystal, W. W. Norton, 1991, p. 28.
5. "Continental Divide over Executive Pay," *Business Week,* July 3, 1995, p. 41.
6. "France's Boardroom Revolution," *Wall Street Journal,* October 17, 1995.

they invest, some director pay goodies that had been safely obscured in the past are coming to light. However, there is also no doubt that European boards and managers are deciding that, since they must compete with the United States, maybe they should start paying like the United States as well.

44

Flash Forward: The High-Tech Board

"The future is not what it once was," said someone quicker with a snappy quote than I am. To put it in a more roundabout manner, many of the wonderful ideas that were going to recreate our future have become amusing artifacts at best, and embarrassments at worst. At the end of his six-hour workday, twenty-first-century Dad flies home in his supersonic heli-car to the family's nuclear-powered suburban ranch house. Mom gives him a peck on the cheek at the door and taps a few buttons on the kitchen wall so the robot chef will start supper. While waiting five minutes for the synthetic steak to perfectly cook, Dad sneaks in a few last-minute work details through a videoconference between his office in the den, the corporate headquarters, and a factory on the other side of the world.

We know what's wrong with this picture, but did you spot the part that's *right* with it? The videoconference. Because, despite all our lost hope in the other streamlined details, twenty-first-century Dad very well could attend a corporate board meeting from his den. And as a high-tech corporate director, he will probably have to.

Service on a corporate board of directors has become much more demanding of time, but for most top executives today, time is a rare commodity. Boards seek directors who are engaged, successful leaders in their fields: CEOs; CFOs; divisional presidents; legal partners; top marketing, entrepreneurial, and consulting talent; name academic and civic leaders. Good governance requires much more of them than ever before with committee meetings, consultations, review of materials, fact-finding, and research. Modern legal and regulatory standards today impose great time and efforts to meet even the minimum levels of due care. According to Korn/Ferry, the average hours a director commits yearly to a board seat shot up 58% in just one year, from 1994 to 1995.[1] However, these same people face unprecedented demands from their "day jobs." They must meet ever higher levels of productivity, deal with endless restructuring, and be on the scene for quick-paced decision making.

While corporations seek new and better faces for their boards, these very boards are just as likely to frown on their CEO adding any more outside commitments to his or her own busy schedule. Dennis Carey, of the SpencerStuart executive search firm, reports that director candidates carefully weigh the time demands of any new board offers—and if those demands are seen as excessive, the offer receives a turndown. "More directors are pushing CEOs to meet fewer times. I know of one corporation that held board meetings 10 times a year. The directors voted to cut that to five times yearly, and now they're talking about cutting back to four."[2] In board searches today, red flags go up if a candidate already has more than two or three directorships. Yet these high-achieving directors are often the most desired.

Corporate boards, then, do not demand anything unreasonable today. They just want to have it all. The very best executives and leaders, available for their boards, when they want them. Technology is making this possible.

Computer and communications technology allows us to break down time and space, two of the factors that have traditionally kept corporate boards stunted and parochial. The growth in cellular telephone and fax communications is already factored into business decisions. Board discussions regularly occur with directors on jets, on ski slopes, at the beach, and in traffic jams. But computer and video technology are pushing out the boundaries of high-tech governance. Rather than serving as a stopgap for quick consultations, expect technology to become an integrated tool in how the board meets, when, and how often, and how governance is conducted.

The first application would be to put computer technology to work. There are a number of ways computers can be used to speed the director's work and improve results. Nell Minow has suggested

---

1. *Korn/Ferry International Board of Directors Survey*, 1995.
2. Author interview, January 1996.

that corporations make sure their directors have access to the company's internal E-mail system. The results of this move alone could be dramatic. Information technology is highly egalitarian and free-flowing. A wonderful way to assure that the CEO is not "conditioning" the board information that passes through his or her office would be to let directors exchange E-mail with any person in the company. Financial information can travel directly from field offices to directors' addresses. Shareholders can send messages directly to the board. Updates and reports from within the company can be instantly "CCed" to all the directors or the members of specific committees. Directors on the other side of the world can check their board messages over breakfast. The ability to attach files to E-mail messages opens even greater horizons. Rather than fax a lengthy report or complex display to directors, the material can be piggy-backed onto an E-mail note. It transmits almost instantly, has less chance of error than a fax, and can be downloaded by the director at leisure.

For the CEO/chair, tapping directors into the corporate E-mail system brings a moment-of-truth decision. Many old-line CEOs (and not a few new-line ones) will recoil from the idea of letting the board send (and receive) E-mail from just anyone in the company. How will the CEO know what is going on? What if the directors start asking the wrong people the wrong questions? God knows who might be communicating with them. The entire medium would be *outside the CEO's control,* and thus dangerous. Yet information flows in just such a democratic, elusive manner. Is the company open, empowering, driving decisions down to the lowest levels, and all those other noble-sounding buzzwords? Then the CEO should welcome directors to the web and not worry what they may learn. Is the company centralized, controlled, and authoritarian? Then the E-mail revolution will be delayed a bit. But it will not be stopped.

The most innovative boardroom technology application is probably videoconferencing. As I mentioned earlier, this would be most practical for smaller, briefer, tightly focused meetings, such as board committees. Suppose the audit committee needs to hold a quick session to discuss a critical auditor opinion. One member drops in at the videoconferencing center at corporate headquarters. Another, on the road, visits one of the commercial centers that are popping up in most cities. A third schedules the facility at the university where she teaches graduate business courses. And the committee chair strolls down the hall from his or her own CEO office to the company's videoconferencing room. The committee members are hundreds of miles apart but hold a brief, vital strategy session, set a course of action, and head back to their other business, all within 15 minutes. A speakerphone conference might have had the same result, but would the chair have been able to read the professor's body language, suggesting that she was uncomfortable with the course they were discussing?

Videoconference technology is rapidly making its way into the boardroom because it meets such an obvious need. Rather than cramming committee sessions in around the (ever fewer) main board meetings or convincing themselves to spend at least a day flying in, conferences can be held wherever the participants happen to be and can be wrapped up over a lunch hour. Presentations from company staff or outside resources can be included with ease. Committees may limit their face-to-face meetings to one or two a year. For example, the audit committee might need only an annual pre- and post-audit "physical" meeting.

Meetings of the total board would not as easily lend themselves to this high-tech approach but could still benefit. A core of the board might assemble at corporate headquarters or at satellite locations, and straggler directors could then teleconfer with the main group. Although I mentioned dedicated teleconferencing facilities above, personal computer technology is rapidly making it possible for real-time sight and sound conferences to be as near as our desktop PC. Also, as the technology improves, large-scale video meetings of the board might become more practical. Eventually (and sooner than we think) virtual reality meetings will allow directors to convene, chat, shake hands, and whisper asides to each other thousands of miles apart.

Aside from the "holodeck" gizmo I just mentioned, the technology discussed above is readily available. Indeed, in some companies, particularly those with a strong technology base, teleconferencing is old hat. However, its use in the boardroom is only now catching on and has yet to reshape boards in the dramatic manner that will come. The pressure to hold fewer board meetings will ease and may even reverse as the average board or committee meeting goes from a one- or two-day event to a one- or two-hour camera chat. The travel expense and time costs of collecting bigwigs for board business will drop to negligible levels. Think of the effect that the steady, sharp price declines for computing power have had on our use of this technology. In three decades computers have evolved from multimillion dollar creations worshipped in a few clean rooms to dirt cheap throwaway pocket calculators and sport watches. A similar, though less extreme, process could occur with boards, and particularly committee meetings.

For a moment, completely rethink what a board meeting must be. What if board committee meetings need not be limited to a few legal necessities widely spaced throughout the year? What if they were so inexpensive, practical, and quick that you could convene one just because it seemed like a good idea? An audit committee that met twice a month? Why not? But what would it do if it met so frequently, you wonder? The answer: A lot more than it does now. What if a governance committee of outside directors could assemble painlessly once a month on-line to review key results and get a personal update from the CEO? Could a pending disaster be detected a lot sooner?

And who would be able to join your board once most meetings could be called to order by tapping a mouse key? International talent from overseas can bring great dividends in broadening the board's horizons and adding insights on foreign markets. But flying someone in from the other side of the world for board meetings is expensive for the corporation and off-putting for the potential director. With teleconferencing factored into your board charter, however, the time shift of a few hours is all that prevents you from adding a director anywhere in the world. This, then, is the greatest, most breathtaking aspect of what will happen when high-tech meets the corporate board. To paraphrase Bill Gates's famous thought-starter on computing power—what if corporate board meetings were free? What new, bold things could you do with them?

45

Why Boards Are Illogical

A da Demb, one of our most respected academic thinkers on corporate governance, has written of the "paradoxes" inherent in our hopes for corporate governance.[1] The board is responsible for the corporation—yet must not trample on the toes of management. The board must exert critical independent judgment—yet must be close enough and involved enough to be effective. Boards consist of high-achieving, independent individuals—yet must function smoothly as a team.

These paradoxes become most apparent when we examine how the modern board of directors functions, and will become even more obvious as we look down the road. As I said earlier, the United States is trying to create a corporate creature that has never actually existed here before—a board of independent, outside corporate directors that is powerful, well-informed, responsible to dispersed shareholders, and able to exert control over management. This definition may itself be a paradox. Yet, as the above board administrative trends suggest, boards are slowly gearing up the structure and procedures needed to make it work.

This process brings us to two more paradoxes of the new corporate board. The first was suggested above by Demb, the board that is involved, yet independent. Follow that problem to its functional quandary: How can a board prevent and fix problems if it is part of the problem? Boards are becoming more engaged, more active, and more aware of company operations. They are passing

---

1. *The Corporate Board,* Ada Demb and Friedrich Neubauer, Oxford University Press, 1992, pp. 4–7.

judgment on strategy, evaluating the job done by management, and pitching in on special assignments. By becoming part of the flow and process of guiding the company, they are gaining in power, value, and responsibility. So what happens when profits sag? When the stock price wilts? When an acquisition comes a cropper? No need asking "where was the board?"—the board was in the thick of it and is as responsible as management. The board must then either give itself a good talking to or, more likely, hunker down and join the CEO in trying to stonewall a defense. Once again, the board would have been co-opted by the CEO.

Or suppose the board has trimmed its sails a bit differently, kept above the bad decision making. In this case, investors will be quick to note that the board *could* have done something, but failed. Possibly, by keeping its hands off of management, the board has isolated itself from the real sources of power and failed to act because it lacked the information and muscle to do so. Thus, the board would either be part of the problem or arrive with too little and too late to be part of a solution.

I am reminded of the opposing criticisms of government regulatory agencies, such as the Environmental Protection Agency, the Federal Trade Commission, and the Food and Drug Administration. Those who run businesses and advocate deregulation regularly complain about the burdens, inconsistencies, and harsh measures that these agencies impose. Liberal consumer groups, however, condemn the "regulatory capture" of these agencies, faulting them as having become not business watchdogs, but lapdogs. Likewise with boards, these bodies cannot win, slammed as being either too removed from those they regulate or too cozy with them.

The disadvantage of a paradox is that by definition, it is irreconcilable. In the case of corporate boards, we either condemn ourselves to muddling through or use the tension of such contradictions to rethink what we really want boards to do.

46

Deconstructing "Pay for Performance"

There is one more paradox of corporate boards, and this is probably the most current, the thorniest, and the one most concerned with nitty-gritty reality. How do you pay these folks to encourage them to think like shareholders?

Certainly there is no end of recent discussion on this topic. If
anything, the mid- to late 1990s have seen more media, academic,
investor, and consultant debate on paying the board than any other
single governance topic. As an indicator of how boards have suddenly begun to matter, this is a good sign. The $20 gold pieces
of yore were probably fitting both for the ritual and value-added
aspect of the era's directors. Even in those distant pre-inflation
days, $20 did not buy you a whole lot of governance wisdom. The
steady rise in director pay and perks over the past two decades have
brought us to an era of what *Forbes* magazine calls the "cosseted
directors."[1] Korn/Ferry found that average 1995 director compensation came to $39,707.[2] This does not include pension plans,
stock options or grants, insurance, charitable donations, or other
benefits. Neither does it account for some of the less-noted perks,
such as free travel, use of company products or facilities, or consulting opportunities.

Looking at such numbers from a very bright-eyed free-market
perspective, we should applaud them as a sign that we are finally
willing to pay for good governance. Rather than treating the board
as a slightly more prestigious form of Rotary Club, we now foot the

---

1. "The Cossetted Directors," *Forbes,* May 22, 1995.
2. *Korn/Ferry International Board of Directors Survey,* 1995.

bill for the best. But we have already seen the holes in that idea. The link between growing board independence and greater pay are likely a sign that if the CEO cannot pack the board with employees anymore, at least the CEO can pay them as such. As Graef Crystal wrote, "If the CEO is on the ball," he or she commissions an outside pay consultant to prove that the board is scandalously undercompensated and will then "suggest that the board approve an increase in its pay."[3] The board furrows its collective brow just enough for propriety and then approves. As the next item in its agenda, the board moves on to examine the adequacy of the CEO's pay.

With a single stroke, then, critics see the CEO not only raising the board's sights on what constitutes adequate compensation, but making himself or herself the cornucopia for their goodies. Directors, say the quibblers, have had their virtue compromised and will allow themselves to be rolled by the chief executive.

The problem with these (I admit, oversimplified) views is not that they are nonsense but that all have elements of truth grained within them. The $20 a pop days were based on the idea that board service was an obligation and duty. If not solely service to the cause of free enterprise, then at least the duty of investment bankers to watch over and build relationships with the company. Board pay indeed soared in tandem with the rise in director independence, but it also matched the increase in director workloads and liability dangers. On the other hand, we have adequate evidence that at least some CEOs, consciously or not, realized that a fat and happy board was more likely to tolerate a fat and happy CEO. Codependency was a boardroom hazard long before it made the TV talk show circuit.

The above scenarios, however, miss a crucial aspect of the governance transaction—they concentrate only on what is paid to directors. The issue is not *how much* we pay directors, but *why* we pay directors—what exactly do we pay them to *do*? Even the patrons of activist boards are at great pains to say that it is not the board's business to manage corporate affairs. Yet the traditional, stripped-down board job description—to hire and fire management—has been superseded at all but the most Cro-Magnon corporations. It allowed management to do far too many things wrong for too long. Adrian Cadbury offers a dandy board acronym: NIFO—nose in,

---

3. *In Search of Excess,* Graef S. Crystal, W. W. Norton, 1991, p. 229.

fingers out. But how do you know that you are sniffing out all the problems unless you poke into operations a bit? And does such a strictly observational board really use the talents that good directors have to offer? Board activists may be forgetting that the Heisenberg uncertainty principle affects governance, too—by being in a position to observe the process, the board invariably affects it.

Precedent on board pay is not much help, either. Most of the history on board compensation, right up to the present handsome packages, tells us no more than that how we pay boards seems to have little to do with company results. Academic and author Stanley Vance for years offered compelling cases of companies with insider majority boards (who presumably received little or no pay for their board duties) that had booming productivity and results. Robert Pearson, CEO of Lamalie Amrop, notes that the very Graef Crystal who slammed board pay-setting decisions has also concluded that there is no statistical relationship between director shareholdings and company performance.[4] Anecdotal evidence abounds to prove that paying directors in almost any shape or quantity aligns with improved corporate performance—and also with corporate failure.

As we end the current millennium, this anarchy of incentives is no longer enough. We seek director rewards that directly encourage certain results. Shareholder activists, who are always handy with sound bites, call this "pay for performance." But paying directors for company performance is also a very confused issue. Performance for shareholders? This certainly is reasonable and is indeed the group to whom directors owe their strictest fiduciary duty. But which shareholders? Robert Kirby, senior partner with the Capital Group Partners, points out that shareholders cover a spectrum from Warren Buffett at one end of the scale to hedge funds and arbitrageurs at the other. Warren Buffett buys and then never sells, sticking with his companies like a mother hen and accepting short-term inefficiencies for what he sees as long-term gains. The arbitrage folks are financial engineers seeking the greatest profit as quickly as possible. For the latter group, Kirby opines that if directors "thought like these shareholders, I believe something approaching chaos would rapidly ensue."[5]

---

4. *Directorship Magazine Special Report, 1996,* Robert L. Pearson (contrib.), p. 7–11.

5. *Directorship Magazine Special Report, 1996,* Robert G. Kirby (contrib.), p. 6–1.

Most equity is held by major institutions, the mutual funds, and pension funds, who are not found at either of these extremes but are scattered along the continuum between them. Their needs and agendas vary widely, from strong short-term results, to safety, to steady returns, to a solid change of control premium. In discussions of paying for governance, we tend to denigrate investors with the shortest-term interests. They are seen as greedy, strip-mining gamblers who drive directors and managers to make poor decisions for short-term payoffs. Indeed, many commentators maintain that such investors are not "good" shareholders. Their quarter-to-quarter (if not hour-by-hour) focus makes them illegitimate as investors. Robert Monks and Nell Minow go in search of the "ideal owner" for governance purposes in their book *Corporate Governance,* and see the ideal owners as pension funds and major institutional investors, such as their own LENS fund.[6] These holders, it is argued, bring the patience, governance savvy, and critical mass that make them worthy of board consideration.

However, investor reality tends to run with the strip miners. Albert Dunlap took over as chairman and CEO of Scott Paper in April 1994 and immediately set to firing employees, cutting one-third of the company's total workforce, over 11,000 people. When he took office, Scott Paper was worth $2.8 billion. The stock price climbed steadily, and when Scott was sold to Kimberly-Clark in 1995, the company brought $6.8 billion (with Dunlap's severance package worth a whopping $100 million). However, a 1996 article in *Business Week* claims that under Dunlap the company had received only a hasty "slash and burn" fix-up, weakening its core structure while prettying it up for a quick sale.[7] *Newsweek* calls Dunlap "the poster boy for the folks who say that CEOs have gone too far."[8] Investors in Scott Paper certainly made out well over the short term, but did the company's board select the wisest long-term course? Some shareholders were relationship investors displeased with the company's poor performance in 1994. They were no doubt glad to bet on new leadership, if uneasy with the massive cutbacks. Others bought in after Dunlap was hired because they suspected a quick sale and sought resultant quick profits. Both groups are sharehold-

---

6. *Corporate Governance,* Robert A. G. Monks and Nell Minow, Blackwell, 1995.
7. "The Shredder," *Business Week,* January 15, 1996, pp. 56–61.
8. "The Hit Men," *Newsweek,* February 26, 1996, p. 48.

ers. Each has a very different agenda. Yet the board is to be rewarded for delivering value to both.

Which leads to another quandary. If we have difficulty pinning down something as material and legally recognized as a "shareholder," how do we define a concept as vague as "performance?" Some companies are valued as income producers, others for growth. Some will require enormous amounts of cash to produce profits down the road. Some are cyclical. There are times when the breakup or sale value of a healthy company will be greater than its present stock value. Corporations that are instantly, constantly frangible could be a great way to deliver value to shareholders—if we ignore all the other costs. In 1989, the board of Time hastily restructured its merger deal with Warner Communications specifically to avoid a higher-priced offer from Paramount. Did this deliver maximum performance to Time shareholders? The Delaware Chancery Court said it did, by preserving the strategic value of a Time and Warner combo.

The shareholder performance that we pay directors to deliver, then, is certain only at the extreme ends of the scale. A company that is obviously a mismanaged dog has no business making either its executives or its board wealthy. A company like Disney has made Michael Eisner a very wealthy man over the last decade, and the board also deserves its share of Disney World passes. Yet in between are many very lightly delineated shades of gray.

47

Directors Discover Serious Money

Despite the difficulty in defining what we want to pay directors for, there is no doubt that the *amounts* we pay them are hitting unprecedented highs, with little sign of slackening. Korn/Ferry's 1995 directors survey shows that average cash retainers plus meeting fees totaled $31,415, up from $26,190 in 1990, roughly $1000 more each year excluding stock gains. These averages show great variation, though. The 1994 numbers indicate that at midcap industrials with sales under $1 billion, the directors' cash take totaled only $25,490 per year for retainer and meeting fees. At corporations over $5 billion this soars to $41,111. Committee fees add to this figure. Committee meeting fees on average are very consistent across the range of company sizes and categories at $1000 per meeting. Committee chairs earn slightly more per meeting but are often paid retainers for their committee service. These, according to Korn/Ferry, vary widely by company size, more than doubling from $2,995 at the under $1 billion industrials to $6,259 at those in the $5 billion range.[1]

Board benefits, although widely attacked, are not as common as some believe. Directors and officers' insurance is so necessary today that many observers do not even count it as a benefit. The most popular benefit after that, deferral of board fees until retirement, is found at only about half of corporations, though it is much more common at the largest companies. Following closely in popularity are retirement pension plans, which vary widely in the amount of income provided and in their benefit terms.

---

1. *Korn/Ferry International Board of Directors Survey,* 1995.

The typical director pension program offers periodic payments to the director upon retirement from the board. Age of the director is also a factor, especially if the board has a formal (or even informal) retirement age, which is usually somewhere between 65 and 70. A minimum length of board service is another normal requirement, most often five or ten years. Some boards (if they do not mind courting controversy) require as little as three years for their directors to receive pensions.

The amounts paid to retired directors vary greatly, with almost every corporation using a different formula. The annual retainer and fees paid to the board member at retirement is the starting point for calculations, although few companies offer to continue the total amount. A percentage deal is most common, often based on the number of years the director served. The longer the retired director's tenure, the higher the percentage climbs. Although some board pension plans are good for the remainder of the director's life (and a few even continue payments to a surviving spouse after death), most cover only a limited term. A typical formula here is to pay for the same number of years that the director served on the board, although some plans pay all retirees for a set number of years.

The idea of pensioning directors is one of the little ideas that causes a lot of discomfort to shareholder activists. In 1995, 48% of B. F. Goodrich shareholders voted to end director pensions, a remarkably high figure for such a technical proposal. Over the past several years, shareholder proposals to cut pensions have been the second most common, after those related to staggered boards. Pensions are seen as weakening director independence, making it too dangerous to oppose management and risk losing one's board seat.

Board pension programs and deferred payment of fees are usually lumped together, with the deferral often taking the place of a pension. This can have strong tax and accounting advantages for both the corporation and the director. The intermixing of pensions and deferrals has likely helped keep board cash retainers from rising faster than they have. As an author in the *Corporate Board* subtitled his article on director pensions, "Pay them now or pay them later."[2] Also, directors cannot count on a cozy sure thing in looking forward to their board pension or deferred board fee check. These are not

---

2. "Rethinking Director Pensions," Edmund Schwesinger, *Corporate Board*, September/October 1995, p. 7.

held in trust like employee pensions and do not have to meet any ERISA rules. A change in control or company difficulty could leave the former director high and dry.

The Conference Board found charitable "matching grant" benefits at a third of surveyed corporations in 1995, though this was down from 36% the previous year. Straight charitable giving plans were offered at 8% of corporations.[3] Charitable donation assistance is a board benefit that would seem hard to argue with. Who doesn't want to do good? Yet shareholders are also curious as to why their money is being used to do this good, usually with no input from themselves. In a typical usage, noted by Graef Crystal, the company purchases a life insurance policy on a director and, on the director's death, endows the benefits on a major university to fund an academic chair. While there are certain tax benefits to the company in such a program, they only apply if we assume that we *have* to deliver boodle to directors in some form and that this is at least the most deductible.

Charitable beneficence reached its extreme in the case of Armand Hammer and Occidental Petroleum. In 1989, Occidental's board, handpicked by chairman and founder Armand Hammer, approved a donation of $95 million to build an art museum specifically to house Hammer's art collection. Though presented as a boon to the people of Los Angeles (where the museum was to be built, next to Occidental headquarters) and a deductible public relations coup for the company, a number of shareholders sued. The case was ultimately settled. Occidental was burned by the bad publicity (it turned out that shareholders had also footed the bill for much of the art collection itself). For their part, shareholders felt forced to compromise because it appeared that the courts would approve the board plan as being within their business judgment ambit. If charitable giving plans are supposed to be an all-around feel-good exercise, the Armand Hammer museum was a distinct failure.

---

3. *Corporate Directors' Compensation*, 1996 ed., Conference Board, p. 31.

48

Paying the Board in Stock:
The Cheers . . .

Pay and perks for the board have, as I noted, been the spark point of recent corporate governance debate. But the nucleus, the epicenter of this board pay debate consists of one word—stock. Investor activists, again showing their talent for bumper sticker phrasing, put it thus: If we want directors to think like shareholders, they should *be* shareholders. The tools to achieve this end come under two main headings—paying directors in varying degrees with stock, and then making sure that they own and retain a substantial amount of equity.

Director stock ownership has not always been a governance ideal. Newton Baker, Woodrow Wilson's secretary of war and a noted corporate statesman, was quoted as frowning on outside directors owning stock in their companies. Those rascals in the boardroom would promptly take the inside information they held, trot off to their broker, and make a killing. At the least, their judgment would be clouded by personal interests. Baker was not alone. In *The Modern Corporation and Private Property*, Berle and Means write from a 1930s viewpoint on how United States Steel Chairman Elbert Gary would carefully keep his directors in the boardroom after a dividend vote until the move was publicly disclosed. Gary wanted to be sure "that no individual could take advantage of the information."[1]

---

1. *The Modern Corporation and Private Property*, Adolf Berle and Gardiner Means, Harcourt, Brace, & World, 1932, p. 330.

Writing in 1947, Copeland and Towl decried the "myth" and "misconception" that "a man who holds a large block of stock will be a better director."[2] In 1971, however, Myles Mace observed that directors who held substantial chunks of equity in a company "are much more likely to ask discerning questions of management than an outside director who does not own stock."[3] It is interesting to note that both of these sources, and other early observers on board stock ownership, based their thoughts on *large* owners of equity. Both dismissed board ownership of nominal shares as irrelevant, and most of the levels projected by current board stock advocates, even in the thousands of shares, would have been viewed as too small to matter.

The early commentators discussed director stock ownership as a percentage of *total* company equity and seemed to view it as a factor only when it approached the 5% to 10% range. Their view was the reverse of most modern advocates, who want good people to join the board and then make certain they buy or are paid enough stock for governance to be personal. Writers of the past saw the pattern the other way around, harkening back to the days of major financiers and investors on the board calling the shots. In those cases, directors already held a large piece of the company and stayed on the board to guard their assets.

By the mid-1970s, though, the idea of directors as shareholders (rather than shareholders as directors) was gaining attention. In 1977 Myles Mace described a new Mallory corporation plan granting directors stock options as "the first option plan for directors I have encountered," and quite a bold novelty. But he also recalled that when interviewing top executives of the 1960s for his book *Directors: Myth and Reality*, "They expressed instantaneous, vigorous and unqualified disapproval" of any plans to put stock in director hands.[4] A stockholding board, the managers feared, would prove a meddlesome board. Certainly, the idea of requiring board members to hold a certain amount of equity and that this level

2. *The Board of Directors,* Melvin Copeland and Andrew Towl, Greenwood, 1947, 1968, pp. 145–146.
3. *Directors: Myth and Reality,* Myles Mace, Harvard University Press, 1971, p. 61.
4. "Stock Options for Outside Directors," Myles Mace, *Harvard Business Review,* July/August 1977, p. 47.

should be broadcast to the whole world would seem shockingly intrusive, not just to the CEOs but to the directors themselves. It would be almost like insisting that directors publicly donate a pint of blood once a month.

With the 1980s though, the idea of shareholding directors was gaining converts. Steady increases in director pay and benefits, combined with the changes in shareholder power and makeup, were making board pay as much an issue as board performance. Still, there were concerns about what sort of shareholders directors would prove to be. A 1988 article in the *Corporate Board* by A. W. Smith Jr. found the author cautious on the idea of paying directors with stock options. He voiced a common fear that options gave the appearance of self-enrichment and would tempt directors toward short-term decision making solely to goose stock prices. Besides, he noted, "Options do not equal ownership." Rather, Smith, a noted pay consultant, advised payment with restricted stock, though once again concerned about the appearance of self-dealing.[5] In the 1989 *Pawns or Potentates,* Jay Lorsch endorsed the idea of paying directors at least partly in stock, although admitting that his research had found that stock ownership was not a prime motivator for board service. Rather, he supported the idea "for psychological reasons,"—it would give directors a yardstick to measure their results and increase identification with shareholders.[6]

With the boardroom revolts of the early 1990s, director stock pay and stock holdings became a part of many activist manifestos, but the issue remained at the rear of the pack. With the pace of corporate change from 1989 through 1993, there were so many governance items on the investor's menu that a sort of corporate triage was required, attending first to such major concerns as take-over defenses, director independence, proxy reform, and cumulative voting. Most of this shareholder agenda of the early 1990s was aimed at immediate results and focused on entrenched, unresponsive management. This meant that investors such as CalPERS needed to build their bridges with corporate boards for success. Cracking down on how those boards were paid would hardly have

---

5. "Stock Options for Directors?" A. W. Smith Jr., *Corporate Board,* March/April 1988, p. 14.
6. *Pawns or Potentates,* Jay Lorsch, 1989, Harvard Business School Press, p. 177.

been good politics at that stage, so the issue of board compensation was temporarily shuffled to the back of the room.

By 1993, however, as the investor agenda gained victories on most of its basic items, the issue of board pay was recalled from the farm team. The first major battle cry on the topic appeared in the *Corporate Board* for July/August 1993. Nell Minow of LENS wrote an article for us on her concept of "The Ideal Board." Leading off her checklist: "The single most important requirement is that all directors have a significant and personal stake in the company." She defined this stake with one word: "Stock." Although Nell and her collaborator Kit Bingham offered 15 further characteristics of the ideal board from an investor viewpoint, all that followed would inevitably "come about on their own if directors become shareholders."[7]

The issue began to find its way into shareholder resolutions and governance discussions—and also into real action. In 1994, Campbell Soup updated its corporate governance standards to include a requirement that directors own at least 1,000 shares of company stock within one year after election to the board. The year's biggest news, however, came among the turmoil at Scott Paper after Al Dunlap was named CEO and chairman. In August of 1994, Dunlap presented his board with a proposal to pay themselves *totally* in Scott stock. No meeting fees, no retainers, no pensions, nothing in cash. Strictly stock—1,000 shares per year. According to legend, the board not only approved the proposal at that August meeting, but all the directors present promptly handed their meeting checks back to be exchanged for stock. Dunlap, who never shrank from assigning heroic status to his ideas, has observed, "I have passionate feelings about boards of directors. I do not think a person ought to be on a board to get a big, fat paycheck. . . . The ideal of paying stock to directors . . . should be up for a proxy vote at every company each and every year."[8] Scott thus became one of the few companies (Travelers Insurance is another) to pay its board wholly in stock.

The Dunlap proposals also included hefty stock ownership targets for senior management as well, though Dunlap put his own money where his mouth was, personally accumulating four million

---

7. "The Ideal Board," Nell Minow and Kit Bingham, *Corporate Board,* July/August 1993, p. 11.
8. Albert J. Dunlap, speech, Stetson University, 1995.

shares. When the company was sold to Kimberly-Clark in late 1995, the $9.4 billion agreement reflected a 225% increase in value since Dunlap took over. Although I have noted the controversy about the harshness of Dunlap's measures (and the true long-term value of his results), those who were force-fed Scott stock received a rich diet.

In May of 1995, *Forbes* magazine hit the newsstands with its cover article on "The Cosseted Director." The cover shows a gloriously decadent boardroom Nero swinging his ewer of wine, happily oblivious to the mischief the CEO is no doubt cooking up on his watch. "Pigging it up . . . Corporate managements who seduce their directors into submission," says the headline. Inside it got worse, with steamy revelations of board perk and pay scams. Golden board parachutes, lavish pensions, sinister consulting contracts, and the heftiest pay packages around were examined in lurid detail. "How motivated can a board be to get tough . . . when the chief executive showers it with goodies?"[9] Many directors were outraged over what they saw as a slanted attack with unrepresentative cases of board excess. One of the directors profiled as particularly well-paid told me that "the substance is accurate, but the tone was very negative." Yet the *Forbes* cover was another sign that boards had truly arrived as a business media topic—and were now fair game.

A final nudge on the board pay in stock matter came in June 1995, with the National Association of Corporate Directors Blue Ribbon Commission report on director pay. The commission was chaired by Robert Stobaugh of the Harvard Business School and included 19 other noted corporate governance thinkers, including Jay Lorsch, Nell Minow, and Ira Millstein. The 41-page Stobaugh report offered five principles for director pay setting to be enacted through six "best practices." Although a bit light on specifics (inevitable if you try to put 20 corporate governance experts in a room and get them to agree on anything), the theme of aligning the interests of shareholders and directors came through strongly. Director compensation disclosure, motivational value, and integration were other key points.

The most newsworthy aspect, though, dealt with practices and targets for board stock pay and board stock holdings. Best Practice #2 calls for boards to set a substantial target for director share own-

---

9. "The Cosseted Director," *Forbes*, May 22, 1995, p. 169.

ership and a schedule for reaching this target. The most quoted provision, however, was Best Practice #4, that boards pay their members solely in equity and cash, "with equity representing a substantial portion of the total up to 100 percent."[10] The same provision also called for dismantling all board benefit programs.

By the end of 1995, the movement to make directors into shareholders had turned into a stampede. In a December update on its May article, *Forbes* magazine found that substantial movement had already occurred on the issue of director pay and perks. "Behind closed doors, many companies—including Bell Atlantic, Brunswick and B. F. Goodrich—are now giving consideration to paying their boards more heavily, or entirely, in stock."[11] The 1995 Korn/Ferry survey found that 62% of companies studied pay their directors with some form of stock, and 28% said the percentage of stock pay had increased within the last year. This rose to 38% at the largest corporations ($5 billion and over), which are usually the trendsetters. Sixteen percent of companies set stock ownership targets for directors. Although the average for this target figure was 1,413 shares, the median figure for actual director share ownership was 4,000.[12]

Directors quizzed by Korn/Ferry agreed overwhelmingly (89% to 11%) that directors should be paid partially in stock. (Interestingly, the same percentage mix, 89% to 11%, overwhelmingly *disagreed* with the idea of paying directors totally in stock.)[13] A study by McLaughlin and Company puts a dollar figure to the average director holding: $123,000 excluding options, an impressive 4.6 times the average board retainer.[14] This could suggest one reason why directors have proven to be largely unexcited by the directors-as-shareholders issue—they already *are* shareholders.

As we speed downhill toward the year 2000, the idea of paying directors at least partly in stock and requiring them to hold more than nominal amounts has become a staple of the push for improved governance. Indeed, the twin concepts are gaining the status of dogma, their rightness and logic difficult to marshall any arguments

10. "Director Compensation," *Director's Monthly*, August 1995, p. 4.
11. "Off with Their Perks," *Forbes*, December 4, 1995, p. 60.
12. *Korn/Ferry International Board of Directors Survey*, 1995.
13. Ibid.
14. *Directorship Magazine Special Report, 1996*, David J. McLaughlin (contrib.), p. 7–22.

against. Nell Minow, who helped launch the current campaign, remains certain that down the road "the number one agenda item will be stock ownership. . . . Everything else is secondary. A hundred thousand dollars worth of stock is the point where [directors] start thinking about their own pocketbooks." Nell also sees a second stage over the horizon with indexed options for directors. The value of the stock they receive would be linked to the company's performance compared to its competitors.[15]

Carolyn Brancato, editor of the *Brancato Report on Institutional Investment,* sees the board pay issue as a growing sign that the big investors are "looking away from structural issues to performance. Pay in stock is definitely part of this trend. The key is to align directors with the downside as well as the upside."[16] A 1996 survey of institutional investors by Russell Reynolds Associates found that 61% consider company stock the ideal form of pay for directors.[17] The Investor Rights Association of America in 1996 offered shareholder resolutions specifically to pay directors in stock at 30 companies, including Dow Jones, Bausch & Lomb, Dexter Corporation, and Heinz. The proposals typically called for half of board compensation to be paid in equity. In 1995 only eight such proxy proposals had been filed by *all* shareholders, and in 1994 only three.

Campbell Soup, which several years ago was a pioneer in setting director stockholding targets, in 1995 raised the crossbar. In November, shareholders voted to pay board retainers exclusively in stock, a combination of 1,200 shares plus 1,000 options. The company also cut its board retirement benefits and upped its director stockholding requirement from 1,000 to 3,000 shares. Campbell is gaining company. A 1996 study of 350 major corporations by pay consultant William M. Mercer finds that 26% are now offering their directors stock replacement grants, which either allow or require directors to substitute equity for some portion of their pay. Of companies that do offer these grants, almost half make the grants voluntary, but 37% require at least some portion of director pay in stock.[18]

Such research suggests that the issue of paying boards in stock

15. Author interview, November 1995.
16. Author interview, January 1996.
17. *1995 Survey of Institutional Investors,* Russell Reynolds Associates, p. 14.
18. William M. Mercer Co. press release, January 1996.

is evolving into the next logical stage, from the question of *should* we do it to the question of *how* to do it. The Mercer results find that most directors currently swap cash fees for either restricted or unrestricted stock. This is tougher than the traditional use of straight grants, with their emphasis on options. Only about 15% of the companies gave their stock-paid directors any premium discount to soften the change.

In the *Corporate Board* for March/April 1996, Don Gallo of Sibson & Company offered one of the first blueprints on how to design a practical board stock pay plan. Care must be taken to structure stock payments in ways that avoid SEC short-swing trading rules, for instance. Boards can find great flexibility in stock payment plans, however. Gallo notes that 3M corporation still pays a $30,000 annual retainer to its directors—however, $5,000 is diverted into 3M stock until board members reach a target holding of 10,000 shares. Gallo also notes that deferral of board stock pay into share accounts can not only avoid regulatory hassles but makes an excellent substitute for the pension plans that are under such fire. Using such accounts, or the more common alternative of simply restricting stock until retirement, "makes the value of [director] pensions dependent upon a strong stock price."[19]

Directorship magazine has also addressed the issue in a special report on the incentives and rewards for board service. An article by David McLaughlin showed how substantial board stock payments can rapidly accrue into substantial equity for directors. At Pepsi, directors receive an annual grant of $30,000 in stock. The median holding of Pepsi board members is now 10,500 shares, worth about $400,000. Contributors to the *Directorship* report chorused their support for the idea of paying directors in stock. Thomas Flanagan, president of the Investors Rights Association of America, opined that "when directors have their own stock at stake, decisions regarding profitability and shareholder interest will be managed in a way more favorable to shareholders." Charles Elson of Stetson University (and a member of the Stobaugh panel) finds the concept "simple and obvious. . . . Companies should compen-

---

19. "Paying in Stock: A Board Blueprint," Don Gallo, *Corporate Board*, March/April 1996, p. 13.

sate their outside directors primarily in company stock." Noted pay consultant Pearl Meyer adds "when good corporate governance is critical, companies can't afford not to pay directors in stock."[20] It would seem that the idea of board stock pay and holdings is a sure bet for the future.

---

20. *Directorship Magazine Special Report, 1996,* various authors.

49

. . . and the Jeers . . .

A nd yet . . . A low murmur of criticism over turning directors
into substantial shareholders continues up to the present. The
Directorship report prompted a fierce 1996 debate between academics and writers questioning and supporting the stock pay theory.
Some of these objections are old ones, yet they raise still-unresolved
questions about board stock pay. These concerns may be sorted out
as we build experience with turning directors back into owners.
However, this very process of taking director stock pay from the
academic journals to wholesale reality could turn any unforeseen
flaws or motivators into major problems.

Objections to turning directors into major shareholders come
under several headings:

Short-termism. If we look at the rewards and disincentives that face
corporate managers, most relate to short-term or intermediate results. Share prices and quarterly results are what draw the attention
of analysts and, whether we like to admit it or not, usually determine
how we judge the value of a management team. No one suggests
that board members with hefty amounts of stock in their names will
immediately turn into scavengers, eagerly selling the corporate seed
corn needed for future growth. But such an extreme reaction would
not be necessary for a stock program to bring a deterioration in the
board's role. Perks, corporate waste, and weak divisions would no
doubt draw a more critical eye from a stockholding board, but so
would major capital projects, R&D, and new product launches. The

board of directors is the singular body in a company that is supposed to worry about long-term perspectives. Paying them in stock could start them running with the rest of the corporate herd.

Shareholders may think this is just fine, but will they like the ultimate results? For all the investor activist talk of "good" long-term relationship investors and "bad" quickie arbitrageurs, we should bear in mind Gresham's law of good and bad money—the bad will drive out the good. Robert Gumbiner, former chairman of FHP International, writes that "ownership of stock options by members of the board has a strong tendency to compel them to act in a short-term, deleterious manner."[1] Advocates of paying the board in stock will counter that safeguards can be built in to assure that directors become long-term shareholders. But this leads to the next objection . . .

The millstone theory. Although payment in stock, and substantial holdings, can be a potential gold mine for directors, you would not know it from most of the writings on the theme. Lax boards will instead be "forced" to pay attention to the shareholders, will be "in the same boat" with them, and will "keep their priorities straight." Stock pay will shine "sunlight" on the dubious world of director rewards and sever their "dominance" by management. Too often, the rush for board pay in stock is presented not as a perk but as a punishment, a financial version of the electronic ankle bracelets required for probationers. By mandating that the board hold certain levels of equity and putting strong written or unwritten restrictions on when the director can sell the stock and how much, are we compelling a shotgun marriage? Even the big funds get to sell *some* of their holdings when the fund manager wants to.

Noted pay consultant Charlotte Armstrong suggests that board payment of retainers in stock does not really offer an incentive at all, but is simply compensation for services rendered, though in a very illiquid form. Stock payments that are not in themselves an incentive and which are limited through sale or deferral restrictions

---

1. "A Contrarian View," Robert Gumbiner, *Director's Monthly,* December 1995, p. 13.

"impose an unfair penalty. They put the director in an economic straitjacket."[2]

Stock sales by these insiders would be frowned upon in most of the stock pay plans discussed. Such sales bear heavy SEC reporting burdens, with the risk of short-swing profits or even insider trading charges. They can also draw lots of attention, most of it negative. Notice how often C-page articles in the *Wall Street Journal* headline "heavy stock sales by company insiders" as a sign that trouble is brewing. In discussing the Scott director pay plan before the company's sale, Albert Dunlap voiced the punitive aspect of director stock schemes. "Our directors cannot sell their stock right away. They have to notify our general counsel if they are going to sell. And if they do that, they are not going to have any longevity on our board."[3] Of course, it turned out the Scott directors did not have much board longevity anyway.

Deferred stock, which might be forfeited through board ouster, could even backfire in its purpose, giving an incentive for the director to not make waves and endanger his or her nest egg. No doubt investors need better tools to battle poor governance than "the Wall Street walk." But do we benefit by forcing directors to the opposite extreme of being "chained for life?"

Board pay is not all that rich to start with.   What? With all those perks, fees, freebies and stock options? As noted earlier, Korn/Ferry found that director pay averages over $39,000. Let's raise the ante and look at board pay for only the very biggest industrials, where cash compensation alone averaged over $49,000. Such a figure is . . . Well, frankly, it is barely enough to put the average 1990s U.S. family into the middle class. In the professional stratum that provides most of our corporate directors, $49 grand might attract some attention but is more likely seen as part of a retirement nest egg or a helper for junior's third year at Princeton.

The same issue of *Forbes* that groused about directors' fat paychecks and perks also listed America's 800 top-paid CEOs for 1995. The median for salary and bonus was $993,000. Aerospace CEOs

---

2. *Directorship Magazine Special Report, 1996,* Charlotte P. Armstrong (contrib.), p. 7–33.

3. Albert J. Dunlap, speech, Stetson University, 1995.

did even better, bringing home an average of $1.6 million.[4] That was *before* any stock sales or dividends. Since the gold standard for Fortune 500 corporate directors remains CEOs and other top execs, it is uncertain how tempting board pay is in turning anybody's head. It is money, no doubt, but for most of Our Gang not *serious* money.

Even some of the people who are most concerned with tying board pay to performance will admit that the raw numbers themselves are not that big of a deal. "On one hand, directors get paid too little for what we ask them to do. On the other hand, they get paid far too much for what they actually do," wrote Robert Monks in 1991.[5] John Pound, although he too seeks to tie board pay more closely to results, believes that "director compensation has to skyrocket. . . . We're now pushing board service toward the level of charity work."[6] Fears that director goodies are breaking the corporate bank are far out of line. For a better perspective, board pay should be viewed in context of how much a good board can earn for shareholders with a single crucial decision—and how much it can cost the company with a bad one. No doubt $49,000, plus options and benefits, might appear pretty good wages for about three weeks' work yearly. But if a board performs its monitoring job well, delivering the perspective and power only they can at crucial moments, the price is actually a bargain.

I am reminded of an old auto mechanic joke. Guy's car starts sputtering, so he chugs it into his local mechanic's shop. The mechanic pops open the hood and raps a strategic spot with a screwdriver handle. Instantly the engine starts purring. The mechanic then presents the owner with a bill for $50. Considering how little effort was actually required, the owner considers the price outrageous and demands that the mechanic at least itemize the bill. The mechanic promptly jots on the bottom, "Rapping the engine—$1; knowing where to rap—$49."

---

4. "Payday for America's 800 Top Chief Executives," *Forbes,* May 22, 1995, pp. 184–185.
5. *Power and Accountability,* Robert A. G. Monks and Nell Minow, Harper Business, 1991, p. 174.
6. "Corporate Governance as Strategy," John Pound, *Corporate Board,* July/ August 1994, p. 3.

Does board pay in stock really motivate? The problem here is not a lack of answers; rather, there are too many of them, and they contradict each other. Charles Elson conducted a 1992 study of *Fortune* magazine's most admired corporations and found that those with the highest reputations for results, performance, and quality management boasted boards with the highest shareholdings.[7] A study by Robert Stobaugh, leader of the NACD director pay commission, found a more direct correlation between board ownership of company stock and company performance.[8]

However, a 1996 study by Leslie Levy's Institute for Research on Boards of Directors surveyed over 300 directors of top corporations and found that the directors rated themselves and fellow board members little motivated by material rewards. Only 7% said that "the opportunity to increase cash income" was a top reason for joining a board. Even less exciting were board benefits, given as an important consideration by only 1% of directors. On the other hand, 74% cited "the opportunity to contribute and be part of a force for change" as the board motivator that swayed them, followed by "respect for the CEO" (61%) and the chance to be "part of a winning team" (38%).[9]

This may sound a bit overly noble to some observers (and it brought guffaws from many stock pay advocates). However, the directors were also asked to rank the same motivators for *other* directors, and the results were similar. It is human nature to assign ourselves high ideals, but we are not so sure about the other guy, so this tends to validate the findings. *New York Times* writer Judith Dobrzynski, a longtime supporter of board reforms, was so impressed with these findings as to ask, "Are shareholders barking up the wrong tree when they pressure companies to pay board members in stock, not cash?"[10]

Research by academic Jay Lorsch on the subject of board motivators is also enlightening and shows the quiet divisions within the governance community on the effectiveness of stock pay.

---

7. "The Duty of Care, Compensation, and Stock Ownership," Charles M. Elson, *University of Cincinnati Law Review,* 1995.
8. "Director Compensation: The Road to Better Governance," *Directorship Magazine Special Report,* 1995, p. 50.
9. Institute for Research on Boards of Directors press release, January 1996.
10. "Directors and Investors at Odds over Pay," *New York Times,* January 12, 1996.

Lorsch was a member of the NACD Stobaugh commission, which wholeheartedly endorsed the idea of paying board members in stock up to 100%. However, in a piece for the *Directorship* report on board incentives, he expressed personal ambivalence on the Stobaugh findings. "My endorsement of the commission's report . . . is qualified for several reasons. I know of no systematic evidence that stock ownership by directors will lead to more effective boards."[11]

Lorsch questions the survey conclusions of Stobaugh and others by noting that even in cases where director stock ownership correlates with higher company performance, no one can find any cause-and-effect relationship. "More than a few academics are arguing based on their hopes and beliefs, without any supporting data." Lorsch's own study of director motivation, conducted for his 1989 book *Pawns and Potentates,* found little relationship between material rewards and board service. "Our findings suggest that directors are far less motivated by financial incentives or stock ownership than by less tangible rewards." Indeed, his 1989 survey found compensation and major stock ownership as respectively the next-to-last and last cited reasons for joining a board.[12]

Who will we attract to the board? A wholesale switch to board pay in stock would be tossed into the turmoil of changing board membership that I discussed earlier. More technical expertise, heavier time requirements, greater diversity, and increased independence would have to compete with an interest in, or even willingness to, accept stock as pay and greater company holdings.

One of the concerns raised by such a change is that it might harm board recruitment efforts for minorities, women, and people from outside the executive offices. Many people in these groups have fewer resources, lower cash flow, and greater interest in immediate rewards for their commitment. Though not paupers, they might be less willing to accept their pay in the form of illiquid equity and even less able to make large personal investments in company stock. Others, however, see such cases, in Albert Dunlap's words, as an unrepresentative "red herring" that will prove

---

11. *Directorship Magazine Special Report, 1996,* Jay W. Lorsch (contrib.), pp. 3-2–3.
12. Ibid.

few and far between. Janice Hester-Amey, corporate affairs advisor for California's teacher retirement fund, brings a black and female perspective to this objection and is likewise unimpressed. Since our current pay system has as yet done little to expand minority board membership, she asks, "Why worry about the ability of stock payments to interfere with the board diversity when it scarcely exists anyway?"[13]

However, the factors that go *into* a process affect the final *outcome* of that process, and stock demands would be a definite factor in who joins boards. High-growth technology company directors would realize the greatest bonanza due to their stock's volatility (indeed, stock has long been a major factor in paying both high-tech directors and employees). Big, old-line industrials, however, would have a less tempting motivator. General Motors has shown solid results from its recent turnaround and restructuring efforts, but during 1995 its stock performance did little more than follow the rise in the market. What director would find this appealing?

If directors are truly motivated to join boards due to the stock considerations, the best and brightest candidates would likely grab for the growth opportunities in high tech. Would they not also be less willing to invest their valuable time (and money) in an ailing metal bender with a stock price they could not lift with a hoist? That is the whole point, some reply, to get them working, building value to boost the stock price. Indeed they might, but as the case of Scott Paper shows, there are both good and not so good ways to jump the stock price, depending upon one's values.

There is a final aspect of who would show up on boards if strong stockholding requirements come to pass. If we seek to turn directors into shareholders, will we eventually turn shareholders back into directors? The major institutional shareholders, particularly the public pension funds, have long been among the most active in calling for improved governance and closer director identification with shareholders. If we seek directors who own substantial chunks of equity and are in for the long haul, why try to create

---

13. *Directorship Magazine Special Report, 1996,* Janice Hester-Amey (contrib.), p. 7–5.

them from scratch? Why not just add a representative from CalPERS or the Wisconsin state pension fund?

At present, the main problem is that these bodies truly do not want to be on the board. They want to monitor the board, communicate with it, and be taken seriously as owners, but shy away from the final step of taking a seat at the table. While they have a fiduciary duty to their holders to vote their proxies, be active, and seek improved value, they would face serious clashes with director duties if they joined the board. A pension fund director could learn in advance that the next quarter's earnings will not meet analyst expectations, that a much-vaunted new drug failed its clinical trials, that talks on a hot acquisition are about to break down. The stock price will surely take a hit. Does the fund director seek to cut the fund's losses? That would transgress his or her duties of loyalty to the board—as well as blatantly violate insider trading laws. But standing pat would in turn be a breach of fiduciary duty to the pension fund.

This offers institutional investors a no-win choice between which laws to break, and they have wisely stayed outside the boardroom door. But does the push toward substantial director holdings, along with other board shifts, leave institutions as reluctant but ultimate candidates? Consider the politically correct directors shaping up for the next century: strongly independent of management yet with enough equity to take a personal interest, knowledgeable on the company, diverse, serious in their fiduciary duties—sure sounds like the institutions. We may already be seeing hints of this. Peter Lynch was eagerly sought by boards after leaving the Fidelity Magellan Fund, and in February 1996 Chrysler stymied investor Kirk Kerkorian by naming to its board noted fund manager John Neff. Neff recently retired from the Vanguard/Windsor Fund but still consults with Wellington Management. A *Wall Street Journal* piece on Neff's election debated how he would maintain a proper Chinese wall between his Chrysler inside knowledge and duties to his Wellington clients.[14]

No doubt CalPERS, TIAA-CREFF, and the others truly are loathe to leave their fingerprints on the board minutes. Nell Minow

---

14. "Neff's Chrysler Post Pins Him to the Wall," *Wall Street Journal*, February 13, 1996, p. C29.

observes that "I'm very respectful of the expertise needed to be a good money manager, and of that needed to be a good director, but they're not the same."[15] However, director stock pay and substantial holdings could be another step toward leaving no other volunteers.

---

15. Author interview, February 1996.

50

. . . and the Common Ground

Admittedly, the negative points above take some issues to the extreme. Also, most have readily available solutions. Holding and retention periods can be set and enforced to avoid short-term temptations. Stock pay can be combined with cash to give directors both liquidity and a piece of the action (proxy proposals on board stock pay usually seek just such a half-and-half approach). And more research can (and should) be done to find solid evidence of what motivators stock holding brings to the board and what if any causal effect it has on company performance. But these factors are not independent of one another. Some fixes for one objection would aggravate another. For example, any move to more firmly wed directors to a long-term interest in their stock would worsen the ball-and-chain punitive effects of their holdings. None of the objections are fatal, but all suggest that on the issue of boards and stockholdings, our agenda has outstripped our present knowledge base.

There are strong feelings and arguments on each side of the issue of paying boards in stock. However, it is an idea that lends itself to compromise. Most of the people who have raised objections to aspects of the push for board pay in stock, including Charlotte Armstrong, Leslie Levy, and Jay Lorsch, nonetheless endorse the idea in principle. Some who are dubious about director shareholding nonetheless apply something like the "Pascal's wager" of Christian belief to the idea. If it works, you will win big, and if not, hey, at least it won't hurt you.

Leslie Levy's research, which shows that material gain is a low board motivator, can be read for an inverted message—if directors are not interested in joining boards for cash income, why *not* go ahead and pay them in stock (or wampum beads, for that matter)? Also, as noted, the basic problem of convincing directors to hold more than a handful of shares is already curing itself. Most corporations already offer some form of stock compensation, average director holdings are surprisingly high, and both of these figures are on the rise.

The phenomenon of paying some fees in stock and requiring some level of director holdings is also working its way down from the largest corporations to the midcaps. Unlike most outside governance reform brainstorms, board stock ideas seem to generate little resistance from managers or boards. While boards have so far resisted (and will continue to resist) measures based on firm guidelines and absolutes, they seem willing to experiment with the form their rewards take. Perhaps, as Jay Lorsch observed, the biggest value of paying directors in stock is psychological.

I believe that, going forward, we will see board pay with a substantial stock element become the standard. Unlike other governance crusades of the past few years (such as the separate chair), board pay in stock and director equity holdings lend themselves to gradualism. In 1996, proxy resolutions on director pay, which usually serve only as preliminary warning shots to boards on a topic, typically look for no more than half of pay to be delivered in stock. Requirements that directors reach certain levels of shareholding can be eased in over a number of years. They could also be made flexible, based on the director's other sources of income, though such an attempt to be fair would itself bring some inequities.

Speaking of inequities, we will also need to watch how stock pay formulas play out. At first glance, it would seem simple; we just substitute stock valued at the same price of any cash compensation we eliminate. But most observers note that the risk, illiquidity, and long-term nature of stock justifies at least a minor premium over exact replacement value. In the world of compensation, though, minor premiums over time tend to grow into major booty. Some of the arguments used for paying directors in stock today are the same ones used 20 years ago to launch director stock option programs. They would hold cash pay down and, best of all, would compel directors to think more like shareholders. Yet over the years, the value of board pay has steadily increased—while the value of board options has soared. Research by Handy HRM finds "that many boards are devising creative strategies to encourage director stock ownership while avoiding cuts in cash."[1] The temptation of such double-dipping could offer a cynical clue as to why at least some directors are not opposed to stock pay programs. The majority of directors may indeed be disinterested in how they are rewarded. But those who like the dollar signs are pleased at the idea of a new income venue that turbocharges their current pay package.

While there remain unsolved problems in the quandary of how we will pay our directors in the future, the concept of paying in stock has none that are insoluble. Despite the punitive tone of some of their proposals, proponents seem realistic and openhanded on the matter. For example, the idea of direct performance-based board incentives, such as cash bonuses for annual results, are dismissed as too dangerous, encouraging an extremely short-term view and tempting the board to meddle in management decisions. And if advocates stress shareholder identification as first on their list of reasons for stock pay, board motivation is second. If directors grow rich by making the shareholders rich, everyone cheers at the annual meeting. Precisely how we *motivate* directors to *monitor*—offer a reward based on action for behavior that is essentially passive—I am not quite sure. But as board pay for performance becomes a twenty-first-century reality, as our knowledge of what works and does not work in board pay grows, and as tools to monitor and communicate become more certain, boards *themselves* will tell us how they are best inspired.

---

1. *Directorship Magazine Special Report, 1996,* Greg Keshishian and Paul Lydon (contrib.), p. 7–17.

51

A New Era in Suing the Board

O f course, there's one sure way to motivate our future directors—sue them. Modern corporate directors face an intimidating level of regulatory and liability constraints, and these burdens
seem to grow no matter which way the winds of deregulation are
blowing. In 1995, the Wyatt D & O Liability Survey found that the
average settlement cost of lawsuits against directors had reached a
new high, $4.6 million, *excluding* legal defense costs. This was over
$1 million higher than the previous year's figure. The cost of settling
a typical shareholder's suit (and these make up 41% of the total) has
hit $7.7 million.[1] Another 1995 survey, this one by Lou Harris &
Associates, found that 42% of Fortune 1000 company directors have
been sued in connection with their board service.[2]

But dollar figures tell only a part of the liability burden facing
directors today. The subtlety and weight of legal and regulatory
dangers have increased. Conduct and mechanisms that a few years
ago would have created a snug, safe harbor today seem increasingly
perilous. Regulatory offenses and even simple oversights that in the
1980s were almost a cost of doing business can today be a cost that
undoes the business. Board compliance procedures and strong,
watertight directors, and officers' insurance coverage are vitally important, but each time directors believe they have mounted the ultimate defense, liability lawyers discover a new ultimate weapon.
And, as with any arms race, costs grow exponentially.

---

1. "In Review," *Corporate Board*, May/June 1995, p. 26.
2. "In Review," *Corporate Board*, November/December 1995, p. 27.

The great legal precedents that defined board takeover duties in the 1980s, Trans Union, Revlon, Unocal, and Time Warner, left plenty of unexplored room for reinterpretation and liability. A series of cases in the 1990s involving the takeover of Technicolor left a patchwork of precedents involving board duties in a takeover. The Technicolor case goes back to 1983, when Ron Perelman's Mac-Andrews & Forbes Group purchased Technicolor, reselling the company five years later for a profit of $650 million. An angry group of original shareholders sued, claiming that the Technicolor board had obviously done a shabby job of gaining maximum value for the company.

A 1993 Delaware Chancery Court decision found that the board had indeed failed to use a proper process in evaluating the deal. The Revlon duties to auction the company to the highest bidder were found to have been triggered in 1983. But the court ruled that the Technicolor board had muffed the subsequent search for top shareholder value in several ways. It had failed to do a thorough search for alternative bids, several of the directors did not know about the deal until the meeting at which they approved it, and Perelman seemed to have an effective lockup before the board even voted on his bid. This shifted the burden of proof from the plaintiff to the board. The court found that when selling the company, directors "have the burden of establishing that the price offered was the highest reasonably available,"[3] which would seem to have settled the matter.

However, in wending its way through the Delaware courts, the Technicolor case gained some odd second-guessing. While not contradicting the Trans Union precedent, some of these decisions sure did muddy the waters. In 1995, the state's supreme court held that even if a board breached an aspect of the business judgment rule, this breach did not *automatically* create liability. Rather, other factors could be considered that would indicate the overall adequacy of the deal. This "entire fairness" doctrine of how the board handled its duties is less a checklist of procedures than an atmosphere of process and intent. The Delaware court decided that the Technicolor board had, in its favor, gained an increase over the initial

---

3. "Duties in Sale of the Company," R. Franklin Balotti and Joseph F. Johnston Jr., *Corporate Board,* January/February 1995, p. 6.

offer price, had shown good faith throughout the process, and had worked closely with legal counsel. Therefore, the problems with shopping the company did not add up to a fatal flaw. A breach of fiduciary duty, yes, but liability, no.

At first glance this ruling seems to turn the Trans Union precedent on its head, saying that results, not process, determine liability. Rather, though, it offers the board a bit of breathing room in handling a takeover bid. Rather than the ever-growing list of legalistic minimums that most 1980s case law encouraged, Technicolor offers a more humane approach to judging how a board handles itself in the pressure cooker of a takeover. Instead of demanding that a series of steps be present to prove the board met its duty, courts will look at the overall menu of choices the company could have made. Though a welcome message to corporations, Technicolor's drawn-out litigation offered little comfort to companies that hoped to sneak by with any dubious takeover moves. Rather, it just told boards they did not have to be perfect.

Though not perfect, boards must also stay disinterested, and failure in this brought Paramount directors to grief in a takeover war between Viacom and QVC. In September 1993, the Paramount board approved a $69 per share merger bid from Sumner Redstone's Viacom. Redstone would gain majority control of the company, but he had driven a hard bargain with the Paramount board to keep competing bids away. There was a "no-shop" clause that limited Paramount to doing no more than the legal minimum to entertain other suitors. If Paramount should have any second thoughts on the marriage, it would have to pay Viacom a $100 million consolation fee to break the agreement. This breakup would also trigger an option allowing Viacom to purchase 19.9% of Paramount stock at its original offer price, which could be paid for with a senior subordinated note.

Such conditions should have ended the matter right there, but QVC media company immediately launched a counteroffer for Paramount, upping the price to $80 per share. Viacom matched the offer with a bid for 51% of Paramount stock, and a bidding war was on. The Paramount board favored its original match with Viacom, however. It refused to bargain with QVC and in November voted to formally pursue the Viacom deal. QVC sued in Delaware Chancery Court, claiming that the termination fees and option deals gave an unfair edge to Viacom. The court agreed and ordered the Paramount board to hold off on the wedding with Sumner Redstone. In December the state supreme court backed this decision and delivered an unusually harsh criticism of the Paramount board, stating that it was doing a very poor job of seeking shareholder value. If Viacom gained majority control, shareholders would lose their last chance to seek top dollar. Either a change in control or a breakup of Paramount was a foregone conclusion, said the court, so the Revlon duties to get the best deal for investors had kicked in. It also threw out the termination fee, as well as the options and no-shop agreements.

With little choice in the matter, Paramount opened a formal bidding process. After several weeks of rough-and-tumble, Viacom finally emerged the victor with a bid of $107 per share. Although the harsh judicial spanking the Paramount board received drew most of the attention, the main effect of Paramount was to push the Revlon duty to auction a bit further into deal making. At first it had seemed limited to sale or breakup of the company. But now it appeared that effective change in control to an acquiring entity was trigger enough to demand bidding.

So if Technicolor slackened the rope a bit on one side, Paramount took some of it back on the other. The effect of such decisions has been to make boards more circumspect about takeover activity. They are making sure to dot their i's and, more importantly, to do deals that offer strong strategic value all around. A change in the atmosphere of takeovers has also helped lessen legal battles. The 1980s milieu of raiders, plunder, and leverage offered rich hunting for plaintiff lawyers. A no-holds-barred mind-set among raiders led to a no-holds-barred approach by litigants.

But in the 1990s, if a deal benefits everyone, offers a strong strategic fit (and is seen as such by analysts), and will improve productivity and earnings per share, legal challenges are less likely. The strong stock market of the mid-1990s is leading to a boom in such "safe sex" mergers. In 1995, a record $458 billion in M & A deals was set, with such headliners as Disney buying Capital Cities/ABC, Chemical Banking buying Chase, and Time Warner acquiring Turner Broadcasting. Most of these deals went off quickly and smoothly. They tend to be stock based, making them less costly (fewer banker and consultant fees) and less burdened with debt. Of

279 corporate mergers between 1994 and 1995, 128 were straight stock-for-stock deals and 57 combined stock with cash.[4] Stock swaps have great tax advantages as well. Legal challenges of today are more likely to be based on minor, technical issues, drawing less attention, smaller damages, and thus less interest from the plaintiffs' bar.

---

4. "Deals Using Acquirer's Shares Surge," monograph for clients, Stephen I. Glover, January 1996.

52

The Board Liability Christmas Gift

The biggest director liability issue for the rest of this century will be working out the impact of the Securities Litigation Reform Act of 1995. It is not often that technical, procedural legislation dealing with such a wildly unsexy topic as securities law draws such headlines, or such high drama in Washington. Debate on the legislation was sharp and tended toward the extreme, with supporters seeking to curb the greed of predatory strike suit lawyers and opponents fighting an open season for corporate lying. The bill was passed by the United States House and Senate in early December 1995. Though he had earlier remained neutral on the bill, President Bill Clinton, after some wavering, announced his opposition and vetoed it. However, the law had strong bipartisan support (including sponsorship by Democratic Rep. Christopher Dodd, who was miffed at the president for his opposition). The veto was overridden by a narrow majority in the Senate, was overridden by a large majority in the House, and became law on December 22, President Clinton's first veto override. "Congress Sends Business a Christmas Gift," headlined the *Wall Street Journal*.[1]

But what sort of a gift is it? The law was designed to cure a number of perceived flaws in our private litigation system for securities. While private securities law is designed to encourage corporate honesty and disclosure, a number of abuses by plaintiffs seemed to be not only hobbling this disclosure, but forcing corporations to settle suits with little merit. Whenever a corporation

---

1. "Congress Sends Business a Christmas Gift," *Wall Street Journal*, December 26, 1995, p. A2.

had a drop in stock price, no matter the cause, lawyers would rush to sign up shareholders and file suit, alleging fraud by the company. Some suits, in the names of "professional plaintiffs," would feature almost identical filings from case to case (and in one infamous suit, the attorneys so rushed their word-search duties that some names *were* the same). Though a final verdict against the company might be unlikely, corporate boards facing prolonged, expensive litigation would often settle, essentially extorted into giving the plaintiff money to go away.

Boards of directors are personally in the crosshairs of such filings. Although they have rarely been liable for personal damages, they face high anxiety, great potential liability, time and effort in discovery and depositions, and tainted reputations. Estimates vary on how strongly liability influences decisions to join a board. But even if liability is not a large factor, it could well be *the* factor that tips a potentially excellent candidate, who could greatly benefit the company and its shareholders, toward a "no" decision. Certainly in some industries, such as chemicals and technology, it is an even bigger risk factor. The directors of high-tech corporations on the West Coast tell me that they view getting sued by a shareholder as a matter of *when*, not *if*.

The securities suit reform act was designed to change this, and radically. Attorney Harvey Pitt calls the reforms "the most comprehensive revision of private litigation under the federal securities laws since the New Deal."[2] The reforms offer corporations real relief from some of the most egregious abuses under securities law but will also demand new oversight by boards and serious changes in how they do business.

Just listing the major provisions of the law suggests its eye-popping impact on director liability. First, it sets tougher pleading requirements for securities lawsuits against public corporations; a drop in stock price is no longer enough. Second, policies have changed on how a "lead defendant" is appointed when (as is usually the case) multiple defendants are involved. There are now limits on attorney's fees. The "joint and several" liability faced by uninvolved corporate directors is largely abolished. Burdensome discovery stan-

---

2. "Promises Made, Promises Kept," monograph for clients, Harvey Pitt and Karl Groskaufmanis, December 27, 1995.

dards have been tightened. And there are now far more clearly defined safe harbors for projections.

Perhaps the most substantial of the new reforms kicks in at the very beginning of the process, the appointment of who serves as lead plaintiff. One of the most repellent aspects of strike suits has been the "race to the courthouse" to see which plaintiff's attorney can be first to file. This has given the winner power and priority in negotiating a settlement for all members of the class action. But it has also triggered a feeding frenzy in which professional plaintiffs, who might own a company's stock solely for this purpose, team up with hard-driving counsel to file the instant a stock price slips, with no time to evaluate the real cause of the price change. The old system rewarded haste over legal merit.

The new rules relieve the land rush aspect by requiring the first plaintiff who files to widely circulate a notice to all other potential members of the class identifying the claims involved and notifying them of his or her attempt to represent the class. Within 90 days, the judge in the case will select "the most adequate plaintiff," based on who in the class has the greatest financial interest at stake. This will in most cases give big institutional investors a strong say in whether and how the case proceeds (and is also another reason why boards and managers should make nice to those investors). This plaintiff will then be responsible for selecting counsel (no matter who originally filed the case), further weakening the clout of professional plaintiffs and their professional plaintiff attorneys.

Speaking of professionals, lead plaintiffs must file, along with their complaints, certification that they did not buy their securities at the direction of counsel, or as an attempt to "buy in" to the suit, and are receiving no added fees for serving as lead plaintiffs. In one of the law's more controversial aspects, people are prohibited from being plaintiffs in more than five such class actions in the previous three-year period. While this can limit access to the courts, it should not apply unless someone is a professional at the strike suit business or else was born under a very unlucky financial star.

The law also offers reforms in the actual filing of a securities suit against the company and its directors. A problem faced with most attempts to clean up strike suit abuse has been that a plaintiff need not actually win the case to come out a financial winner. The costs, burdens, and aggravation of defending a securities suit against a tough, professional litigator—even if the case is meritless, even if the defendant can win in the end—are such that almost everyone settles. A drop in the stock price was enough to launch a suit with vague allegations of "fraud." This warning shot was often adequate to coerce a settlement. If not, the threat of a massive discovery process to fish out a reason for suing would usually bring a surrender. The company or its insurer paid, the the plaintiff counsel took a generous cut, and the lawyers went home happy because they were the only clear winners.

The reform hits such strike suit piracy at the very beginning by demanding "particularity" from the plaintiff's plea. Every company statement that is supposed to be misleading must be specified, along with why it is deceptive—and why such a fib or omission makes any difference. Defendants can move to have any suit that lacks these specifics thrown out. While this move for dismissal is under review, the discovery process is put on hold, crippling the previous temptation to sue first, subpoena everything in the defendant's files, and then sift through until some justification is found.

The reform law gives boards and executives a new safe harbor provision for forward-looking projections. This provision prompted much argument and name-calling during debate on the bill, with opponents condemning it as a loophole big enough to drive a double-bottom lie through and proponents concerned that the provision was too weak to be of real value. Regardless, the law now shields companies from private liability for projections and disclosures, at least as long as a few crucial asterisks are included. Shielded statements can now be oral as well as written and can include management plans and objectives, as well as projections of future performance. However, they must be clearly identified as projections, not facts, and be accompanied with language that "bespeaks caution," in the phrasing of a precedent-setting 1977 Eighth Circuit Court decision.[3]

This suspiciously vague concept has actually been pinned down a bit over the years. As Harvey Pitt notes in a monograph on the reform law, a statement that bespeaks caution

- is tailored to the specific statement and context (i.e., vague boilerplate will not do);

---

3. *Polin v. Conductron Corp.*, 552 F. 2d 797, 806 n.28 (8th Cir. 1977).

- conveys the general magnitude of the risk (is it minor or major?);
- is prominent, is reasonably close to the projection itself, and is easily understood; and
- includes any underlying statements of the risk involved.[4]

As noted, oral communications are also allowed to dock in this safe harbor. The law recognizes that cautions here will not be as specific and thorough as the written ones, but if detailed written information exists on the disclosure, it can be referenced. Of course, the new law requires that any projections be made honestly and without conscious attempts to mislead. It puts a burden on plaintiffs to prove scienter here.

As a final benefit of the reform law, there are a number of damage limits both on who pays and on who receives. As a last disincentive in the rush to be lead plaintiff, this plaintiff's share of the judgment or settlement must be allotted on a proportional basis with everyone else in the class. No more lion's share for pushing your way to the head of the line. Attorney's fees awarded to plaintiff counsel also will face a judge-set "reasonability" cap.

On the supply side, the law enacts a "fair share" rule that ends the all-or-nothing aspects of the former joint and several liability concept. In most cases, joint and several liability is eliminated for innocent outsiders, specifically directors. Should directors be found liable but not a knowing party to the tort, they are, in most cases, responsible only for their proportionate share of damages.

---

4. "Promises Made, Promises Kept," monograph for clients, Harvey Pitt and Karl Groskaufmanis, December 27, 1995.

53

Tort Reform Meets the Audit Sleuths
(and Other Problems)

The new tort reform law sounds like a good deal, and it is, all in all. However, the new law has its share of downside aspects. Oddly, most of these recognize the growing role and authority of the board of directors in a particularly backhanded way—by making the board more responsible.

Foremost of the new law's tougher elements is a major change in the audit regimen. The role of auditors in detecting and reporting financial fraud has been debated for years in legislatures and accounting rule-making bodies. The new law comes down strongly on the side of whistle-blowing and mandates it for auditors as a sort of trade-off for the fair share provision. Major audit groups and the big accounting firms have long lobbied for such relief from the joint and several liability provisions of financial fraud. Many firms have been badly hit with damages for claims that they either ignored or even acquiesced in company swindles.

The reforms give auditors some "hand-washing" protection from client misdeeds—at a price. The corporation's outside auditors must now develop and include in their audits procedures to sniff out illegal corporate acts that would have a material effect on financial statements. There is no firm standard of proof; the law says only that the client *may* have committed an illegal act, and this transcends accounting matters to include "an act or omission that violates any law, or any rule or regulation having the force of law."[1]

---

1. Securities Exchange Act §10A (1995).

Auditors are even expected to evaluate whether the company is in danger of going under. The corporation's outside auditor will now become the government's cop on the beat, paid for by the company.

The implications and practicality of auditors having to play detective will require much working out over the next few years. Detecting illegal acts outside their expertise might prove far-ranging combat duty for a financial auditor (though some accountant with a literary flair will no doubt do for auditor crime fiction what Scott Turow and John Grisham have done for lawyers).

If the auditor should uncover suspected illegal activity, he or she is required to first inform top management of the corporation. If not convinced that remedial action has been taken, the auditor must then inform the audit committee of the board, and then the full board of directors. The corporation must inform the SEC of its little discovery within one business day. If the company's board fails to report, the auditor is to resign the job and make its own report of findings to the SEC within the next business day.

The long-term implications of this policy have been little discussed so far, but could have devastating implications if not monitored by the board. The ultimate act of this process, auditor notification to the SEC that something smells bad at the company, would be a major legal and investor relations disaster for the firm. Such a danger signal should be avoided at all costs. As the first line of notification, management must take steps to build communications with the auditor, designate an executive contact person, and lay out steps for managing a claim once it is made. As with so many other legal flash points, procedure will count for as much as the final results, so each step of the notification must be carefully documented and handled with the utmost seriousness.

Although management is the first line in dealing with audit fraud allegations, the new law places ultimate responsibility on the board of directors, and specifically the audit committee. "The Act imposes a heavy burden on audit committees," observes Attorney Harvey Pitt.[2] Pitt advises that the board enact a strong compliance program going in to assure that the auditor has no bloody gloves to find, and that "the audit committee reviews the operation of the compliance program on an annual basis to ensure that all potential

---

2. "More than Classical GAAS," monograph for clients, Harvey Pitt and Karl Groskaufmanis, February 5, 1996.

violations have been addressed."[3] An audit compliance program requires two major components.

First, the committee should review its charter to make sure that it is up to the new demands. As I mentioned earlier, a strong, comprehensive audit committee charter is vital anyway. The new auditor notification rules show how important this charter is and also the need to keep it regularly updated. The committee must develop (and show) a structure for working with management to detect, investigate, and deal with illegal acts in the company. The committee must not only assure that management and auditors have the tools in place to discover mischief, but must have its own board mechanisms. The current audit committee charter should already lay out powers to launch investigations, hire outside support, and talk to whomever it deems appropriate, but the new auditor law makes this authority even more crucial. As part of the charter, or as a codicil, the audit committee should spell out its procedures for handling allegations of hanky-panky—and then make sure that they are followed to the letter.

Second, the legal changes put a premium on the audit committee building contacts both inside and outside the company. The new law requires major judgments on the importance of illegalities and reporting to the SEC within a 24-hour time frame. This leaves no time for tracking people down, catching up on events, and working out a fire drill. The audit committee needs to build ongoing, personal dialogue with both management and the outside audit firm. This will help them gain a "heads up" on any potential problems. It also builds the informal relationship that makes raising such unpleasant matters easier, and will save time when (and if) the alarm is sounded.

Of these two dialogues, that between audit committee and outside auditor will take on the greatest legal importance. The audit provisions of the lawsuit reform law are at once so sweeping and yet ill-defined that endless misunderstandings are possible. For instance, the new law offers an exception to the auditor's reporting requirements, excluding matters that are "clearly inconsequential." How "clear" this is might have been obvious to those who drafted the law but is dangerously vague to those who must operate under it.

---

3. "Promises Made, Promises Kept," monograph for clients, Harvey Pitt and Karl Groskaufmanis, December 27, 1995.

And the price of misunderstandings is high. Auditors, not eager to run afoul of the law, will be tempted to throw in every speeding ticket unless they can come to an early consensus with the committee on what matters and what does not. Before the annual audit begins, the committee and the outside auditors should discuss what sort of legal transgressions will and will not be consequential. Not only will this limit surprises at audit time, but decisions made in advance will gain more legal respect than those made on a hasty ad hoc basis.

Along with the truth-or-consequences dialogue, the committee and the auditors will need to agree on how ground rules for the audit itself will change. By turning accountants into detectives, the law compels them to poke into many new areas, including some that may take the company by surprise. Company hot lines, confidential reporting mechanisms, and internal complaints may or may not be of interest to the auditors. Internal legal and financial reports or opinions might also seem relevant, and auditors could seek personal access to key people from these areas.

The audit committee is a good negotiator for such delicate disclosures. Some of the work products or records sought could bring out confidential matters far beyond the traditional auditor purview and would expose material the company reasonably wants to keep under wraps. There are even concerns that attorney/client privilege could be lost. Stonewalling the auditors on such material might lead them to report that the company cannot prove a good internal mechanism for spotting violations. At the least, the auditor could claim they were unable to conduct a proper audit.

There are other questions that an audit committee will need to broker between management and the audit firm. What happens if the auditor stumbles upon an illegality outside the scope of the audit? What is the reporting chain for any problems discovered? Can the auditors contract with their own outside sources for investigation and counsel? What are the disclosure and confidentiality obligations of these secondhand resources? Does the corporation have a firm policy of getting back to the auditor on any concerns (so the auditor does not go notifying the SEC about a problem that is already solved)? The board's audit committee, already facing great new pressures, has gained yet another pivotal role under the new securities suit reforms.

There are further land mines hidden in the reform law. For

instance, the new safe harbor for projections and disclosure is less safe than it first appears. A problem with such sweeping, omnibus packages as the new law is that they offer many new opportunities for the courts to sort out the precise meaning of their often obscure provisions. The reform law is unusually general in many of its terms, and how the "safe harbor" for written projections will shake out must likely be settled by case law. For example, we can assume that the company need not reveal *everything* about itself in its forward-looking statements. But what happens when the only nuggets it chooses to reveal are positive ones, while ignoring the negative? Does such duplicity deserve a safe harbor?

Also, with managers and particularly directors now more free to give spoken projections, exactly how they parse their cautions will receive a close hearing. Precisely what constitutes a proper caution in a conference call to analysts or discussion with a reporter is still being worked out in the courts. Few corporations want to be named in legal citations that show what *does not* constitute "bespeaking caution." Plus, the new law makes clear that corporations have no duty to update old or inaccurate projections, but phrases it in such a way that you wonder if it might not be a good idea anyway. There are also a number of exceptions to the safe harbor provision, including forward-looking comments on IPOs, tender offers, attempts to take the company private, and financial statements. And the safe harbor is out of bounds for companies that, in the previous three years, were guilty of certain crimes and misdemeanors, such as federal antifraud provisions. Although the new law would appear to give companies new safety in talking up the company, it is likely that plaintiff attorneys will busy themselves for some years trying to find breaches in the safe harbor provisions. Do not expect investor relations staff, executives, or directors to become blabby anytime soon.

The discovery process reforms also have a few bugs. While discovery of evidence can be delayed by defendant companies, the firm now bears a new duty to preserve *all* documents and data that might prove to be evidence. In short, the plaintiff may not be able to discover it yet, but that does not mean the defendant is free to get rid of it. Document retention schedules and procedures need review to assure that something required as evidence next year is not shredded this year.

As a final negative on the new shareholder liability law, the gauntlet of challenges a case must face before being filed will show the truth of Nietzsche's adage, "That which doesn't kill me makes me stronger." Strike suits that survive the process and are ultimately filed will be much more estimable and well designed than those of the past few years. This strengthening process should bring a final dose of realism for any corporate directors who believe that the reforms will completely cure the wasting illness of rampant shareholder litigation.

There is no doubt the new laws will bring justice and balance to a process too long based on bad ethics and blackmail. However, the strike suit industry has built too much of a strong, well-funded infrastructure to go away quietly. There will be continued legal challenges, attempts to sue in state courts, and an ongoing search for loopholes. Boards have gained some powerful tools for fending off unmerited liability suits, but the problem is unlikely ever to disappear.

54

The SEC and Boards: "How *Not* to Avoid Indictment"

The securities suit reform law shows one of the ways the federal government, particularly the SEC, is inserting itself more deeply into the governance process. In the new law, the commission does this by using outside auditors as a proxy enforcement mechanism. However, the SEC is also taking a more direct approach. It has made it clear that it will demand more accountability and oversight by boards in the future and fired a recent warning shot on the issue in case its intent was not obvious.

The strike suits and takeover liabilities mentioned above often pivoted on minor technical points. Reform advocates could cite them as proof that plaintiff lawyers were running amok and that the courts and SEC were willing to let them. Businesspeople, even given their personal interests in the matter, usually give other businesspeople the benefit of a doubt, if not their outright sympathy. But a recent, heavily cited case had none of these gray areas. In the matter of Cooper Companies, the corporation's—and the board's—behavior was so bad as to be indefensible. And the SEC made clear that it held the Cooper board responsible for the disaster that resulted.

At the start of the 1990s, Cooper Companies was a major manufacturer and marketer of contact lenses, incorporated in Delaware with headquarters in New Jersey. In the 1980s two major shareholding families named Singer and Sturman gained control of the company and named two representatives, Gary Singer and Bruce Sturman, as cochairmen of the seven-member board. A restructuring and sale of company assets left Cooper with up to $100 million in liquid capital to be invested, a responsibility handled by Cochairman Gary Singer. But Singer, along with some family members and several friends at two mutual funds, set up a "front-running" scheme for the early purchase of high-yield bonds that the funds planned to recommend to their major clients. The front-running operation netted the Singer family approximately $3 million in ill-gotten gains. Singer also fraudulently traded these bonds back and forth between accounts in his name, that of his wife, and the Cooper company itself, draining $560,000 in profits from the firm into family coffers. Apparently to prove his continued interest in the welfare of the company, Singer also illegally manipulated the price of some company debt instruments to avoid an interest rate reset obligation.

The monkey business at Cooper Companies came to the attention of the SEC in early 1992, apparently because Cochairman Bruce Sturman informed. In January, the SEC launched a formal criminal investigation of Cooper, Gary Singer, the Singer family, and the two funds. In March, the United States Attorney's office for the Southern District of New York also began investigating.

Suddenly, the board of Cooper Companies faced allegations of massive criminal fraud extending to the very top of the corporation. How did it respond? First, it suspended and then fired Sturman, apparently for disloyalty. It also expressed its continued confidence in Gary Singer. This was not only a matter of business principle, but family pride. Of seven board members, four were in the Singer family. In February, under questioning by the SEC staff, both Gary Singer and his brother Steven (also a Cooper director) invoked the Fifth Amendment. Four days later, the Cooper board, seemingly unconcerned, named Steven Singer to the position of chief operating officer.

In March 1992 the board, after a briefing on the various federal probes, voted to name an independent counsel to conduct an internal investigation, but this counsel was soon stymied when the Singer brothers refused to cooperate. However, the counsel did uncover a few nuggets, such as the outlines of the bond front-running scheme. This information was reported to the board—which did nothing. In May, the SEC filed criminal charges against the contacts at the two funds, one of whom swiftly implicated Gary Singer in the scheme. The indictments also prompted a number of shareholder suits against Gary Singer and other members of the board.

With legal and media queries flying about them, the Cooper board put the best face on things by issuing a press release firmly stating that "The Company denies any wrongdoing and is unaware of any wrongdoing on the part of its officers or employees."[1] This press release was apparently written by Steven Singer, with the knowledge of Gary Singer, who a few months earlier took the Fifth Amendment on these same charges. Both were members of the board, which had been recently told by its independent counsel extensive details on Gary Singer's bond hijinks and how much they had cost the company. Yet the company remained "unaware."

The pressures that had prompted the press release continued to build, and on May 28, Gary Singer agreed to take a temporary leave of absence from Cooper. Singer continued to receive pay and benefits however. Also, though the announcement of his leave indicated he would immediately relocate his office away from Cooper headquarters, five months later he was still there several times weekly. And Singer remained as a board member.

In late July 1992, the SEC informed Cooper that it would bring charges against the company and against Gary and Steven Singer for the bond scam, violation of various securities laws, and for the "false and misleading" press release feigning ignorance. The Cooper board responded by keeping Gary Singer on leave and cutting his salary, though continuing his benefits. These included insurance, support services, and a car, a package worth about $80,000 per year. However, at the same board meeting, Gary and Steven Singer finally resigned their board seats, though Steven Singer continued as executive vice president and chief operating officer. New directors were added to the board at this time—Singer family neighbors and allies, Steven Singer's father-in-law, and an attorney representing the family.

On November 10, 1992, the SEC filed its charges against Cooper and the Singer brothers. At this time, the supposedly exiled Gary Singer was still in the company headquarters regularly, taking care of business and even calling securities brokers about Cooper accounts. And though the board on November 16 formed a management committee to serve the CEO function, it chartered itself

---

1. Cooper Companies press release, May 21, 1992.

to work through the COO—Steven Singer. In the months leading up to trial, the position of Cooper's board became more untenable, but there remained a strong Singer family influence right up to January 1994, when Gary Singer was found guilty on 21 counts and the Cooper company itself guilty of seven counts of fraud. Indeed, Gary Singer's benefit package continued until his formal resignation from the company—a week after the conviction. Various fines, restitution, and disgorgements cost the company over $3 million. At Gary Singer's sentencing in 1995, Federal Judge Robert Ward found Singer's crimes so blatant that he rejected a plea for home detention and sentenced him to 28 months in prison.

The Cooper Companies case is one of those incidents that drop into our midst every so often to keep us from growing smug about how advanced and independent corporate boards have become. The actions of the company's board were so egregious, brazen, and destructive of company and shareholder interests that a law review article on the case summed up their actions as "How *Not* to Avoid Indictment."[2] The SEC, aside from its investigation and prosecution of the case, was so disturbed by the specific failings of Cooper's board that in December of 1994 it took the unusual step of issuing a public report on its findings. The SEC report was a strongly negative critique of the Cooper board's performance.

This was a rare SEC essay into the internal relationship between a board and management, usually a matter of state incorporation law. Rather than attaching responsibility solely to individuals, or the larger corporate entity, the SEC report sought to show how the board as a fiduciary failed in its oversight duty—and to hint that it was starting to actively monitor how boards behave. "The Commission is issuing this report to emphasize that corporate directors have a significant responsibility and play a critical role in safeguarding the integrity of the company"[3] The commission found several aspects of the Cooper case particularly outrageous:

The company board either did not notice or ignored the problem for ages. The SEC traced Gary Singer's bond mischief as far back as

---

2. "The Saga of Cooper Companies," Richard Thornburgh and Roger Adelman, *SEC Enforcement & Litigation Update,* spring 1994, p. 1.
3. *Report of Investigation in the Matter of the Cooper Companies, Inc. as It Relates to the Conduct of Cooper's Board of Directors* (after, *SEC/Cooper*), Securities and Exchange Commission, December 12, 1994.

1988. This meant that by the time the commission launched its query in early 1992, some high-level chicanery had been under way for almost four years. If the board was truly in the dark, should it not at least have had some suspicions?

The internal investigation was a lax dead end.   Although the Cooper board named an independent counsel to investigate the allegations, the Singer brothers informed the counsel that they would not give interviews or information on the matter. Thus, a cochairman and COO of the company, implicated in serious felonies, told their board that they would not cooperate with the board's own investigation. The directors took no action on such dangerous defiance and essentially bypassed the issue. Although the independent counsel did uncover some damning information, several months later he informed the board that the investigation could not "progress further" without testimony from the Singers. The directors chose not to force the matter.

Nothing was done to "quarantine" the accused.   The idea of treating suspects as guilty until proven innocent is no doubt repugnant to most of our Western notions of justice. But, in matters of corporate governance, don't directors face an even higher standard of appearance and investor confidence? The Cooper board confronted allegations that their cochairman was committing felonies involving company assets, knew that he was pleading the Fifth Amendment to federal investigators, and knew that his brother the COO was also heavily implicated. Yet for months they did nothing more than keep Gary Singer on a leave of absence, and a paid leave at that. He was in the office regularly, was conducting company business there (including securities business), and continued to serve on the board. Steven Singer was not even suspended, but continued to operate the day-to-day operations of the company he was accused of bilking.

Why were the brothers not removed from company operations? Why were they not kept from company headquarters? Why did they continue as board members, still attending meetings? And why, after Gary Singer finally eased away from his executive post (at least in title), did the board transfer authority to Steven Singer, who was himself under the same cloud?

The company lied in its public relations.   This might seem a minor point to some of us, but the SEC found Cooper's May 21, 1992, press release that denied any knowledge of wrongdoing to be particularly galling. The commission saw this "false and misleading press statement" as a distinct offense beyond the bond and financial shenanigans. It was also a violation of Section 10(b) of the Exchange Act, sending misleading public information to investors. To tell the public that the company denies any wrongdoing and has no knowledge of wrongdoing by anyone in the company is not just a matter of putting on a brave face. When the people who issue the press release are facing federal charges, stonewalling, and keeping vital information from the board, it is downright dishonest. Cooper Companies would be placed in danger of bankruptcy when the full scope of the Singers' activity became known. This is something investors might like to know about, but they would learn nothing of it from the company's statements.

The board itself was part of the problem.   Up until July 1992, the Singer brothers stayed on the board as part of the family majority (indeed, a third brother, Brad, was also a member up to that time). After they left (they neither resigned nor were expelled, but chose not to stand for reelection), the board was repacked with family members, friends, and neighbors. Indeed, to fault such a board for failing to act against the Singer brothers almost seems naive. How *could* such a board show any semblance of objectivity and responsibility to shareholders when it was a corporate family reunion?

"Cooper's board failed to satisfy its obligations when confronted with serious indications of management fraud," concluded the SEC report. The board seemed to "prefer management's interest in keeping the facts secret over the investors' interest in full, fair and accurate disclosure."[4] The board had made the disastrous mistake of casting its lot with one of its managers rather than its shareholders. Unlike some corporate crime, such as pollution or foreign bribery violations, the board could not even hide behind the dubious fig leaf of breaking the law for short-term company profit. The Singers were stealing from the company and its shareholders, yet the board did nothing. Well, almost nothing. One of its first acts when the allegations broke was to suspend Cochairman Bruce Stur-

---

4. *SEC/Cooper,* Securities and Exchange Commission, December 12, 1994, p. 7.

man as the suspected squealer. Though not mentioned in the SEC report, this move alerted the commission that something was rotten in the state of New Jersey and helped start their investigation on the wrong foot for Cooper.

The SEC and the federal courts threw the book at Cooper and Gary Singer, at least in part because of its somnolent board. Much of the tone of the SEC report suggests federal irritation at the many ways and opportunities the Cooper directors had to cooperate and lighten the consequences, but did not. Otto Obermaier, U.S. Attorney for the Southern District of New York, complained that up until the time of the indictments, the board had "done little, if anything, to rectify" the situation.[5] Federal sentencing guidelines make a great deal out of the value of corporate compliance programs and cooperation, but the Cooper board snubbed each of these opportunities. At worst the Cooper board was an active participant in the misdeed; at best it took a "don't ask, don't tell" attitude that almost ruined the company.

---

5. "The Saga," Thornburgh and Adelman, p. 2.

55

Why the Commission Now Thinks Your Board Matters

The SEC report served its purpose of making an example of Cooper Companies, and has drawn wide attention from governance thinkers and corporate counsels. But the SEC does not make an example of someone, especially such a stark, unrepresentative case as Cooper, without the intent of sending a message to everyone else. Securities fraud and market manipulation are traditional concerns of the SEC, but for the commission to insert itself into how effectively a corporation is governed is quite new. Most law on the role and responsibilities of a board of directors is state based. With its Cooper comments, the SEC seems to be staking a new federal claim in the boardroom.

Increased enforcement powers given the SEC in the late 1980s and early 1990s have broadened the scope of its powers. The commission is now able to pursue activities and corporate entities that help "cause" violations, rather than just those directly committing the violations. Did the Cooper board cause the company's violations by being (and choosing to stay) asleep at the switch? Did it help cause the illicit press release that put a smiley face on the affair? Without running the risk of an actual indictment in this uncertain territory, the SEC has notified the corporate world that it now takes an interest in how effectively boards do their job—and that it has the authority to act when they fail.

In the 1990s, the SEC has set out further signal flags on federal involvement in governance that will bring implications for the next decade. The 1992 Caterpillar case, though far less dramatic, showed that the SEC now assumes that boards play a central role in corporate decision making. In early 1990, the Caterpillar company's top management was concerned over economic instability in Brazil that could affect company profits. Although Brazil was a fairly minor part of total Caterpillar operations, hyperinflation in the country, combined with exchange rate oddities, made Brazilian subsidiary operations unusually profitable. Though accounting for only 5% of Caterpillar revenues in 1989, Brazil contributed 23% to total corporate net profits.

So in early 1990, with an imminent change in the Brazilian government (and, most likely, economic policies), Caterpillar management grew concerned. It developed a separate analysis of company operations in Brazil (a departure from usual procedures, which consolidated all operations) and briefed the board in February 1990 on its findings. The board and management discussed the potential effects of change in Brazil and the serious hit this change could bring to Caterpillar profitability. Sure enough, in April, major economic reforms in Brazil sharply cut inflation, and in a board meeting that month management predicted that 1990 profits would fall as a result. Not until June, however, did Caterpillar go public with its predictions of substantially lower profits due to the change in Brazil. Company stock promptly fell by ten points in one day.

During early 1990, Caterpillar had made its usual 10K and 10Q filings. The Management Discussion and Analysis sections of these reports said nothing about the company's exposure in Brazil, its potential effect on profits, or the fact that the matter had been a subject of boardroom discussion. This oversight drew the interest of the SEC, which in March 1992 issued a cease and desist order that essentially told the company to improve its MD&A procedures and not to do it again. Just what "it" was is unclear, but with time we have seen how the commission's interest in the Caterpillar MD&A affects the board. The SEC's follow-up comments fault Caterpillar management, legal counsel, controller, treasurer, and finance staff for signing off on the MD&As without mentioning the Brazil exposures, a conclusion that seems hard to argue with. But to the commission, the most compelling proof that the neglected information was in fact vital was its regular discussion among the Caterpillar corporate board. The board was briefed, subsequently discussed the matter, and asked to be kept informed. Therefore, the subject was important—important enough to tell investors.

56

The Director as Inside Trader

Although regulatory actions on boards send the message of more
toughness and responsibility, the federal courts have given hints
that they may take a less expansive view of director duties in the
future. In April 1994, the United States Supreme Court set the
pattern by decreeing that shareholders could not hold directors liable on an ill-defined charge of "aiding and abetting" an alleged
securities fraud. In the *Central Bank of Denver v. First Interstate
Bank* case, the court faced a situation common in shareholder securities suits. The corporate directors (in this case for a bank) were
included in a shareholder suit because they "aided and abetted" an
alleged securities fraud perpetrated by the company.

Sounds terrible, but many of these actions have been the sort
the new securities suit reform was designed to cure, and directors
were included solely to cast the liability net as widely as possible.
Directors have at times "aided and abetted" alleged fraud by being
present at the board meeting where a financial statement was discussed, because company sales results were a board agenda topic,
and because they approved a positive earnings projection (which
later was not met). In these cases the company's stock price subsequently fell or a management fraud was uncovered, suits were immediately filed, and the board members were included because . . .
well, because they were the board. For some 30 years, federal courts
have allowed plaintiffs to cast their securities net over the board
because they were presumed to have made the fraud possible just
by being in the room.

The Central Bank case narrowly overturned this presumption,
and at the highest judicial level in the land. Directors usually play

only a peripheral role in the company's securities transactions, and the Supreme Court acknowledged this. Even if dishonesty lurked somewhere in the company regarding securities, the board was guilty only of bumbling oversight, not active conspiracy, and active conspiracy is where fraud becomes a federal case. The implications of this decision are only now becoming apparent, as many years of precedent at all federal courts must be rethought.

Many of the legal and regulatory traps that face directors today remain uncommon and theoretical. Cases as outrageous as the Cooper Companies are rare, and although I may be an optimist, stock or accounting fraud among directors and top executives are the exception rather than the rule. But what of insider stock trading? The very words cause business readers to recoil, stirring images of tippees, disgorgements, and suitcases full of illicit cash. Yet insider trading, defined for our purposes as buying and selling of stock by those who are also involved in corporate governance, is as common as changes in the weather, and usually as benign. Millions of shares of public corporations are traded daily by executives and directors of those corporations. As the idea of paying directors in stock and requiring them to be major holders of their corporations heats up, the mass of company shares involved, and the frequency of inside trades, will grow even larger.

The rules and theory of corporate insiders trading in their own stock bring many difficulties. As noted, insiders accumulate substantial holdings and buy and sell them regularly. They also know all sorts of nonpublic information about a company as a matter of course. That is their job. There is nothing legally wrong with this in the vast majority of cases. And in the vast majority of the cases where there is a legal problem, it is a minor reporting matter, failure to file within the proper time window after a legal trade or such (although the penalties for these paperwork gremlins have grown harsher of late). But then there are the cases that make the SEC Federal Securities Law Reports and the *Wall Street Journal*, with insiders and directors making illicit profits by trading on their inside knowledge of upcoming takeovers, losses, acquisitions, and corporate shifts. They take "material, nonpublic information" as the SEC phrases it, use it in their trading decisions, and often spread the information around to cronies. Shame on them.

To the layperson coming across this matter from the outside, this raises a puzzling question. Most trades by corporate insiders are harmless matters of buying and selling, no worse than what happens at any stock brokerage office across the United States. Some are venal attempts by an insider to turn privileged information into personal profit. Yet both transactions are being performed by someone who has inside knowledge of the company and its prospects. How could a corporate director *not* have inside information on a company? Even the most abandoned of sleep-through-it, uninformed directors from the bad old days would know things about the company not known to the average outside stock trader. There is a popular investment newsletter called *CDA/Investnet* that analyzes insider stock trade filings specifically to glean insights on a company's prospects. According to publisher Bob Gabele, the directors and officers of a company base their trades on factors and intelligence that most outside analysts have not yet seen. But the SEC is not dragging these insiders into court. Where is the line between simply shuffling one's portfolio on the one hand and disgorgements and community service on the other?

Lots of company directors and executives ask themselves that question. It is hard to imagine an area of business where the line between behavior that is expected and even encouraged and that which is criminal is so treacherously vague and variable. Corporations set up policies on trading by company insiders, addressing trading windows, notifications, and holding periods, but there is enormous variation in these from company to company, suggesting the level of uncertainty that exists.

When corporate directors violate all these unwritten rules they are often seen as particularly venal by the courts and the commission. "With directors we're more likely to pursue misconduct, and be fairly aggressive, even if we're only talking about 100 shares," says Bill McLucas, SEC Enforcement Division head. "If their fiduciary duty has been breached, we don't sit around debating whether to prosecute."[1] In 1992, Bruce Dines, a director of Colorado National Bank, was charged by the SEC with tipping his brother that CNB was a takeover target. Commission and NASDAQ computer work tracked the connection and filed charges in federal court that Dines had breached his fiduciary duty to the bank. The brothers ended up settling for $655,000 in civil fines. In 1994, Edward Downe was found guilty of SEC charges that he used his

---

1. Author interview, February 1996.

position as a corporate director of two companies, Kidde and Bear, Stearns, to use inside information for illegal trading. The penalty was unusually stiff: Downe was required to pay over $11 million, requiring liquidation of most of his personal assets, and was also sentenced to three years' probation and 3,000 hours community service.

The SEC has proven famously unwilling to pin down an exact definition of inside trading over the years, but has been increasingly zealous at tracking and punishing it. Deceptive or manipulative stock practices have been outlawed since the Great Depression, but for years only the most blatant of inside trading cases were discovered. Over the years, however, case law and SEC rule making pushed the boundaries of what was privileged information and who bore duties to guard that information.

Beginning in the mid-1980s, the boom years on Wall Street, especially with big takeovers, made the quick profits to be had with a juicy tip irresistible. The result was a number of new laws expanding the powers of the SEC, particularly when it came to insider trading. The 1984 Insider Trading Sanctions Act allowed the commission to seek treble damages for profits gained or losses avoided. In 1988 the Insider Trading and Securities Fraud Enforcement Act expanded these damage provisions to "controlling persons"—the corporation itself. The 1988 act also compelled not only corporations, but brokers, dealers, and investment advisors to develop and enforce written procedures to prevent the misuse of nonpublic information.

In 1990 the Securities Law Enforcement Remedies Act and the Penny Stock Reform Act gave the SEC far more tools and muscle to fight inside trading. Financial penalties were greatly increased, even for minor reporting technicalities. It became much easier for the SEC to seek to bar officers and directors. Combined with the new federal sentencing guidelines, it also became much easier to send them to jail. Basic SEC filing forms for insider holding and trades, the SEC forms 3, 4, 5, and 144, have been around for decades. However, 1991 rule changes made the penalties for errors, omissions, or late filings much harsher, with fines up to $75,000. Between 1986 and 1992, the SEC increased the number of cases it litigated fivefold.[2]

---

2. "The New Environment," William McLucas, SEC, *NSCP Currents Newsletter,* November/December 1992, p. 4.

SEC tools and technology are also making it easier to track insider stock transactions—and to set off warning bells if something looks fishy. Computer watchdogs at the SEC and the major stock exchanges, as well as greater cooperation from foreign governments, makes it much more likely that Big Brother is watching your trades, no matter where in the world they occur. In early 1995, the SEC announced the results of an incredibly byzantine investigation into inside trading of the Motel 6 company that encompassed 29 people and went through nine generations of tipper to tippee. According to an SEC enforcement official in New York, the case "is indicative of the commitment the agency has to see [a case] through."[3] And the SEC headaches are in addition to private actions against the trader. Shareholders, other contemporaneous traders (who presumably lost by the insider's gain), and even the corporation itself can sue for damages.

Very noble, but what exactly *is* insider trading? Despite the case law and regulations spelling out duties, mechanisms, and, certainly, penalties, Congress and the SEC have studiously avoided ever stating a precise legal definition. There is no "Thou shalt not trade on inside information" to be found in any statute book. Said author Stan Crock in *Business Week,* "Depending on the precise circumstances, an investor who trades on a hot tip can end up either lauded in the financial press for his prescience or sent off to prison."[4] The SEC has opposed any black-and-white definition for years, fearing that to proscribe all known examples of insider trading would give our ever-inventive financial crooks permission to create a whole raft of new scams, which would then be legal, at least until lawmaking caught up to them. The SEC believes that it would be trapped in a never-ending arms race against clever traders if it were to pin down solid insider stock rules.

However, basing prosecution on the shifting sand of judicial opinion can be dangerous when the sand starts shifting under your feet. The SEC has found itself in such a spot in recent years as the agency's expansive stands have begun to conflict with a more conservative judicial system. The SEC goes to trial in an average of 35 to 40 cases per year and has a strong record when it takes alleged

---

3. "The Labyrinth of 2 Insider Cases," *New York Times,* March 3, 1995, p. C1.
4. "Insider Trading: There Oughta Be a Law," Stan Crock, *Business Week,* December 12, 1994, p. 82.

perps to court. "We win far more cases than we lose," says Bill McLucas, "probably three out of four."[5] But when the SEC loses a case the opinions increasingly seek to reign in the commission's ill-defined powers.

A 1995 decision in the Second United States Circuit Court would seem to have delivered to the SEC its ultimate weapon, an opinion saying that anyone who trades while in possession of insider information is violating the law. But over in the Fourth Circuit, another opinion has questioned the commission's "misappropriation" rule, that if a trader gains inside company information, use of that information is a theft of company property. This was a major setback for the SEC and shows the disadvantage of depending on case law. Also, juries can get lost in the maze of insider trading regulations and intricacies. When forced to choose between someone who is supposed to have grabbed illicit boodle and an all-powerful federal Big Brother, they can have their sympathies pulled either way.

Lack of a consistent rule of law for insider trading has also made SEC efforts more dependent on internal commission vagaries. While the SEC has steadily sought to expand its powers to go after inside trades over the years, the actual priority and pursuit of such cases has blown hot and cold, depending on commission leadership. If the SEC chair or enforcement division chief decides to make insider trading prosecutions a priority, we see more aggressive action. But if new leadership chooses to concentrate the commission's limited resources on other areas, the emphasis slips.

These difficulties have increased the SEC's willingness to consider a formal insider trading law. The last major initiative for such a law came in 1987, at the heart of the '80s takeover fury. A group of securities lawyers led by former SEC General Counsel Harvey Pitt drafted an outline for a law that would have finally codified inside trading. The proposal would have prohibited misappropriation of information, trading based on breaches of fiduciary duties, and tipping that was intended for trading. Although legislation based on this blueprint was introduced in the United States Congress, it went nowhere, and the idea has languished.

Today, the SEC remains formally standoffish to a national law. "Our approach has won pretty widespread support, and there's no

---

5. Author interview, February 1996.

groundswell for change," observes Bill McLucas. Still, with judicial decisions continuing to raise uncertainty both for the enforcers, and worse, for directors who must navigate this minefield, the SEC is melting a bit in its opposition. "The Commission would be inclined to flexibility on an insider trading law. And we'd look favorably on a definition that codified the misappropriation theory, one that would overrule the Fourth Circuit court decision."[6]

With the burst of takeovers and acquisitions we have seen in the mid-1990s and suggestions that the trend will continue for the foreseeable future, there are many fresh opportunities to make a killing on inside tidbits. "Inside trading is a growth industry," says McLucas. Look for more major prosecutions as the takeover wave continues.

---

6. Ibid.

57

How Many Stakeholders Can Dance on the Head of a Pin?

The earlier discussion over "good" shareholders versus "bad" shareholders, or, simplistically, those with long-term versus short-term interests, should not detract from the legal issue that *all* are still shareholders. The board's fiduciary duty of loyalty to them has been repeatedly, painfully enforced by state and federal courts. Directors, and especially managers, win praise for seizing the most value for shareholders, and short of fraud or violation of regulatory standards, the courts will back a board decision if it is proven to deliver value to the shareholders.

But are the people who own company stock certificates really the only critics who matter? When facilities are closed, divisions sold, and thousands laid off, shareholders benefit from increased value. But does the rest of society pay the price? That is the argument of those who support "stakeholder" concerns in corporate governance. The legal duty to maximize value for shareholders can too often leave others out in the cold. With the massive shifts caused by restructurings and job cuts in the 1990s, employees have gone from being viewed as expendable overhead to being treated as a damned expensive nuisance. By the mid-1990s, the push for downsizing and greater productivity found us with laudable corporate profits—but also sluggish wages and living standards. What about the corporation's duty to its employees? And by extension, what about other stakeholders in the corporation's success? What about the communities where plants are located (and that includes the greater community of the United States, at least when facilities move to lower-wage nations)? What of suppliers, customers, and creditors? Should these interests be stirred into the pot with those of the shareholders?

Over the past decade, many people have thought so, and their efforts to mandate such stakeholder considerations have touched directly on how the board does its job. In the 1980s, 28 states passed stakeholder constituency statutes that allowed (and in some cases, required) boards of directors to factor stakeholders into their decisions along with the stockholders. These laws are usually limited to major structural decisions of the board, such as takeovers, mergers, divestitures, or plant closings, but can extend to other financial and strategy matters. Boards are encouraged to heed the welfare of these nonowners and to take them into consideration as long as their needs do not conflict with those of shareholders.

Stakeholder concerns have exploded during the past year as "corporate responsibility" issues have grabbed the headlines—and the political agenda. President Clinton addressed the need for corporations to "share the benefits" with their employees in his 1996 State of the Union Address. In May 1996, the Clinton administration convened the first annual Corporate Citizenship Conference at the White House to bring stakeholder issues to the national policy level. The conference grabbed national business news attention and featured over 100 corporate attendees selected, in the words of the president, because they "prove [business] can do the right thing and still make money."[1] CEOs and corporations such as UAL, Patagonia, and Corning were highlighted for their antilayoff policies, their worker retraining efforts, and their "lifework" concerns, such as child care and paid time off. President Clinton even proposed a Ron Brown Corporate Citizenship Award, named for the late Secretary of Commerce, to be granted annually to companies recognized for their responsibility. Summing up, Secretary of Labor Robert Reich said that corporate responsibility "will continue to be an issue after the November elections."[2]

In the United Kingdom, Labour Party leader Tony Blair has made a "stakeholder society" a plank in his efforts to return Labour to power. A 1996 *Newsweek* cover story on job-cutting CEOs styled

---

1. Remarks by President Bill Clinton, White House Corporate Citizenship Conference, May 16, 1996.
2. Author interview, June 1996.

them as "The Hit Men," irresponsible greed-heads who are stoking a populist backlash against Wall Street. "Doing the right thing for your people," the author scolds, "is often the best thing you can do for your business."[3]

Bringing stakeholder concerns into the boardroom stirs strong debates and unusual alliances. While some view the issue as a communitarian must, others sense a scam in the making. In 1990, Pennsylvania pushed the stakeholder issue to its current summit with its Public Act 36. Act 36 mandated that corporate directors consider the interests of affected parties in their decisions as they feel appropriate—and in a new twist, were not to view any one group, including shareholders, as "a dominant or controlling interest or factor." Directors were not to face liability for their stakeholder decisions. Corporations were, however, allowed to opt out of the bill's provisions within 90 days of its passage.

Talk about strange bedfellows . . . Pennsylvania's State Chamber of Commerce and an AFL-CIO coalition heartily endorsed the bill, but many shareholder activists and business conservatives were appalled. The "notorious" Act 36 brought "usurpation" of shareholder value, according to Robert Monks and Nell Minow.[4] The *Wall Street Journal* editorialized against such an "awful piece of legislation." British governance observer Jonathan Charkham saw Act 36 as "extreme."

How could such a noble-sounding law provoke such strong, divergent reactions? Primarily because the board decisions it sought to protect involved takeovers. The bill was passed specifically to aid Armstrong World Industries fight off a raid by an out-of-state company. It would allow the board of Armstrong, as well as other targeted Pennsylvania firms, to legally consider factors other than shareholder value in weighing a takeover bid. The public list of these factors included the effect on Keystone State communities, employees, citizens, and suppliers. The not-so-public agenda worked to entrench management and directors. This hidden antitakeover agenda showed through in such less-noted provisions as making it clumsy to accumulate more than a 20% hostile stake and forcing "disgorgement" of any profits gained in a run on the company.

---

3. "The Hit Men," *Newsweek*, February 26, 1996, p. 48.
4. *Corporate Governance*, Robert A. G. Monks and Nell Minow, Blackwell, 1995, p. 39.

Investor and media pressure were brought to bear in urging Pennsylvania companies to opt out of Act 36, and the campaign proved surprisingly successful, with almost a third of state corporations declining its questionable embrace. They had a few sound business reasons for doing so. A study by Wilshire Associates traced a 4% stock price decline for Pennsylvania companies to passage of the bill. Investors as a group viewed the law as an antitakeover tool that blatantly diluted their rights as owners, and they responded accordingly.

Boards have other reasons to approach corporate responsibility considerations with caution—they create a liability minefield. James Hanks, a noted Maryland corporate attorney, wrote a piece for the *Corporate Board* that pointed out some of the most painful contradictions in stakeholder legislation. Despite their communitarian sheen, "These statutes have gone too far, and may do more harm than good."[5] Hanks notes that despite the liability shields offered by laws such as Pennsylvania's, there are still plenty of legal traps when boards mix stakeholder and shareholder needs:

If boards "may consider the needs of stakeholders," almost every word is freighted with controversy. What does "may" mean? Up to the point where it would harm shareholders? Only if stakeholder consideration would eventually dovetail with those of shareholders? What does the board do when it is a coin flip? The words "consider," "needs," and, of course, "stakeholder" itself also open themselves up for similar deconstruction. Can the board ignore stakeholders for years but then seize upon their needs when facing a raider? How does the board switch on and off this factor? What happens when different stakeholders have different needs? Do stakeholders within the state of incorporation gain extra points over out-of-state stakeholders?

Just how does a board consider the stakeholders? Should it form a committee on stakeholder relations (Oh, God, not another committee," moan the directors)? How does the board define its stakeholders, define their interests, and weigh them within a governance

---

5. "Non-Stockholder Constituency Statutes," James J. Hanks Jr., *Corporate Board Special Report,* July/August 1991, p. 6.

context? At exactly what point does the balance tip from stakeholder to shareholder?

What happens when the lawsuits hit?   Directors can and will be sued if they pick the wrong definition. The moment a board makes a choice on a takeover offer or restructuring or plant closing because stakeholder needs outweigh those of investors, it can expect a flood of lawsuits from those investors. Even laws such as Pennsylvania's leave duties to stakeholders vague and undefined, while those owed to shareholders are rigidly laid out—and legally enforced. Pennsylvania recognized this problem in drafting its law and specified that the board would be held harmless for factoring in stakeholders. But plaintiff attorneys have proven endlessly inventive at finding ways to sue corporations and their boards. No doubt they will eventually go over, under, around, or through the Pennsylvania defenses, as well as other formal stakeholder statutes. "Such weapons pose more dangers to directors than to raiders," wrote James Hanks.[6]

What is the value to the corporation?   Obviously, the stronger a stakeholder rule is, the better it serves as a takeover shield. But is the cost worth the benefit? As discussed, the Pennsylvania law depressed stock prices for state companies, at least temporarily. It is not hard to see why. Investors and analysts encounter a law that will allow state corporations to shuffle their interests as owners into the crowd with everyone else. Their stock holdings thus become a devalued currency. Who wants to pay top dollar for a corporation with weaker ownership rights? This, rather than philosophical reasons, is probably why so many companies opted out of the Pennsylvania statute.

In a recent cover story on the corporate responsibility/stakeholder quagmire, the *Economist* painted the concept as "astonishing" and "wrongheaded" for several other valid reasons. First, attempts to make boards and managers accountable to everyone make them accountable to no one. Shareholders lose a tool to enforce stronger productivity and returns if management can point to vague, even if legitimate, stakeholder considerations. Thus a source for investor pressure would be lost. "Managers are insufficiently accountable to anybody in particular. That is why the next surprising thing

---

6. Ibid, p. 7.

you will hear is a lot of bosses enthusiastically embracing the language of stakeholding."[7] Even if the board sought to keep management's eye on shareholder value, its hand would be weakened.

As a final argument, precedent on stakeholder value is not conclusive. Japan and many European countries, particularly Germany, have long practiced a form of social responsibility governance in running their corporations. The social contracts in both Japan and Germany make it difficult, expensive, and unseemly to fire employees, especially in large numbers. In Japan such lifetime employment has been the rule, at least for major corporations. In Germany there are restraints on layoffs, mandatory retraining programs, and support mechanisms that make major cutbacks very sticky. As to the rest of these companies' stakeholders, tight, overlapping long-term relationships with suppliers and investors form a close web of interests around major corporations, both supporting and constraining the corporate family.

Yet this foreign stakeholder model has shown severe drawbacks over the past few years. It has proven inflexible and stifling for corporations that must compete globally. Ongoing recession in Japan has weakened the idea of lifetime employment and led to strains on the *keiretsu* system of cross-ownership, as well as previously unthinkable plant closings. German industry is striving mightily to cut its labor costs, battling with unions, making major layoffs, and trying to trim a bit of its extensive (and expensive) social welfare net. Even the indignant *Newsweek* article on stakeholder concerns confessed that Germany and Japan offer no answers: "They're more messed up than we are."[8] While the rights of stakeholders are catching on in the United States, the battle cry overseas is shifting to shareholder rights—the right of owners to demand higher productivity and profitability from a business investment.

Stakeholder concerns, despite their many unanswered questions, will become a growing issue for corporate boards in the future. Although laws and political pressures may continue to seek stakeholder consideration, there is very little legal reason why boards cannot already take the wider world into account in their deliberation. The 1986 Revlon decision in Delaware is best known for triggering the board's Revlon duties to seek the best price for

---

7. "Shareholder Values," *Economist*, February 10, 1996, p. 15.
8. "Hit Men," *Newsweek*, p. 48.

shareholders once sale of the company becomes inevitable. But Revlon also made clear that, before this point is reached, the board is free to value other considerations—as long as they do not conflict with shareholder needs. The 1990 Time Warner decision, despite its controversies, affirmed this concept. Despite our infatuation with restructuring and productivity, directors can, and often do, consider the effect of their actions on those beyond immediate shareholders. Shareholder challenges to such honest consideration are rare.

Indeed, much of our legal climate already compels boards to look beyond simple profit maximization. Laws on the environment, equal opportunity, restraint of trade, and labor relations are among those that force boards to trade off short-term shareholder value for longer-term social good. Yet without the single, overriding goal of shareholder value, the board loses its true North Star to steer by. Director consideration would become subject to the vagaries of interest-group consensus politics, weighted by personalities and public pressures. Or the board would again retreat to the role of distracted sheep, led by the firm hand of the CEO, because without a strong shareholder base, the board would lose its mandate to govern. Corporations do not tolerate a leadership vacuum, and in any contest of many divided interest groups, management has shown an ability to come out on top.

The interests of stakeholders will become a greater part of the board's deliberations in the future. But it is, oddly, in our long-term social interest to keep this concern strictly advisory. The true benchmark must remain shareholder value. Evidence tells us that both shareholders and society do well by boards doing good. As the *Economist* summed up, "Only an agitator or an academic could seriously claim that big American and British corporations are fixated exclusively on maximising returns for their shareholders."[9]

---

9. "Shareholder Values," *Economist*, p. 15.

58

Flash Forward: Federal Incorporation?

The legal and stakeholder turmoils I have discussed show some common factors. Perhaps the foremost of these is that while corporate governance in the United States has long since outgrown the control of state law, federal law is still struggling to take custody. Major transactions and legal precedents involve some of our largest corporations, with revenues in the billions, global operations, and thousands of employees. Yet they are sorted out at a state court in Delaware, one of our smallest states. A massive overhaul of the federal shareholder tort system has passed into law, but plaintiff lawyers will respond by hustling their strike suits into state courts. The Securities and Exchange Commission tries to impose a national, if unwritten, standard for insider trading but has to keep putting out fires among contrary district court decisions. While these are federal courts, they still suggest that behavior that is a felony in one district is no big deal in another. And stakeholder battles threaten to become civil wars between competing states.

So why not *federal* incorporation for companies? Rather than 50 competing units of government chartering, supervising, and regulating the heart of our economic system on a piecemeal basis, why not handle the entire process out of one federal office in Washington?

Among the "big ideas" on corporate governance, federal incorporation is one of the oldest. Federal chartering of banks extended back even before passage of the U.S. Constitution, to the Articles of Confederation in 1781. James Madison proposed an overall federal chartering provision during debate on the Constitution, concerned that states would lack the authority to properly regulate a corporation (a fear that has survived for two centuries). However, the Constitution's drafters still associated the corporate charter with a grant of monopoly and chose to keep the national government out of the matter. Incorporation would be handled at the state level.

Aside from the various essays into federal bank chartering in the nineteenth century, there was little more discussion of federal incorporation until late in the century. However, over the decades, corporate charters had shifted. They became much more elastic, allowing corporations to expand their lines of business, accumulate great sums of capital, and reach across state lines, becoming national and even international in scope. First the railroads, then major industries such as oil, chemicals, and consumer goods, became far too large, powerful, and wide ranging for any single state to manage. The rise of trusts and the populist movement in the early 1900s stirred demands to bring the "rapacious corporations" into line. Populist William Jennings Bryan called for federal licensing of any business that sought to conduct interstate business, and Theodore Roosevelt imposed minor reforms on corporations early in the century. But most of these early reformers were more concerned with ending corporate abuses than tinkering with the corporate form.

However, the idea that a federal law of incorporation would offer the ultimate reform caught fire in top circles in the years before World War I. State incorporation had taken a decidedly free-market turn—a turn downward. In the 1890s New Jersey abolished all antitrust laws for companies incorporated in the state. It threw out many of the traditional fetters on corporations, such as limited life spans and lines of business, loosened capitalization requirements, and gave more powers to corporate officers. The result? Companies flocked to incorporate in the Garden State, and by 1905, New Jersey had an almost $3 million surplus in its treasury.[1]

Other states busied themselves condemning New Jersey as hanging a "for sale" sign on its state capital, at least until they could prepare bigger "for sale" signs of their own. Delaware, a tiny, largely ignored state out of the flow of most capital, out–New Jerseyed New Jersey with its 1899 General Corporation Law. A few years later, when then-New Jersey Governor Woodrow Wilson led a corporate reform campaign, companies looked around for a new, more hos-

---

1. *Taming the Giant Corporation*, Ralph Nader, W. W. Norton, 1976, p. 47.

pitable home and found Delaware waving a welcome. State incorporation gained a bad name that it is still living down.

Presidents Roosevelt and Wilson publicly supported some form of federal chartering, and President Taft in 1910 proposed that Congress pass a federal licensing bill for business. Planks supporting federal incorporation appeared in both the Democratic and Republican presidential platforms between 1904 and 1912. A number of federal bills were introduced, though none advanced very far, and momentum cooled with passage of the Federal Trade Commission Law in 1914. Once again, the reformers headed off the revolutionaries.

The Great Depression brought a fresh chance for the Jacobins. Franklin Roosevelt's National Recovery Act paved the way for government to take a stronger role in how businesses operated, and the Securities and Exchange acts in 1933 and 1934 were viewed by many as laying the groundwork for a final federal takeover of the corporate form. In the late 1930s, with the strong support of liberal SEC Chairman William O. Douglas, a serious move to enact federal chartering began. Senator Joseph O'Mahoney of Wyoming launched a National Charters for National Business campaign, and in 1938, he introduced SB 3072, which would have required all corporations with assets over $100,000 to obtain a federal license for interstate trade. However, the New Deal juggernaut was losing steam, and the O'Mahoney bill, still highly controversial, died away.

The federal charter concept slumbered for decades but, with the corporate and government scandals of the 1970s, again stirred to life. Ralph Nader's Corporate Accountability Research Group in 1976 proposed a far-reaching legislative package to take the federal chartering concept further than ever before. "State chartering is a costly anachronism—as logical as the state printing money or passports."[2] The Federal Corporate Chartering Act of 1977 would apply to all corporations with over $250 million in goods and services, including those privately held, and would serve as an additional level of chartering on top of present state provisions. Shareholders, but also citizens, would gain expanded rights of action against the corporation.

Boards would be made up of paid professional directors nominated directly by shareholders, with specific areas of representation,

---

2. Ibid., p. 70.

including employee welfare, consumer protection, and the environment. Much broader corporate disclosure would have been required, with specific public and shareholder reports on pollution, equal employment, advertising, lobbying, and much more vigorous financial disclosure. An employee bill of rights would be required in every corporate charter. And once a U.S. company was federally incorporated under the rules, it would not be allowed to change its mind and incorporate in another country. The race to the bottom would end abruptly at the Potomac River. In short, a package that any Naderite would love. Although there was no Federal Corporate Chartering Act of 1977, the Carter administration of the late 1970s offered a haven for similar business thinking.

Some of the same impulses showed up a couple of years later in two bills that actually made it into Congress. I discussed these two 1980 packages, the Corporate Shareholders' Rights Act and the Corporate Democracy Act, earlier, but their federal chartering provisions deserve special attention here. The Shareholder Rights Act, introduced by Sen. Howard Metzenbaum, would have sidestepped the issue of federal chartering by making national standards de facto rather than de jure. It sought to impose strong federal standards on all corporations with over $1 billion in assets, including a majority of outside directors, independent audit and nominating committees, and direct shareholder nomination for the board. Though the feds would not handle chartering, they would set most of the standards for how all state chartered corporations did their business.

The Corporate Democracy Act, sponsored by Rep. Benjamin Rosenthal, abandoned such moderation and hewed much more closely to the Ralph Nader blueprint. Indeed, Nader's Corporate Accountability Research Group was a major booster of the bill, along with the AFL-CIO. Specific qualifications for director independence were set, and board constituencies for employee well-being, consumer affairs, the environment, and so forth were mandated. Company auditors would gain specific reporting requirements for wrongdoing. Employees could be fired only for "just cause," and directors were limited to two directorships. Although the Rosenthal bill also did not mandate federal charters, Section 702 made clear that its provisions overrode all state incorporation laws unless they were stricter than its own provisions. By thus imposing a national floor on corporate structure and behavior, it would effectively federalize major corporations. As Mark Green, one of Nader's Raiders and a specialist on corporate law, wrote, "There is already a kind of federal chartering law, only drafted in Wilmington, not Washington."[3]

Both of these bills brought intense debate between the business and government communities, but any hope for their passage melted when Ronald Reagan took the oath of office in 1981. During the 1980s and 1990s, the subject of federal charters would pop up every time a state or major company offered what shareholder activists saw as a fresh example of corporate outrage. Delaware court decisions (particularly the 1989 Time Warner opinion) and the Pennsylvania corporate stakeholder law of 1990 brought renewed rumblings that state incorporation law was an increasingly embarrassing anachronism.

Beyond this, however, there has been no serious push for federal incorporation since the Carter years. Today, as we sputter into the next century, we have federal courts, legislators, and presidents competing to downsize the central government and turn back more authority to the states. Many provisions of the last spate of federal chartering proposals sound bizarrely liberal and intrusive to contemporary ears. Federal chartering of corporations would seem to be a stunted perennial of political discourse, like the much-discussed shift from an electoral college system to direct popular voting for our presidents. Both are ideas that pop up in regular cycles, like presidential elections or Halley's comet, and then fade away. So why should I think that federal chartering is even worth discussing today?

Because, whatever the extremes of earlier proposals, there is a logic to federal chartering. There are some good arguments in favor of requiring at least our larger corporations to be chartered federally—a few that even businesses will like. Here are the essentials:

- Regarding the "race to the bottom." In a perfectly free-market society, a company would like to have its legal presence in a place where it faces the least regulation, the lowest taxes, and the lightest liability danger. By being able to choose among at least 50 jurisdictions for housing this legal

---

3. "The Case for a Corporate Democracy Act of 1980," Mark Green, *Americans Concerned about Corporate Power*, 1979, p. 2.

presence (never mind offshore options), there are thus at
least 50 bidders seeking corporate business. By making the
actual state of incorporation easily changeable and almost
totally divorcing it from any physical presence, states are
tempted to give corporations whatever they want with little
risk to themselves. The states benefit by incorporation fees
and taxes but can push the costs of polluting factories, layoffs, or board sloth onto the other 49 states.

However, the ease with which the state of incorporation can
shift means states must always strive to keep corporation-friendly
laws. That means limiting liability, making hostile takeovers difficult,
and not delivering any laws or judicial decisions that hobble how
the company runs itself. While competitive bidding is to be applauded, are the costs in this case too high? Enacting a law of federal
incorporation might not please Delaware, but it would keep states
from trying to out-debase one another. It would enforce a uniform
code of corporate conduct.

- Ease of accountability. If we look back 70 or 80 years ago,
  there was hardly any federal crime. That was not due to any
  lack of interstate bad guys, but rather to a lack of federal
  laws. One reason outlaws like Bonnie and Clyde and John
  Dillinger were able to wreak such havoc was their ability to
  rob a bank, skip across the state line, and go on their merry
  way with impunity. To some thinkers, corporate law in the
  United States has long looked like that. A motley collection
  of weak state laws and thin federal enforcement race their
  jalopies in futile, endless pursuit after corporate America. A
  federal law of incorporation would impose uniform rules
  that could not be avoided, laws that would be debated,
  passed, and enforced with a national consensus.
- Bringing management to heel. Many of the corporate goodies the Delaware courts and legislature hand out exist to
  make life safer for management. In 1989 Steve Ross sought
  to keep the Time Warner merger out of the hands of shareholders because he had a long-term strategic vision for the
  deal—and also because he would pocket some $190 mil-
  lion. The Delaware courts gave him and the boards involved

the benefit of a doubt. In the 1980s, legislative protections, antitakeover laws, and shareholder constituency statutes saw states outbidding each other to keep home-state corporations safe from raiders—and firmly in the hands of current management. "Management picks the state of incorporation," writes Robert Monks, "and, to the extent that there is competition, the result is a contest to see who can treat management the best."[4] With federal chartering, it would be easier to codify and enforce the powers of boards and shareholders.

No doubt there have been too many political activist garnishes on the federal chartering concept over the years. Still, the idea that world powers like General Motors, AT&T, or DuPont are granted their legal framework out of a tiny office in Delaware seems ludicrous, especially as we are about to start a new, global millennium. Also, federal chartering has a cyclic nature. This suggests that at the very point when the idea seems least likely, we are most certain to begin a swing back toward it.

Despite our current national push back to the states, power over the longest of hauls tends to centralize, and corporate matters are no exception. Even in cases of true gains by the states, it has been a matter of two steps toward the feds followed by one back toward the hinterlands. The very Congress that gained power in 1994 by proclaiming a return of power to the states passed the Private Securities Litigation Reform Act of 1995. This law not only preempts a number of state powers in shareholder suits, but adds strong edicts on corporate auditor disclosure—disclosure to the *federal* government.

Among the few realistic aspects of the late 1970s rash of corporate federalizing ideas was that they avoided formal federal chartering. While federal regulators would gain all manner of new oversight rules and enforcement powers, the Metzenbaum and Rosenthal bills did not actually call for someone at a bureau somewhere in D.C. to formally grant national charters of incorporation. Rather, federalizing the corporation became an overwhelming regulatory force. Federal chartering will likely take such a route in the

---

4. *Power and Accountability,* Robert A. G. Monks and Nell Minow, Harper Business, 1991, p. 137.

future, an ad hoc noncharter that looks, walks, and quacks like a charter.

Arguments over the intrusiveness and usurpation of earlier federal chartering schemes have also sorted themselves out over the years, usually in favor of the feds. The late 1970s proposals were obviously punitive measures, designed to keep these no-good corporate rascals from polluting, bribing, discriminating, and generally being illiberal. The roster of those opposed were obvious, were powerful, and had good arguments. Why should the government be mandating that a member of your board represent tree huggers?

Yet some of the less repressive provisions have trickled their way into subsequent legislation. The Foreign Corrupt Practices Act of 1977 predated the Metzenbaum and Rosenthal bills, but its full implications took awhile to be felt. It not only outlawed most commercial bribery, but mandated internal corporate structures (including those at the board level) to sniff out illegalities. Federal sentencing laws, plant closing laws, civil rights reforms, and the expansion of director liability also made life hot at the national level for the renegade corporation. These earlier reforms (and recent moves, right up to the shareholder lawsuit changes) defused the movement for such a radical overhaul as federal chartering. Yet they have also brought us closer and closer to the de facto federal system. More of the rules for how a corporation manages its equity and finances, what and how it discloses, the duties it owes shareholders, and how it behaves as a corporate citizen come from the federal government. Why not end the piecemeal approach and enact a single, omnibus federal standard of corporate governance?

There is another factor that could boost future federalizing efforts: the renaissance of shareholder activism over the past decade. While federal chartering waves of the past century were stirred by politicians, jurists, and consumer advocates, a renewed effort would likely be led by shareholders. As we have seen, institutional investors over the past decade have built a formidable structure for making their wishes known to corporations and their boards. They have gained communication and proxy tools, established their clout, and developed statistical and public relations savvy. With each passing year these big investors are better able to hold managers and boards accountable.

Shareholder advocates still have some major beefs with corporations, though. One of these is the way state lawmakers and judges sometimes let management get away with murder at share-holder expense. To the investor, a tighter national standard on what corporate governance can and cannot do (which could include national chartering) would have strong advantages. It would strengthen corporate accountability and encourage boardroom backbone. None of the major thinkers in governance have brought federal chartering back out of mothballs yet, but look for it to show up on activist agendas soon.

One final element would be needed for an effective federal law on corporate governance—the consent of those affected, in this case, corporate leadership. Although such a law would seem a sure-bet golem to the corporate community, the history of federal chartering shows surprisingly mixed reviews. In 1908 the *Wall Street Journal* endorsed a then current federal corporate licensing bill, and the National Association of Manufacturers supported such a law as "a national blessing."[5]

It is easy to see why there could be business support for some form of federal chartering. The 1908 "blessing" from the NAM went on to expound that a national corporate license would "protect one corporation from the oppression and rapacity of another."[6] In short, federal chartering would not bust monopolies but would license them. Since then, there have been many occasions when big business has seen big government not as an oppressor but as a savior, and it is possible that the future environment could open another such window. If federal corporate certification could supersede state lawsuits, coordinate often contradictory federal regulations, and set clear standards for board behavior, it might well draw new fans from the business sector.

Now the consumer activists and politicos who are veterans of the chartering movement 20 years ago might well object to such a protective view of federal regulation, seeing it as "regulatory capture" at its worst. And no doubt any such massive legislative package, after traveling through a hotly debated legislative process and then being interpreted by regulators and the courts, could bring an end result to frighten any sane businessperson. But Ralph Nader might have to wait until he is old and gray for the zeitgeist to cycle back to his vision of chartering as a form of corporate probation. If

---

5. *Taming the Giant*, Nader, p. 68.
6. Ibid.

federal incorporation could instead be limited to a uniform, omnibus "hold harmless" standard for governance, there just might be a future to it. Unlike some of the other big ideas of corporate governance, the licensing of directors, stakeholder concerns, or paying directors in stock, federal chartering has no real boosters at present. But that doesn't mean it won't in the future.

59

The 21st Century Board:
Sorting out the Trends

S o where does the U.S. board of directors stand as we look toward a new century? The pace of change in how boards function, their membership, and their responsibility has accelerated steadily since the 1970s. I am reminded of Moore's law of computing—that chip speed doubles every 18 months. Likewise, board shifts that would have been unthinkable at the beginning of the 1990s—like paying directors in stock—are popping up all over today and may become the commonplace for the year 2000. Also, some of the hotter board trends—including, again, board pay in stock, as well as splitting the roles of chair and CEO—have unresolved questions or may prove self-limiting.

Others, such as board makeup, feature a clash of competing trends and ideologies that will fight for top status. Boards face pressure to add more women and minorities—but also to increase top executive membership, where women and minorities remain scarce. They are expected to look more at the specific skills a director can bring and beyond titles—but are also to drop directors who lose that outside title, as Chrysler did with Joseph Antonini. Boards are to be much choosier in who they add to their circle—but are finding candidates much choosier in sharing their talents. And we want to pay them to do half a dozen competing jobs at once.

This lack of any certain standards makes projections on corporate governance a decade hence unusually tricky. Tricky, but all the more necessary. Flinging all caution to the winds, here are a few boardroom projections to take us into the next millennium:

- Board membership will stay at around 12 members, with a quarter of these insiders. As solid-gold directors become harder to find and more pressed for time, there will be logistical pressures to shrink the average board size, perhaps closer to ten. While this is feasible, there are counterforces that will keep board numbers up. The rise in committees, their workloads, and proliferation will either work a small board to death or keep minimum membership high. Board technology and streamlining improvements may help a smaller board be more effective, but they can also help a larger board be even more so.

Though good boards can function with the CEO as the only insider, such a purist approach is based not on effectiveness but on faith—faith that insiders do not belong. In truth, there is real value in keeping one or two extra inside members on the board. General Motors, which started the current boardroom revolution, had CEO John Smith as its only inside member as recently as 1995. But when Smith added the chairman's title in 1996, Corporate Counsel Harry Pearce joined him on the GM board.

If we look beyond the standard list of objections, we discover that inside directors oddly fit our growing image of a twenty-first-century corporate director: talented, motivated people who are found further down in a company than the CEO, but are also younger and more motivated; able to bring precise technical skills and wedded to the success of the company; possessing both the time to commit to the company's board and knowledge of the business. If the only thing keeping these people off the board is their employee status, perhaps the board should reconsider its rules. One insider, though, seems doomed to extinction: the former chair. To the modern investor, retired bosses bring none of the advantages of current inside directors, with added political baggage.

- Younger, faster, and more diverse. We can tell how far we have come by looking back on where we were. Any boardroom photo from more than 20 years ago shows precisely what we thought a board of directors should look like: stolid, 60-something white male CEOs, all named George or Fred or Norm. Today, it is impossible for an observer to view such a yellowing photo without thinking how unrepresentative it seems. The modern board of directors simply *looks wrong* without women, minorities, and younger executives at the table. We think of the markets, skills, and perspectives such a company must be missing. As I have noted, the trends toward diversity, new skills, and membership beyond proven CEOs are trends that nurture each other and are rapidly shifting the look of boards. Women are making more progress than minorities at present, though, and this trend will continue into the near future.

Foreign-born directors are speedily becoming popular. The boards of newer, high-tech firms already seem incomplete without some savant from Taiwan or Pakistan or Singapore as a member. But as boards of older firms increase their world presence and global comfort level, they also see a greater need for international directors. Still, it is unlikely that Fortune 500 boards will look like the payoff of an affirmative action program until a couple more decades have passed. Those named to directorships tend to come from the fountainhead of the business pipeline. We can seek shifts in how we define that fountainhead but must still wait for changes downstream to work their way up.

These trends are welcomed by those of us who seek both fairness and talent for boards, but I offer two quick cautions. First, board retirement policies have stiffened greatly in recent years. The era of octogenarian directors is dying faster than octogenarians themselves. Yet any policy that arbitrarily limits the talent boards can choose from will have some negative consequences. As I write this, Sen. Bob Dole is campaigning as the 1996 Republican presidential nominee. Yet at 73, he is too old to sit on many corporate boards. Older directors can bring skills, scope, and gravity to their place at the table. A policy of pushing them out to make way for younger blood can lose the company as much as it gains.

This touches on another concern with reshaping the board demographic. A move away from older, retired CEO warhorses could relieve the board of the very people most likely to get tough with the CEO. In the boardroom CEO coups of 1992–93, these proven veterans, including John Smale at GM, James Burke at IBM, and Rawleigh Warner at American Express, brought the savvy and strength needed to organize a rebellion. The one person on the board least likely to be overawed by the CEO is another CEO. To prevent a board consisting of up-and-coming talents from shunning confrontation, boards will have to strengthen their organization, independence, and oversight powers. In the long term, such structural authority is more reliable than hoping the board has a Godfather when one is needed.

Committee "federalism."   The rise in board committee power is already turning them into the tail that wags the boardroom dog at many companies. This trend will continue as management oversight by the board becomes more structured and prescribed. The vague governance duties of the traditional board, especially in the days before Delaware's Trans Union decision, were easily handled by a group of overall generalists, with the audit committee meeting occasionally to nod over the financials. Tightened duties, with stronger technical oversight and checklists of procedures to prove compliance, have shifted power to committees. This is where the real action is migrating today. The long-term result will be a sort of governance federalism, with the overall board serving as a nexus that unites the power of committees.

This will prove effective for administration of board duties, but we must be careful that it does not dilute the board's power in dealing with the CEO. A board that functions as a confederation of smaller units will be less able to serve as a unified check on the CEO's power, especially when the CEO and chair are one and the same.

The chair/CEO question.   Speaking of which, will the future rend asunder the combined office of CEO and chair? I don't think so. Although the number of separate chairs at U.S. corporations has increased during the 1990s, it remains uncommon, found only at one-fifth to one-quarter of major companies. And, as we have seen, these tend to be either temporary cases of the former CEO on his or her way to retirement, or short-term emergencies. Divided leadership still sends a message to the markets, potential acquirers, and within the company itself that the CEO is a lame duck. The formally elected lead director likewise brings logistical problems, compounded by our inability to precisely define the role. Look for this pattern to continue, at least until the board chair as an independent office brings real power of its own. Although the CEO/chair split will then likely stay uncommon, it will be more socially acceptable.

With the rise of committees, however, there could be a need for an outside director who acts as the coordinator of committees, a committee "wrangler" who serves as their liaison and spokesperson. This, of course, also describes the lead director or separate chair role, but would probably exist on a more informal, consensual basis.

Director pay. Board pay in stock is here, and the arguments against it, though often valid, will not undercut the momentum. Paying a board totally in stock will likely remain rare for all except the most demanding companies, but stock pay is an idea that lends itself to gradualism. A mixed formula, perhaps a 50-50 split between cash and pay or retainer in stock and meeting fees in cash, seems most likely. This would offer the incentives of stock along with enough cash to take care of walking-around money. Board pensions and benefits are on their way out (they were not all that common to start with). However, director stock programs suit themselves to deferred compensation setups, which often serve as a functional pension.

A warning for board pay in stock is to make sure that the elements stay in balance and do not tend to inflate each other. There could be a temptation to treat stock that has long deferrals or vesting periods as far away "funny money" that can cheaply boost director pay. If stock is directly substituted for a percentage of board pay, the resulting shrunken director checks might make future cash increases seem more reasonable.

Board meetings. Of all the paradoxes facing boards today, how boards will actually *work* is the most pressing. Governance demands more time, more effort, and greater access to special skills, often on a hurry-up basis. However, the executives who are board candidates face greater limits on the number of directorships they are allowed to accept. Even when directors do say "yes," there is constant pressure to cut back on the number of meetings. As the director search pool expands into the deeper executive levels of companies, this problem can actually worsen. CEOs have more freedom to juggle their schedules than vice presidents, and will have more clout in pressing their own boards to let them add directorships.

Sooner or later (hopefully sooner) we will have to meet this problem by redesigning how the board works from a clean sheet of paper. There are a number of tools we can use for this task: technology such as teleconferencing; greater use of outside counsel for technical needs like law, compensation, and audit; a core of staff for dedicated board support (most is currently handled by the offices of the CEO, CFO, corporate counsel, or corporate secretary as vital nuisance work); and streamlining board meetings and assignments to improve productivity. Such a rethinking would improve the value of the board and broaden the pool of potential directors. It might, as a bonus, give the board greater presence and clout. Such a modernized board function, particularly the permanent in-house staff, would help establish the board's power as an independent, ongoing entity, not merely a shadow of the CEO's office.

Battling shareholders. As the board gains enough power to be a substantial governance tool for shareholders, look for those shareholders to squabble over how to use this tool. The rise in strength of institutional shareholders over the past decade obscured the fact that these institutions have widely different, and often competing, agendas. Major funds may applaud when a corporation cuts costs through big layoffs, for instance. But public pension funds, particularly those affiliated with labor or progressive beliefs, will scold the board for not properly protecting employee stakeholders. As different investors discover how useful the board has become in enforcing value, they will compete for its favor. Negotiating these conflicts will require the board of directors to take on one more job—power broker.

The danger of legalism. Despite its stodgy, walnut-paneled reputation, the classic boardroom was an informal place regarding duties and roles. Aside from the basics of corporate minutes, financials and approvals, there was little for the board to do and even less that it legally had to do. Today, the corporate board is speeding toward the opposite extreme—rigidly laid out, extensive duties, specific roles for each director, and a checklist approach to ensure compliance. Rather than a social club, the future board will work more like an auto racing pit crew, with each member drilled to perform a specific function with breathless precision. If a member of the pit crew drops a wrench, the race can be lost. The price is much higher, though, should a board member flub due diligence, fail to ask a prescribed question, or say the wrong thing at the wrong moment. Shareholder suits, SEC fines, personal liability, even jail time are possible. The upside of this is a much higher level of professionalism among directors, seriousness of purpose, and, of course, better governance. The downside could be a threat of "by the numbers" rote board function. Directors might decide that their job is done because they did everything on the corporate counsel's checklist. Corporate boards function in a fishbowl today, at least at major companies. While this encourages them to aim for perfection and weigh every act, it also suppresses innovation and risk-taking. The business and personal risks could simply become too high for the director to do anything of which the lawyers will disapprove.

Some compliance programs, such as those for environmental or illegal foreign payment concerns, are to be set up so compliance is automatic. While this makes compliance more foolproof, it also means that directors are fools if they try to improve or question any aspect. I have yet to see such a gridlock set in, but as the road maps of governance become more firmly marked and the penalties grow harsher, conditions are ripe for such a chill. Worse, boards could be encouraged to ignore problems not covered by the rule book. Since the Trans Union case in Delaware, boards have been given the message that process is what really matters in defensible corporate governance. Could process ultimately prove more important than results?

60

New Boards, Old Boards, Your Boards

In trying to offer a glimpse of the future, I am afraid I have given you a few more paradoxes. But these have their roots in a greater paradox. In the United States today, we have two basic board models, what we might call the "old board" and the "new board." The old board is the historical model that has evolved over the decades and is still the archetype at most major companies. It consists of a dozen or so formidable people, mostly older white male CEOs, with a smattering of inside directors and a combined chair/CEO. The directors are busy and work quite hard for the company, though their attention is heavily split between their day jobs and other boards on which they serve. They own at most a couple thousand shares in the corporation. These directors vary from the acquiescent sort to one or two informal leaders, usually seasoned CEOs or CEO retirees. They depend on informal networking among themselves and a few key staff people to keep an eye on the CEO, but they generally back the chief executive up. If the company is in trouble, the CEO can rely on this board, but if they start to lose faith in him or her, some of the board leaders will launch a palace revolution to tighten the CEO's strings, or even oust him or her.

In the new board, directors are younger and own much more of the corporation, either by getting paid in equity or often by investing capital in the company early on. The firm is most often younger as well, typically in a high-tech or information services market. The board is a hardworking one, and members are often as knowledgeable on the company's field, markets, and products as the CEO. These directors own the company and are not going to let any opportunities pass them by. The CEO is probably also chair, as on the old board, but this is less likely. One of the original venture capitalists might serve as chair instead. Directors of the new board are a diverse lot, with more women and far more foreign-born members than the old board. Committees are active and searching in their business. The new board's corporate style is marked by volatility: volatile stock prices (a downside of this is that shareholders often sue), volatile business strategies, and volatile product cycles. Management structure is often volatile too—if results start to slip, the CEO's job is not safe around this board. The company *itself* is volatile. These directors are quite willing to merge or acquire themselves out of jobs, if it is good for shareholders (such as themselves).

Although it would seem at first that we should boo the old board and cheer the new board, both have their advantages, and it is hard to find any board that is purely one or the other. It is easy to imagine shareholders getting rich quick with the new board company (think of Netscape stock in late 1995), but it is also easy to imagine them losing their shirts in a hurry (think of Netscape in early 1996, when tech stocks sagged). Employees at the new board company are more mobile, better educated, and more likely to earn stock options. Employees at the old board company more often value a stable job and are more likely to have union representation.

The road from old board status to new board is evolutionary, with corporations realizing that board restructuring is a final, crucial link in reinventing how we do business. But (in one last paradox), those new, twenty-first-century boards might just be closer in spirit to those that started the twentieth century. Consider a board of hands-on owners and investors, tough-minded, viewing the top executive as an employee whose job is to increase shareholder value— or else. Sounds like the owner/financier boards of a century ago, or even those ancient squires sitting around their corporate plank. As an old, old hymn puts it, "In our end is our beginning."

Recall that I started this book with a brief summary of how the General Motors board, facing corporate disaster and an overwhelmed CEO, launched a coup, fired the boss, and put an outside director in charge. It was quite a revolution when it occurred . . . in 1920. The GM CEO who got bounced then was Billy Durant, the bold founder of the company. Badly underestimating the recession of 1920–21, he had led the firm into a financial black hole and faced personal disaster through his large holdings in GM stock. With the support of the board, Pierre du Pont, a director and major investor, stepped forward to bail Durant out, but took over presidency of the firm in the process. Working with a sharp young GM executive named Alfred P. Sloan, the duo rationalized production and restructured, putting GM on a sound business footing that would last for decades.

So the idea of a strong, active board is not a new one, but the next century demands that we achieve this goal with a new design. The twenty-first-century board will not gain its power through the major investor or inside executive board members of the past. Rather, it must build a new structure of smart, independent directors, leaders who take a strong, personal interest in how the company is managed and will act on that interest. I believe that directors will achieve this. Boards can begin the coming century by reinventing the unique, hands-on authority they held at the start of our passing century. In our end is our beginning. . . .

Index